THE
GLASS CEILING
DELUSION

By Mike Buchanan

For LPS publishing:

David and Goliatha: David Cameron – heir to Harman?
The Joy of Self-Publishing
Buchanan's Dictionary of Quotations for right-minded people
Buchanan's Dictionary of Quotations for right-minded Americans
The Fraud of the Rings
The Marriage Delusion: the fraud of the rings?
Two Men in a Car (a businessman, a chauffeur, and their holidays in France)
Guitar Gods in Beds. (Bedfordshire: a heavenly county)

For Kogan Page:

*Profitable Buying Strategies: How to Cut Procurement Costs
and Buy Your Way to Higher Profits*

THE
GLASS CEILING
DELUSION

The *real* reasons more women don't reach senior positions

mike buchanan

lps publishing

publisher's note
every possible effort has been made to ensure that the information contained in this book is accurate, and the publisher and author cannot accept responsibility for any errors or omissions, however caused. no responsibility for loss or damage occasioned to any person acting, or refraining from action, as a result of the material in this publication, can be accepted by the publisher or the author

this edition first published in great britain in 2011 by lps publishing

lps publishing

isbn 9780956641663

british library cataloguing-in-publication data
a cip record for this book is available from the british library

this edition was printed and distributed worldwide by lightning source inc

I don't want to get to a position when we have women in senior roles because they're women, we want to have women because they are able and as well equipped as men and sometimes better.
Margaret Thatcher 1925- British Conservative politician, Leader of the Conservative Party 1975-90, Prime Minister of the United Kingdom 1979-90

CONTENTS

ACKNOWLEDGEMENTS

My thanks to all the writers whose books I cite in this one. Particular thanks must go to Esther Vilar for *The Manipulated Man* (1971) and to Steve Moxon for *The Woman Racket* (2008). The two books ruthlessly expose the gaps between feminist rhetoric and how men and women act in the real world.

My thanks to Professor Simon Baron-Cohen both for his book *The Essential Difference* and for permission to include his questionnaires on empathising and systemising (appendices 2 and 3). My thanks also to Professor Louann Brizendine for *The Female Brain* which should be required reading for anyone who maintains there are no significant differences between gender-typical men's and women's brains.

My thanks to the senior executives as well as numerous former business colleagues, both men and women, for giving so generously of their limited time, and above all for being candid in relating their experiences over many years of men and women in the world of work.

My final thanks to you, dear reader, for buying this book, or borrowing it from a library. Warmer thanks for the former than for the latter, you understand. I hope the book at least meets your expectations. I should be interested to read of your experiences and perspectives in relation to the topics in this book. Feel free to contact me at mikebuchanan@hotmail.co.uk.

INTRODUCTION

One of the things a writer is for is to say the unsayable, speak the unspeakable and ask difficult questions.
Independent on Sunday 10 September 1995
Salman Rushdie 1947– Indian-born British novelist

A warm welcome to *The Glass Ceiling Delusion*. Let me start by both posing a question and suggesting an answer. What's the difference between the ambitious men and the ambitious women who are disappointed with their career progression? While the men will accept responsibility for their situations, hopefully with good grace, the women can enjoy the luxury of blaming the 'glass ceiling' for their situations *and they will be encouraged to do so*.

We shall see that many women's prime motivation in seeking senior positions is the pursuit of neither job satisfaction nor happiness, but the feminist gender equality agenda; so we should not be too surprised that there is often little correlation between the degree of individual women's ambitions for senior positions, and their fitness for them. The inevitable result? A lot of angry women who appear to think businesses exist to give women positions they deem themselves qualified to fill. They might as justifiably insist on being appointed to the New York Giants American football squad. As a fan of the G-Men for the past 35 years, I have to say I *really* wouldn't welcome that development.

Across the developed world women have enjoyed equality of opportunity with men for many years. This hasn't resulted in equality of gender outcomes so women (or militant feminists, at least) are reverting to their default setting: a demand for special treatment, this time to achieve gender balance in the boardroom. With their customary ingenuity they offer many assertions in support of special treatment. One of their most cherished assertions is that ambitious women seeking senior positions are thwarted by discrimination: the 'glass ceiling'.

But the glass ceiling is a delusion, as we shall see. This book examines 30 assertions put forward by feminists in support of more gender balance in senior positions. I seek to demonstrate that all 30 are variously fantasies, lies, delusions or myths.

If there is to be gender balance in the boardroom on the grounds of merit, this should only result from there being equal numbers of men and women able and willing to take on such roles. But the number of men with the experience and personal characteristics able to take them on greatly outnumbers the number of women with them, and this looks set to remain unchanged for the foreseeable future. But this may be of academic interest only; regardless of experience and personal characteristics, fewer women than men *wish* to take on the roles when offered them. And that too doesn't look set to change any time soon.

We live in an era in which militant feminists – a band I define as those campaigning for gender equality in the boardroom, among other causes – exert an ever-increasing influence over the public and corporate worlds, despite their numbers being miniscule. We shall see that the intellectual roots of feminism are the same as those of Marxism, so it should be a matter of serious concern to all of us that militant feminists exert *any* influence over the public and corporate worlds.

Feminists have been successful in persuading women that their gender's 'under-representation' at senior levels in organisations can be explained by the 'glass ceiling'. In 33 years in the business world, most of them spent in senior positions in major corporations, I never encountered gender discrimination against women. I came across examples of discrimination *in women's favour* but such discrimination is, we must assume, not a problem needing to be addressed.

Does anything drive the feminists' demands for gender equality in the boardroom, beyond their political ideology? Let me say the unsayable. It's perfectly clear that these women – who have little or no understanding of what makes businesses work – are also driven by a chronic childishness; they want to have what men have, even if far fewer women than men are prepared to make the sacrifices necessary to have any prospect of being appointed to the boardrooms of major corporations.

In 2010 I took early retirement to pursue writing full-time. My motivation to write about gender balance in the boardroom came from a growing realisation that the case for this radical change in corporate governance was flimsy at best, and absurd and at worst. The campaign for gender balance in the boardroom is a blatant assault on meritocracy in business, and therefore an assault on a free society.

It suits the militant feminists' bid for boardroom gender equality to assert either that there are no significant differences in the natures of men and women, or that any differences are the results of social conditioning in the family and elsewhere. This is the 'blank slate' theory of human nature and as we shall see, it has been thoroughly discredited. Most men and women are born with gender-typical brains. The book has a good deal to say on the differences between men's and women's natures and how they affect their prospects in the workplace.

It has been my experience in the workplace and outside it that gender-typical men and women are markedly different, have different interests and thought patterns, and given the same life choices, make different decisions. Women tend to be superior in certain areas of life, while men tend to be superior in others. Women's claims to be superior in certain areas, but inferior in none, are simply not credible. It happens that men are more likely than women to have the attributes required for senior positions in business, and it is only to be expected that more men than women will be successful in their bids for these positions.

Militant feminists have done all in their power to bully women out of their traditional roles as homemakers and into paid employment. I couldn't care less whether women choose to be homemakers or to undertake paid work. But why would anyone try to deny a woman the opportunity to find happiness in the role of homemaker, if she wished to choose that option? The world surely has a greater need for well-cared-for families than for more women on corporate boards.

If we are prepared to look at the worlds of the two genders as they really are, we cannot fail to see that women are more likely than men to pay a great deal of attention to their personal relationships: family, friends, and work colleagues. Men tend to be more interested than women in how systems work, and how they might be improved – political systems, mechanical systems, business models, the list is endless. We shall see convincing arguments that these gender-typical differences are 'hard-wired' in most men's and women's brains.

My experience of working as an executive with major corporations in the United Kingdom for 33 years (1978-2010) led me to an inescapable conclusion which was as obvious to me in the later years as it had been in the earliest years:

The number of female executives able and willing to take on senior roles in general, and executive director roles in major businesses in particular, is far lower than the number of male executives able and willing to do so.

We move from business to politics. We should not have been surprised to see militant feminist politicians – notably Harriet Harman – controlling the 'gender agenda' of the previous execrable Labour administration (1997-2010). Perhaps more surprising is that our current Prime Minister David Cameron, the leader of the Conservative party and the leader of a coalition government with the Liberal Democrats, is actively pursuing the same agenda. But evidence existed even before he assumed office that not only does he have a female-pattern brain, but that he's a militant feminist too; not so much 'heir to Blair' as he once termed himself, more 'heir to Harman'.

I worked as a business consultant for the Conservative party over 2006-8 and resigned my membership of the party in October 2009 when Cameron announced his proposal to introduce all-women prospective parliamentary candidate shortlists; the leader of the Labour Party, Ed Miliband, is also a supporter of all-women shortlists. Both Cameron and Miliband read Philosophy, Politics and Economics at Oxford University (graduating in 1988 and 1990 respectively). Their attitudes towards women in the world of work are strikingly similar to Harriet Harman's.

Within eight weeks of coming into office in May 2010 the coalition government signed a Commencement Order bringing into force over 90% of Harriet Harman's brainchild, the Equality Bill 2010. Perhaps the most invidious provision in the Act was the introduction of the concept of 'positive action' through which public sector organisations will 'voluntarily' meet the new 'Equality Duty'. We can expect feminists in the public sector (and especially those in Human Resources departments) to be enthusiastic volunteers, exercising positive discrimination *for* women and *against* men, although both forms of discrimination are illegal under British and EU law. I wrote to The Rt Hon Theresa May MP (appendix 12) to ask whether she personally supported the concept of positive action, and her reply is given at the end of the appendix.

Despite their influence militant feminists are, ironically, highly unrepresentative of women. We shall see that the intellectual sustenance for militant feminism lies within academia and doesn't invite robust debate – or any debate, for that matter. This 'feminist hothouse' fosters deep convictions about some quite extraordinary ideas, held by very few people outside the world of feminist academia. My personal favourite (p.88) is that fatness should be celebrated. You couldn't make it up, could you?

Men have long been manipulated by women at the individual and family levels, and tend not to notice it: perhaps it suits them not to notice it. Militant feminists have extended manipulation of men to the business and political levels, and men don't seem to have noticed that either. Faced with any challenge militant feminists will stridently demand either equality or special treatment for women: whichever one delivers what they deem to be their entitlements.

Fortunately a crucial and perennial problem lies at the heart of the militant feminist mission: the overwhelming majority of women aren't militant feminists. Militant feminists may be likened to a band of generals commanding only a handful of troops. Ignoring the hectoring of their militant feminist sisters, women continue to fall in love with men and seek part-time (and, ideally, emotionally fulfilling) lines of work, even when they're poorly paid, rather than the higher-paid lines of work men typically seek; and they're less likely than men to seek higher incomes through taking on more responsibilities. Women want less work in their work/life balances.

The doors to senior positions in general, and to the boardroom in particular, are open for talented women. But those women need to accept they're more likely to make it through the doors if they're not shackled to less talented women. They have nothing to lose but their chains.

Until the next time.

mike buchanan
bedford, old england
11 july 2011

CHAPTER 1

THE WORLD OF WORK:
FEMINIST FANTASIES, LIES,
DELUSIONS AND MYTHS

He who does not bellow the truth when he knows the truth makes
himself the accomplice of liars and forgers.
Charles Péguy 1873–1914 French poet and essayist: *Basic Verities*

Assertions widely accepted by women including militant feminists –
militant feminists are selective about the equality they want – the 'top 30'
feminist fantasies, lies, delusions and myths – top executives' statements
on gender issues in the workplace are generally public relations exercises
– a female director hears 'blah, blah, blah' – talented women find gender
balance initiatives condescending

I start by outlining a number of assertions about the genders
and the world of work which are widely accepted by women, in
particular by the small band of women I term 'militant
feminists'. Sometimes the assertions are made explicitly by
feminist writers and others, at other times they are implied in
the stances feminists take. For the purpose of this book I shall
define militant feminists as those feminists (usually but not
exclusively women) who campaign not for equality of
opportunity for men and women in the workplace, but for
equality of *outcome*.

Militant feminists are highly selective about the fields in
which they seek equality of outcome with men. They aren't
interested in equality of outcome in unpleasant and poorly-paid
lines of work, nor in lines of work which pose a danger to life
and limb (virtually all fatalities in the workplace involve men).
The equality of outcome of which militant feminists dream,

and for which they campaign and scheme, lies in the boardrooms of major companies. In the United Kingdom they usually mean companies in the 'FTSE100' or the 'FTSE250': the top 100 or 250 companies by market capitalisation, whose shares are readily available to buy and sell.

The assertions made about the genders in the workplace which I contend are variously fantasies, lies, delusions or myths – take your pick – include my 'top 30' outlined below, most of which will be explored over the course of this book. We shall see that feminists draw upon different and sometimes inconsistent assertions to suit differing circumstances and challenges. Some of the assertions might not appear obviously relevant to the 'gender balance in the workplace' question, but their relevance will become clear.

1. Women's progress into the senior reaches of organisations is hindered by overt and/or covert discrimination against them exercised by men (and sometimes women) already holding senior positions – the 'glass ceiling'

2. Unlike men, women are gender-blind when it comes to recruiting and promoting staff. They make selection decisions based solely on individual candidates' merit

3. Talented women with the experience, ambition and qualities required to reach senior positions and the boardroom share a common cause with less talented women, and the career prospects of the former will not be impaired if they campaign for gender balance initiatives with the latter

4. The key psychological differences between men and women result from differences in their social conditioning (nurture) rather than in their biology (nature)

5. The degree of overlap between men's and women's natures, patterns of thinking and behaviour is high enough to make statements about gender-typical natures, patterns of thinking and behaviour unhelpful

6. Women are as likely as men to be ambitious and focused on career progression

7. Gender-typical choices of professions made by men and women (e.g. engineering for men, nursing for women) result from social conditioning

8. A higher proportion of women in senior positions can be expected to enhance organisations' profitability

9. Equal numbers of men and women are able and willing to take on senior positions including board directorships

10. Men and women are equally interested in the world of work; women are not more likely than men to seek a satisfying 'work/life balance'

11. Men are not more likely than women to possess qualities which make them suitable for senior positions

12. Women *are* more likely than men to possess qualities which make them suitable for senior positions

13. Women are unlikely to be either more emotional or less rational than men

14. Women are likely to be more emotionally intelligent than men, and emotional intelligence helps foster a productive working environment

15. Militant feminists are representative of women in general, and are therefore qualified to speak on behalf of women

16. The rate of women's progression into senior positions is being enhanced by the activities of militant feminists

17. Feminist politicians have a democratic mandate to pursue feminist goals through legislation, and to introduce women-only shortlists for prospective political office

18. Where women's responsibilities and interests outside the workplace lead to their commitment to the organisation being reduced – quantitatively or qualitatively – this shouldn't impact negatively on their promotion prospects. In particular, taking time out of the workplace (possibly a number of years) to care for children shouldn't impact negatively

19. Equality of gender outcomes in the workplace is a desirable objective regardless of the proportion of candidates for senior positions who are women

20. Women would be more likely to seek high office if there were more role models to inspire them

21. Equality initiatives and special treatment for women are both valid approaches for increasing the proportion of senior positions filled by women

22. Women are happier in the world of work than they would be (or were) in their more traditional roles as wives, mothers and homemakers

23. Women represent a sufficiently homogeneous and disadvantaged group as to justify positive discrimination on their behalf

24. Businesses have social responsibilities which extend beyond the making of profits for their shareholders and this includes the promotion of gender-balanced outcomes at senior levels

25. If businesses do not pursue gender-balanced outcomes of their own volition, they should be forced to do so through legislation

26. Men and women have no preference for reporting to a male boss rather than to a female boss

27. Men and women are equally resilient and able to weather the stresses and strains of high office

28. Men and women are equally likely to be innovative and risk-taking, and are therefore equally likely to behave in an entrepreneurial manner

29. Men network effectively and 'bond' through activities such as playing golf together; these activities play a significant role in influencing men's decisions about corporate appointments

30. Attractive women don't exploit their attractiveness to give themselves an unfair advantage over men and less attractive female colleagues in the promotion stakes

It doesn't matter in the slightest whether *I* think assertions such as these are variously fantasies, lies, delusions or myths. What *does* matter is that the people running major organisations – the women as well as the men, it must be said – in so far as they consider such matters at all, tend to be of a like mind, even if their public pronouncements on gender-related matters might lead you to believe otherwise. Those pronouncements should be seen for what they are: public relations exercises.

One female director told me that when she hears people put forward arguments for the advancement of women in the workplace she nods encouragingly but all she hears is, 'blah, blah, blah'. She also made an interesting observation. The talented women with the qualities and the drive required to make it to the boardroom find initiatives to advance women condescending.

CHAPTER 2

THE DIFFERENT NATURES
OF MEN AND WOMEN

'Mrs Merton' to Debbie McGee: 'But what first, Debbie, attracted you to millionaire Paul Daniels?'
Caroline Aherne 1963- English comedienne, writer and actress: *The Mrs Merton Show* (1994-8)

Alpha males and beautiful women – gender-typical professions – gender-typical traits – how men and women typically differ – Professor Louann Brizendine and *The Female Brain* – the female brain and hormones – Professor Simon Baron-Cohen and *The Essential Difference* – systemising and empathising – extreme male brains and autism – extreme female brains: do militant feminists have extreme female brains? – the triumph of emotion over reason – the genetic predisposition to Left-wing thinking – Professor Steven Pinker and the 'blank slate' theory of human nature – The Women's Institute – men-only clubs – The Rt Hon Nicholas Soames MP, rhubarb crumble and custard – *Woman's Hour* and the gender pay gap – women crying themselves to sleep – the Prime Minister's ridiculous remark – women's enduring search for 'Mr Right' – the continuing flow of resources from men to women – fairness and equality – why are women bothered about gender balance in the boardroom? – the relationship between female attractiveness and promotion prospects – shopping

There are men among us with faces which (let's be kind) only a mother could love. Some of these men happen to be rich, famous or powerful: 'alpha males'. They commonly share an attribute, having (or having had) remarkably beautiful partners. One thinks of the musical theatre composer Andrew Lloyd-Webber (Sarah Brightman), the magician Paul Daniels (Debbie McGee), the entrepreneur Bernie Ecclestone (Slavica Radić, a former fashion model 11.5 inches taller and 28 years younger than lucky Bernie), the tennis player Andy Murray (Kim Sears) and the French president Nicolas Sarkozy (Carla Bruni). Notably beautiful women do not, it would appear, fall in love with *poor* unattractive men. We shall return to the phenomenon of female attractiveness later in the chapter.

It is necessary, for the sake of clarity, that I explain the terminology I use in this book. When I use the terms 'men' and 'women' I am referring to *most* men and women, those that might be considered 'gender-typical'.

A gender-typical profession for a man is engineering, a gender-typical profession for a woman nursing. There exist, of course, female engineers and male nurses; but they form a small proportion of the total workers in those professions, and this is changing only slowly (if at all).

Why should we have an interest in gender-typical traits? Why can we not treat everyone as individuals, thereby avoiding the cardinal sin of stereotyping? The reason is that women campaign collectively – and effectively – for women's interests at the expense of men's interests, while men rarely campaign for men's interests, effectively or otherwise. So the 'shortage' of female engineers is seen to be a problem requiring to be addressed, while the 'shortage' of male nurses isn't seen as a problem. The inevitable result? A great deal of taxpayers' money has been spent trying to encourage women into engineering, but with minimal impact: even today, over 90% of engineering graduates are men.

I don't consider that either gender is innately superior to the other. But I think it's obvious that the genders are in general *different* in their habits of thinking and acting. I'm now 53, and the different natures of men and women have been clear to me from an early age: their natures haven't changed over that time, nor should we expect them to have changed. 'Nature' being a word whose meaning may be ambiguous, let me state clearly what I mean by it in the context of this book. In general, I believe, men and women differ with respect to:

- their relative interests in interpersonal relationships, in particular those with family members, friends and work colleagues
- their relative interests in work, politics and business
- their attitudes towards taking risks
- their attitudes towards 'work/life balance': the types of work they seek, the hours they devote to work, and their drives to be promoted
- their styles of operating in the world of work: men being more naturally competitive, women being more naturally co-operative

If these differences are real, it follows that they will impact on men's and women's life choices and therefore their average incomes. The most commonly cited measure of the 'gender pay gap' relates to the incomes of male and female full-time workers *regardless of the equivalence of their lines of work*. The gap, while it exists, is not the result of discrimination against women. It is largely attributable to the choices men and women freely make in their personal and working lives, including the greater wish (or possibly readiness) of women to take career breaks to look after babies, young children and ageing relatives. If and when women in significant numbers make different choices, the pay gap will disappear. But there are good reasons for assuming women *won't* make different choices, as we'll see.

If we accept for the moment that, in general, men's and women's natures are different, what might be the source of the difference? Could it be something as obvious as men's and women's brains being different? For answers to this question we turn first to a book written by an American professor of the female persuasion, Louann Brizendine, on the time-honoured 'ladies first' principle. From Wikipedia:

> Louann Brizendine is a neuropsychiatrist and the author of *The Female Brain*, published in 2006. Her research concerns women's moods and hormones. She graduated in neurobiology from UC Berkeley, attended Yale School of Medicine and completed a residency in psychiatry at Harvard Medical School. She is board-certified in psychiatry and neurology and is an endowed clinical professor. She joined the faculty of UCSF Medical Center at the Langley Porter Psychiatric Institute in 1988 and now holds the Lynne and Marc Benioff-endowed chair of psychiatry. At UCSF, Brizendine pursues active clinical, teaching, writing and research activities.
>
> In 1994 she founded the UCSF Women's Mood and Hormone Clinic, and continues to serve as its director. The Women's Mood and Hormone Clinic is a psychiatric clinic designed to assess and treat women of all ages experiencing disruption of mood, energy, anxiety, sexual function and well-being due to hormonal influences on the brain. Brizendine also treats couples in the clinic.
>
> Additionally, Brizendine teaches courses to medical students, residents and other physicians throughout the country, addressing the neurobiology of hormones, mood disorders, anxiety problems, and sexual interest changes due to hormones.

Professor Brizendine is clearly far more qualified than I to make statements about the female brain and to compare it with the male brain. What startled me when I read *The Female Brain* was the sheer extent of the differences between the two brains: men and women truly do inhabit different mental worlds. Brizendine outlines how a range of hormones affect women's brains as they progress through life stages: foetal, girlhood, puberty, sexual maturity/single woman, pregnancy, breast feeding, childrearing, perimenopause, menopause, and postmenopause. She reveals in the book that during her medical education at Berkeley, Yale and Harvard, she 'learned little or nothing about female biological or neurological difference outside of pregnancy', and continues:

> The little research that was available, however, suggested that the brain differences, though subtle, were profound. As a resident in psychiatry, I became fascinated by the fact that there was a two-to-one ratio of depression in women compared with men. No one was offering any clear reasons for this discrepancy. Because I had gone to college at the peak of the feminist movement, my personal explanations ran toward the political and the psychological. I took the typical 1970s stance that the patriarchy of Western culture must have been the culprit. It must have kept women down and made them less functional than men. But that explanation alone didn't seem to fit: new studies were uncovering the same depression ratio worldwide. I started to think that something bigger, more basic and biological, was going on.
>
> One day it struck me that male versus female depression rates didn't start to diverge until females turned 12 or 13 – the age girls began menstruating. It appeared that the chemical changes at puberty did something in the brain to trigger more depression in women...
>
> When I started taking a woman's hormonal state into account as I evaluated her psychiatrically, I discovered the massive neurological effects her hormones have during different stages in life in shaping her desires, her values, *and the very way she perceives reality* [Author's italics]...
>
> Of the fluctuations that begin as early as three months old and last until after menopause, a woman's neurological reality is not as constant as a man's. His is like a mountain that is worn away imperceptibly over the millennia by glaciers, weather, and the deep tectonic movements of the earth. Hers is more like the weather itself – constantly changing and hard to predict.

From the chapter, 'The Birth of the Female Brain':

Common sense tells us that boys and girls behave differently. We see it every day at home, on the playground, and in classrooms. But what the culture hasn't told us is that the brain dictates these divergent behaviors. The impulses of children are so innate that they kick in even if we adults try to nudge them in another direction. One of my patients gave her three-and-a-half-year-old daughter many unisex toys, including a bright red fire truck instead of a doll. She walked into her daughter's room one afternoon to find her cuddling the truck in a baby blanket, rocking it back and forth, saying, 'Don't worry, little truckie, everything will be all right.'

This isn't socialization. The little girl didn't cuddle her 'truckie' because her environment molded her unisex brain. There is no unisex brain. She was born with a female brain, which came complete with its own impulses. Girls arrive already wired as girls, and boys arrive already wired as boys. Their brains are different by the time they're born, and their brains are what drive their impulses, values, and their very reality.

From a later chapter, 'The Future of the Female Brain':

Almost every woman I have seen in my office, when asked what would be her top three wishes if her fairy godmother could wave her magic wand and grant them, says, 'Joy in my life, a fulfilling relationship, and less stress with more personal time.'

Our modern life – the double shift of career and primary responsibility for the household and family – has made these goals particularly difficult to achieve. We are stressed out by this arrangement, and our leading cause of anxiety and depression is stress. One of the great mysteries of our lives is why we as women are so devoted to this current social contract *which often operates against the natural wiring of our female brains and biological reality* [Author's italics].

During the 1990s and the early part of this millennium, a new set of scientific facts and ideas about the female brain has been unfolding. These biological truths have become a powerful stimulus for the reconsideration of a woman's social contract. In writing this book I have struggled with two voices in my head – one is the scientific truth, the other is political correctness. I have chosen to emphasize scientific truth over political correctness even though scientific truths may not always be as welcome.

How, you might well ask, can 'almost every woman' seeking 'less stress with more personal time' be reconciled with women's alleged quests for senior positions in the workplace in general, and for executive directorships of major companies in particular? It can't. Professor Brizendine followed *The Female Brain* with *The Male Brain* (2010). It's larger, but less interesting. The book, that is.

Onto a book written by Simon Baron-Cohen, an eminent British professor. His biography on Wikipedia:

> Simon Baron-Cohen FBA is a Professor of Developmental Psychopathology in the Departments of Psychiatry and Experimental Psychology at the University of Cambridge in the United Kingdom. He is the Director of the University's Autism Research Centre, and a Fellow of Trinity College. He is best known for his work on autism, including his early theory that autism involves degrees of 'mindblindness' (or delays in the development of theory of mind); and his later theory that autism is an extreme form of the 'male brain', which involved a reconceptualisation of typical psychological sex differences in terms of empathizing – systemizing theory.

The professor's book *The Essential Difference* was published in 2003. He starts by summarising the theory to be outlined in the book:

> The female brain is predominantly hard-wired for empathy.

> The male brain is predominantly hard-wired for understanding and building systems.

He describes empathising in the following terms:

> Empathising is the drive to identify another person's emotions and thoughts, and to respond to them with an appropriate emotion. Empathising does not entail just the cold calculation of what someone else thinks and feels (or what is sometimes called mind reading). Psychopaths can do that much. Empathising occurs when we feel an appropriate emotional reaction, an emotion *triggered* by the other person's emotion, and it is done in order to understand another person, to predict their behaviour, and to connect or resonate with them emotionally.

Systemising is described as follows:

> Systemising is the drive to analyse, explore, and construct a system. The systemiser intuitively figures out how things work, or extracts the underlying rules that govern the behaviour of a system. This is done in order to understand and predict the system, or to invent a new one…
>
> Just as empathising is powerful enough to cope with the hundreds of emotions that exist, so systemising is a process that can cope with an enormous number of systems. I will argue that, on average, males spontaneously systemise to a greater extent than do females.

The good professor points out here – as indeed he does throughout the book – that he does not mean 'all males' or 'all females': he is talking about *statistical averages*. I contend that success in senior positions in major organisations requires strong systemising skills, not strong empathising skills: so without positive discrimination for women we shall *never* have gender balance in the boardroom. Gender balance in the boardroom is not of the slightest interest to the vast majority of women; it is of interest only to militant feminists, an assortment of people – almost all women – driven by left-wing ideology. David Cameron, the current British Prime Minister, is a militant feminist despite being the leader of the Conservative party.

Baron-Cohen writes about the advantages of systemising brains to human males early in the species' evolution, which fell under the categories of using and making tools, hunting and tracking, trading, attaining and exercising power, developing expertise, tolerating solitude, being aggressive, and being leaders. The advantages of empathising brains to early females are explored under the categories of making friends, mothering, gossiping, being socially mobile, and reading partners' intentions. I contend that systemising brains are increasingly advantageous to individuals as they climb the hierarchy of major organisations, and this on its own would largely account for the enduring preponderance of men in senior positions.

Questionnaires for self-assessment of empathising and systemising traits are provided in appendices 2 and 3, along with a brief guide to interpreting the results. Why not complete them now, to help you understand where you are with regards to these traits compared with others of your gender, and with those of the opposite gender?

There is a large and growing body of evidence supporting Baron-Cohen's theory that people exhibiting the condition of autism – a spectrum of disorders which includes Asperger Syndrome – have 'extreme male brains'. On average, compared to both men and women on average, they are markedly less empathising, and markedly more systemising. Baron-Cohen points out that these people can lead productive lives if their work plays to their strengths rather than their weaknesses. Some autistic men are found in the top levels of IT companies, for example. Studies of identical and non-identical twins strongly suggest that autism is heritable. In people diagnosed with high-functioning autism or Asperger Syndrome, the sex ratio is at least *ten males to every female*.

Baron-Cohen puts a figure of 2.5 per cent on the proportion of the population born with an extreme male brain, but what about the extreme *female* brain, which theory predicts should be as common? He continues:

> All scientists know about the extreme female brain is that it is expected to arise… Scientists have never got up close to these individuals. It is a bit like positing the existence of a new animal on theoretical grounds, and then setting out to discover if it is really found in nature…
>
> People with the extreme female brain would have average or significantly better empathising ability than that of other people in the general population, but their systemising would be impaired. So these would be people who have difficulty understanding maths or physics or machines or chemistry, *as systems*. But they could be extremely accurate at tuning in to others' feelings and thoughts.
>
> Would such a profile carry any necessary disability? Hyperempathising could be a great asset, and poor systemising may not be too crippling. It is possible that the extreme female brain is not seen in clinics because it is not maladaptive…
>
> A contender for who might have the extreme female brain would be a wonderfully caring person who can rapidly make you feel fully understood. For example, an endlessly patient psychotherapist who is excellent at rapidly tuning in to your feelings and your situation, who not only says he or she feels a great sadness at your sadness or great pleasure at your pleasure but also actually experiences those emotions as vividly as if your feelings were theirs.
>
> However, the contender for the extreme female brain would also need to be someone who was virtually technically disabled. Someone for whom maths, computers, or political schisms, or DIY, held no interest. Indeed, someone who found activities requiring systemising hard to follow. We may all know people like this, but it is likely that they do not find their way into clinics, except perhaps as staff in the caring professions.

I have a strong suspicion that militant feminists have extreme female brains. They have a highly developed sense of empathy, at least towards those of their own gender, and perceive injustice towards women wherever they look. If militant feminists *do* have extreme female brains, they would also have poor systemising abilities, so they could not be expected to understand the evidence that conflicts with their views – in extreme female brains, emotion will always triumph over reason – even if they were willing to try. If feminists *do* have extreme female brains, this might explain why they reject outright the notion of gender-patterned brains, and become emotional when the topic is raised.

Militant feminists might be among those unfortunate souls genetically predisposed to hold Left-wing views. An article in *The Daily Telegraph* of 29 October 2010, 'Feeling liberal? It's in your genes':

> Holding liberal views could be in the blood, scientists said after identifying a gene that makes someone more open-minded. The 'liberal gene' opens up a person to new ideas and alternative ways of living and could influence their belief in Left-wing politics, according to the research. It may mean that liberals are born, not made, although the effect is exacerbated if an individual has many friends during their formative years.
>
> The 'liberal gene' is a transmitter in the brain called DRD4 which is connected to dopamine, known as the reward currency. Dopamine affects the way the brain experiences emotions, pleasures and pain and can therefore influence personality traits.
>
> When adolescents with the gene are also socially outgoing with many friends, they seek and receive other people's points of view, which triggers a pleasurable 'reward' of dopamine. This suggests that, as adults, they will be more open-minded and tend to form less conventional political viewpoints, the study said.

Published in the *Journal of Politics*, the research by scientists from the University of California and Harvard studied 2,000 Americans. It found those with a strain of the DRD4 gene seek out 'novelty', such as people and ways of living different from the ones they are used to. This leads them to have more politically liberal opinions, it found. The person's age, ethnicity, gender or culture appeared to make no difference – it was the genes that counted.

Prof James Fowler, who led the research, said: 'It is the critical interaction of two factors – the genetic predisposition and the environmental condition of having many friends in adolescence – that is associated with being more liberal. These findings suggest that political affiliation is not based solely on the kind of social environment people experience.'

The paper's editorial on the same day contained a piece titled, 'Lifetime cure for Lefties':

Scientists have given mankind many blessings, but the discovery of the gene for Left-wing behaviour must be foremost among them. For now there is a diagnosis, there can be a cure. Just think of it – a quick screening of the unborn infant, a mild course of gene therapy, and hey presto! The disease can be eradicated within a generation.

Perhaps we are getting a little ahead of ourselves. But even if science falls short of an outright cure, it should still be possible to ameliorate the symptoms. The gene does not automatically make the carrier a Lefty; rather, it triggers the adolescent brain's reward mechanism in the presence of novel experiences and viewpoints. The treatment is simple: lock teenage sufferers in a drab room, furnished with the works of Hayek and Friedman. True, their social skills will be somewhat stunted. But the benefits will last a lifetime.

The Canadian-American Steven Pinker is a Professor of Psychology at Harvard University and the author of a number of acclaimed books including *The Blank Slate: The Modern Denial of Human Nature* (2002). He starts the book with the following passage on 'The Blank Slate, the Noble Savage, and the Ghost in the Machine':

Everyone has a theory of human nature. Everyone has to anticipate the behavior of others, and that means we all need theories about what makes people tick. A tacit theory of human nature – that behavior is caused by thoughts and feelings – is embedded in the very way we think about people. We fill out this theory by introspecting on our own minds and assuming that our fellows are like ourselves, and by watching people's behavior and filing away generalizations. We absorb still other ideas from our intellectual climate: from the expertise of authorities and the conventional wisdom of the day.

Our theory of human nature is the wellspring of much in our lives. We consult it when we want to persuade or threaten, inform or deceive. It advises us on how to nurture our marriages, bring up our children, and control our own behavior. Its assumptions about learning drive our educational policy; its assumptions about motivation drive our policies on economics, law, and crime. And because it delineates what people can achieve easily, what they can achieve only with sacrifice or pain, and what they cannot achieve at all, it affects our values: what we believe we can reasonably strive for as individuals and as a society. Rival theories of human nature are entwined in different ways of life and different political systems, and have been a source of much conflict over the course of history. . .

Every society must operate with a theory of human nature, and *our intellectual mainstream is committed to one* [Author's italics]. The theory is seldom articulated or overtly embraced, but it lies at the heart of a vast number of beliefs and policies. Bertrand Russell wrote, 'Every man, wherever he goes, is encompassed by a cloud of comforting convictions, which move with him like flies on a summer day.'

For intellectuals today, many of those convictions are about psychology and social relations. I will refer to those convictions as the Blank Slate: the idea that the human mind has no inherent structure and can be inscribed at will by society or ourselves.

That theory of human nature – namely, that it barely exists – is the topic of this book . . . the Blank Slate has become the secular religion of modern intellectual life.

The Blank Slate theory of human nature is commonly espoused by feminists. Pinker convincingly explains that it is deeply flawed. From the same book:

> Contrary to popular belief, parents in contemporary America do not treat their sons and daughters very differently. A recent assessment of 172 studies involving 28,000 children found that boys and girls are given similar amounts of encouragement, warmth, nurturance, restrictiveness, discipline, and clarity of communication. The only substantial difference was that about two-thirds of the boys were discouraged from playing with dolls, especially by their fathers, out of a fear that they would become gay. (Boys who prefer girls' toys often do turn out gay, but forbidding them the toys does not change the outcome.)
>
> Nor do differences between boys and girls depend on their observing masculine behavior in their fathers and feminine behavior in their mothers. When Hunter has two mommies, he acts just as much like a boy as if he had a mommy and a daddy.
>
> Things are not looking good for the theory that boys and girls are born identical except for their genitalia, with all other differences coming from the way society treats them. If that were true, it would be an amazing coincidence that in every society the coin flip that assigns each sex to one set of roles would land the same way (or that one fateful flip at the dawn of the species should have been maintained without interruption across all the upheavals of the past 100,000 years).
>
> It would be just as amazing that, time and again, society's arbitrary assignments matched the predictions that a Martian biologist would make for our species based on our anatomy and the distribution of our genes. It would seem odd that the hormones that make us male and female in the first place also modulate the characteristically male and female mental traits, both decisively in early brain development and in smaller degrees throughout our lives.

It would be all the more odd that a second genetic mechanism differentiating the sexes (genomic imprinting) also installs characteristic male and female talents. Finally, two key predictions of the social construction theory – that boys treated as girls will grow up with girls' minds, and that differences between boys and girls can be traced to differences in how their parents treat them – have gone down in flames.

Of course, just because many sex differences are rooted in biology does not mean that one sex is superior, that the differences will emerge for all people in all circumstances, that discrimination against a person based on sex is justified, or that people should be coerced into doing things typical of their sex. But neither are the differences without consequences.

By now many people are happy to say what was unsayable in polite company a few years ago: that males and females do not have interchangeable minds... But among many professional women the existence of sex differences is still a source of discomfort. As one colleague said to me, 'Look, I know that males and females are not identical. I see it in my kids, I see it in myself, I know about the research. I can't explain it, but when I read claims about sex differences, *steam comes out of my ears.*'

The phenomenon of women becoming angry and irrational when their viewpoints are challenged is one that men learn to live with, generally by pretending to agree with the women in their lives. One unfortunate consequence is that women are more likely than men to believe things which are patently absurd, as we shall see in a later chapter.

For an illustration of how men and women differ, we need go no further than the Women's Institutes. The combined membership of Women's Institutes in the United Kingdom is around 205,000. They 'play a unique role in providing women with educational opportunities and the chance to build new skills, to take part in a wide variety of activities and to campaign on issues that matter to them and their communities'. Membership is, not unnaturally, restricted to women.

If men had an equivalent body to the Women's Institute – the Men's Institute, say – and excluded women from its membership, doubtless the body would face demands from women to admit them, and change its name to the People's Institute.

Men happily recognise that while men and women enjoy the company of the opposite sex, at times they welcome just the company of their own sex, which is why they have no problem with bodies such as the Women's Institute, or with The Orange Prize for Fiction (a book competition open only to female authors), or women-only competitions in sports, even when men don't enjoy an advantage on physical strength grounds (snooker, darts etc.). But do women accord men the same courtesy? Of course not. The media these days rarely report stories of women's hostility towards men excluding women from their activities – presumably readers are fed up with the subject – so we go back some years for a couple of articles on the matter. The first is titled 'Men-only clubs will not be outlawed' from the 7 December 1999 edition of *The Independent*:

> The Government last night denied reports that it has secret plans to ban men-only members clubs following admissions from ministers that clubs that barred women from membership were 'anachronisms'.
>
> The moves were said to be being discussed by at least four ministers, including the Cabinet Office Minister, Mo Mowlam. They would lead to the end of membership restrictions from every body ranging from the 17th century St James's Club in London to golf clubs and the traditional Labour bastion, the working men's club.
>
> It was claimed that private clubs, exempted by the Sex Discrimination Act, would be modernised under an amendment to the Equal Opportunities Bill in the next

session of parliament. Senior Labour figures are said to be heartened by recent about-turns by men-only stalwarts such as the MCC which last year voted to admit women after 211 years.

A Government spokesman rejected reports of new laws in the pipeline. Many topics were covered in ministerial discussions on equality but Government plans for anti-discrimination legislation did not extend beyond public bodies.

Last night Nicholas Soames MP, the former Tory defence minister, who is a member of White's, Pratt's and the Turf, said: 'This is another sign that living under New Labour is like living in Soviet Russia. What sensible woman wants to be a member of a men's club?'

A good point, Mr Soames, and well made. Now there's a man you can imagine tucking enthusiastically into rhubarb crumble and custard at his club. The following article was printed in the paper the next day, titled 'The Irritations of Modern Life: Men-only Clubs':

I have often wondered what men do in all-male clubs. Million-pound deals? Homosexual rituals? Men, especially if they belong to the Garrick Club, are reticent, giving the impression that it involves little more than long lunches, at which they get slightly squiffy and eat nursery food. Yet, as soon as someone proposes changing the law to force such clubs to admit women, it is as if the very foundations of civilisation had begun to shudder.

'A grotesque curtailment of freedom of association – an almost totalitarian assertion that the state should be able to decide with whom you can spend your own free time on property private to you...' is how *The Daily Telegraph* greeted the news that the Government is thinking of banning men-only establishments. Yikes! Next thing you know, Tony Blair will be personally knocking on *Telegraph* readers' doors, pushing a female across the threshold and instructing them to talk to her.

Of course, there are few subjects so likely to fire up a right-wing leader-writer. The age-old right of the British upper classes to exclude outsiders is slowly being whittled away. The Reform Club has admitted women for years; even Lord's is not the bastion it was. What's left for the man who sometimes feels the need to be with people who, not to put too fine a point on it, aren't going to go all funny and exhibit symptoms of pre-menstrual tension?

Men's clubs are an anachronism. Their very existence institutionalises discrimination, draping it with a veil of respectability. When I witnessed the reaction to this mild move towards equality, I felt as if I'd been transported back to a time when misogyny was so firmly taken for granted that most people didn't even have a name for it. Now we do, and it's not acceptable. The bad news for club bores, tucking into bread-and-butter pudding in Covent Garden – or, indeed, a working men's club in Halifax – is that the time has come to grow up.

Ah yes. 'An anachronism.' 'The time has come to grow up.' I don't suppose the journalist – a lady – is quite so agitated by the Women's Institute, even many years later. And with such arguments women seek to hide the real reasons they want to stop men associating freely with one another, whatever they are. Maybe they've learned of our plan to withdraw voting rights from them. Damn. We've managed to keep that under wraps for *years*. On to *Woman's Hour*, a staple of BBC Radio. From their website:

> October 7 1946 was the start of something big – it was the first broadcast of a programme designed to celebrate, entertain and inform women.

I have never heard a man suggest there should be a programme for men, *Man's Hour* possibly, 'a programme designed to celebrate, entertain and inform men'.

I often heard *Woman's Hour* when driving around the country on business, and did so on 27 April 2009. It's often an interesting programme but some topics come up with mind-numbing regularity. One is the so-called 'gender pay gap', annoyingly – to some people, at least – still a reality 40 years after the 1970 Equal Pay Act. The report concerned Harriet Harman who was putting forward the Equality Bill, which included provisions to require organisations to publicise individuals' salaries. The inference, as always, was that women are discriminated against by men.

But the gender pay gap isn't attributable to discrimination against women once a number of factors are taken into account, such as choice of profession, career breaks for having children, many women preferring part-time work, and women taking earlier retirement than men. Not that you'll ever hear this mentioned on *Woman's Hour*. Or at least *I* haven't heard it in the past 30 years of listening occasionally to the programme.

A later discussion in the same episode concerned women giving up highly paid stressful jobs to enable them to work for themselves, often on low incomes, or to do jobs they found more fulfilling. One of the women had been a 'high-flying lawyer'. The general tone of the discussion was a celebration of women who decided to forsake lucrative but demanding jobs in favour of more job satisfaction. One woman made the following observation:

> So many women I know are crying themselves to sleep on a Sunday night, because they really can't bear the thought of going to work the next day.

No connection was made by the good ladies between the gender pay gap and women voluntarily opting out of highly paid, stressful, unfulfilling jobs. Nor was it considered worth raising that even if a gender pay gap did still exist, it might be attributable to men being more willing than women to continue with such jobs. And so the myths of discrimination against women and the 'glass ceiling' roll on year after year.

The enthusiasm with which politicians – both female and male – keep perpetuating the myth of the gender pay gap is surely a testimony to its enduring vote-delivering powers among female voters. In October 2010 Prime Minister David Cameron, during a major interview on BBC television, made a ridiculous statement: that the difference between men's pay and women's pay was 'scandalous'.

Many women work to achieve financial security, but this is generally not their *preferred* option. Women's search for financial security has traditionally focused on securing a higher status man for a partner, and this has remained unchanged into the modern era. In his 1998 book *The Secrets of Love and Lust*, Simon Andreae had some interesting things to say about women's search for 'Mr Right':

> Handsome men will pass their physical advantages down to the children of whoever they mate with, giving those children a head-start in the race for reproductive success. The indices of conventional male good looks – a rugged jaw, broad shoulders, a full head of hair and a healthy physique – are also indications of genetic health and strength. Yet looks in the opposite sex seem to be less important to women than they are to men, and less important than other factors.
>
> In Douglas Kenrick's study of the percentages required of potential partners before women would consent to dating, having sex, steady dating or marrying them, 'good looks' was the only criterion where women, across the board, were ready to accept a lower percentage value than men. They were even prepared to consider men of below-average physical attractiveness... as long as they had other things to offer...
>
> In Glenn Wilson's study of British sexual fantasies, men were found to fantasise more frequently about group sex than any of the other scenarios he presented to them. But women had a very different fantasy life. For them, by far the most characteristic fantasy was straight, monogamous sex with a

famous personality. The argument runs that famous men today, like village headmen in the past, and successful hunters during the early period in which we evolved, would have acquired the status and resources to furnish a woman and her children with more food and protection than the next man.

Over the incremental advances of time, evolution would therefore have favoured women who developed mental programmes which allowed them to judge the signs of status within their particular environment and culture, and calibrate their desire accordingly.

Fame is not the only indicator of a man who is high in status and rich in resources. In 1986 the American psychologist Elizabeth Hill published the results of an experiment in which she asked her students to describe what sort of clothes they considered high-status men to wear, and what sort of clothes they considered low-status men to wear. Among the former were smart suits, polo shirts, designer jeans and expensive watches; among the latter were nondescript jeans, tank tops and T-shirts.

She then photographed a number of different men in variations of both styles of dress and showed the photographs to a different group of female students, asking them to rate each one for attractiveness. Overall, the same models were found more attractive when wearing the high-status costumes than when wearing the low-status ones.

It's important to note, though, that it's not just status symbols, and resources they indicate, that women find attractive. It's also those personality characteristics which indicate the capacity to acquire such symbols in the future. In most cultures, women rarely have the luxury of being able to wait for a man to achieve all that he sets out to do before pairing up with him; as a result they have to calibrate his desirability partly on unrealised potential.

To find out what these characteristics of future success might be, and to see how they correlated with female desire, psychologist Michael Wiederman examined more than a thousand personal ads placed in various American periodicals between January and June 1992. He speculated that, in an arena where men and women were paying to attract potential mates, they would be more than usually forthright in specifying the attributes they sought, and more than usually direct in how they expressed their priorities.

Taking the various descriptions of what people wanted, and arranging them into categories, Wiederman noticed that terms denoting high status and plentiful resources (terms such as 'business owner', 'enjoys the finer things', 'successful', 'wealthy', 'well-to-do', and 'financially affluent') cropped up ten times as often in the women's wish lists as in the men's.

But there was also a considerable female preference for terms like 'ambitious', 'industrious', 'career-oriented', and 'college-educated'; in other words, for terms which clearly indicated the potential to acquire status and amass resources in the future…

Douglas Kenrick, in his study of how intelligent, attractive and so on men and women had to be before they were considered sexually attractive by the opposite sex, found that earning capacity was much more important to women than to men; and David Buss, in a massive study of mating habits which covered 10,000 people in 37 cultures around the world, found that women rated financial resources on average at least twice as highly as men did.

Some researchers argue that an evolutionary explanation is not justified here. Women only desire wealthy men, they say, because most cultures don't allow women to make much money for themselves. But the female preference for wealth seems to exist regardless of the financial status of the women in question.

There is an unprecedented number of independent, self-supporting women with resources of their own in the world today, yet their mate preferences still seem to be following the age-old, evolved pattern of looking for men who can offer more.

One study of American newly-wed couples in 1993 found that financially successful brides placed an even greater importance on their husbands' earning capacities than those who were less well-off. And another, conducted among female college students, reported that those who were likely to earn more in respected professions placed greater importance on the financial prospects of their potential husbands than those who were likely to earn less. Buss's fellow psychologist Bruce Ellis summed up the prospect for future mate choice by saying, 'Women's sexual tastes become more, rather than less, discriminatory as their wealth, power, and social status increase.'

So there you have it. Even in an era of equal opportunities in the world of work women remain keen that in their relationships with men resources flow in one direction only: *to* them *from* men. Where's the fairness or equality in that? Women seek fairness and equality only when they believe they'll be advantaged by it, *never* when they'll be disadvantaged by it. Which begs the obvious question: why aren't men revolting? Some answers to that question are to be found in chapter 21.

Why are women bothered whether or not there is gender balance in the boardroom? In my view it's the same childish impulse to grasp what men have which lies behind women's claims to half their ex-partners' wealth after a marriage fails: regardless of the woman's contribution to the couple's wealth, the duration of the marriage, or the reason for the marriage failure. And if that's equality, I'm a *crème brûlée*.

Let's consider the issue of female attractiveness in the workplace. While women commonly decry societal pressures to be attractive – although many are evidently immune to the pressures – attractive women themselves don't hesitate to exploit their attractiveness for all it's worth in both their working and personal lives. You have to assume they've figured out that doing that is a great deal easier than working hard to get ahead in the world.

In a career of over 30 years' duration I was fortunate enough to know a number of women who, when younger, progressed further and faster with the help of their looks. Good looks were an advantage for them on at least two grounds. All else being equal, senior executives would promote an attractive women rather than an unattractive one – just as they might reasonably promote a cheerful colleague rather than a miserable one – and clients preferred to deal with, and be entertained by, attractive women. Of course over time these women's attractiveness faded, so I was to enjoy the irony of hearing them later in their careers bemoaning the promotions of younger, more attractive women than themselves.

We end this chapter with something which interests few men but which has been described as most women's favourite hobby: shopping. Women's fondness for shopping is an indicator of at least two ways in which their natures differ from men's. On the one hand it indicates women's preference for spending money over earning it in the first place, which is also evident in their propensity to eschew paid employment or to work only part-time. On the other hand it reveals women's herd instinct, which is nowhere as clearly displayed as in their pursuit of branded clothing, shoes, handbags etc.

At the time of writing – July 2011 – Prince William and his toothsome bride (formerly Kate Middleton) are undertaking a Royal tour of Canada. The tabloid press routinely name the retail outlets from which her clothes are bought, and a television 'fashion commentator' – can there really *be* such a vacuous job? – informs us breathlessly that retailers sell out of stock of the items in question within hours of their provenance being revealed. The retailers favoured by Prince William are never mentioned, and for good reason; who on earth would be interested?

CHAPTER 3

ASTROLOGY, GUARDIAN ANGELS, CRYSTAL HEALING, UNDERPANTS AND STUFF

A good psychic would pick up the phone before it rang. My psychic once said to me, 'God Bless you.' I said, 'I didn't sneeze.' She looked deep into my eyes and said, 'You will, eventually.' And damn it if she wasn't right. Two days later I sneezed.
Ellen DeGeneres 1958- American stand-up comedienne, television hostess and actress

More women than men believe in phenomena with no evidence base – angels – the author's memorable night with Keira Knightley and Cameron Diaz – crystal healing – underpants and stuff – the deceit in *Psychologies* – the ridiculous advert in *The Daily Telegraph* – the dreaded 's' word: 'should'

There are a number of subjects about which men and women typically hold different beliefs. One is astrology. I know a number of otherwise intelligent women who are convinced that the stars, planets, and other heavenly bodies impact on people's personalities and lives in a host of ways. Any man holding such beliefs would be considered simple-minded by other men: the very men who would *not* consider women simple-minded for holding the same beliefs. Why would they judge women by a different standard? Isn't that sexist? Does sexism become acceptable when it *favours* women?

Women are far more likely than men to believe in phenomena for which no good evidence exists, whether it's astrology, witchcraft, crystal healing or guardian angels, to pick but a few examples.

We might reasonably be puzzled by the existence of male astrologers, but the fact that some of them make a handsome living from the mumbo-jumbo should tell us something. I found myself seated next to a male writer on astrological matters at a dinner party recently. About half of the guests were women, and when I challenged him on the evidence base for astrology he was adamant that it was sound. The male guests snorted with derision at the claim, while the female guests appeared pleased.

A good deal of good claret was drunk that night. As the astrologer was leaving we had a few moments together and I asked him again whether he believed in the evidence base for astrology. He laughed and replied quietly, 'No, of course not! It's all bullshit. But women lap it up, and I'm not about to reveal that and put my only source of income at risk, am I?' He then said the most apt book title on the subject was *The Complete Idiot's Guide to Astrology*.

The phenomenon of women saying, 'I think this is true, so it is!' has a long history. Education in the modern era seems to have had little effect on it. To find out what at least some women today believe and read about, I went along to my local Waterstone's bookstore, and to a section I'd never visited before, 'Mind, Body and Spirit'.

The first book I looked through was *Angel Kids (Enchanting stories of true-life guardian angels and 'sixth-sense' abilities in children)* by Jacky Newcomb, 'The Angel Lady'. The back cover describes her as 'one of the UK's leading angel experts'. You couldn't make it up. Text on the back cover of the book invites potential buyers to read about:

- grandparents who visit their grandkids – from the other side!

- the mother who lost her son who was later re-born as her grandson
- the thousands of brilliant and insightful children whom the authorities label as 'learning disabled'

I couldn't see why any intelligent person would want to even *open* the book, let alone buy it or read it. I had an exchange of emails with Ms Newcomb and I'm not proud to say I lost my cool with her. Her position was illustrated by her view that if someone dreamed that his or her dead children or grandchildren visited them, then it was likely *they really did.* Applying the same standard of evidential support, I really do enjoy physical relations with Keira Knightley and Cameron Diaz one or two nights a month. On one memorable night, both of them simultaneously.

The second book was *The Crystal Bible: A Definitive Guide to Crystals*, by Judy Hall. I opened a page at random: page 126, emerald:

ATTRIBUTES: Emerald is a stone of inspiration and infinite patience. It is a life-affirming stone with great integrity. Known as 'the stone of successful love', it brings domestic bliss and loyalty. It enhances unity, unconditional love and partnership, and promotes friendship. Emerald keeps a partnership in balance. If it changes colour, it is said to signal unfaithfulness. Emerald opens the heart chakra and has a calming effect on the emotions.

This stone ensures physical, emotional and mental equilibrium. It eliminates negativity and brings in positive actions. Focusing intention and raising consciousness, it brings about positive action. It enhances psychic abilities, opens clairvoyance, and stimulates gathering wisdom from the mental planes. Traditionally, emerald was said to protect from enchantment and the ploys of magicians, and to foretell the future.

Psychologically, emerald gives the strength of character to overcome the misfortunes of life. It is a stone of regeneration and recovery and can heal negative emotions. It enhances the ability to enjoy life to the fullest. It is helpful in cases of claustrophobia.

Emerald imparts mental clarity, strengthens memory, inspires a deep inner knowing, and broadens vision. It is a wisdom stone, promoting discernment and truth, and aiding eloquent expression. It helps bring to the surface what is unconsciously known. Emerald is extremely beneficial to mutual understanding within a group of people, stimulating cooperation.

HEALING: Emerald aids recovery after infectious illness. It treats sinuses, lungs, spine and muscles, and soothes the eyes. It improves vision and has a detoxifying effect on the liver. Emerald alleviates rheumatism and diabetes. [Author's note: I'm a short-sighted diabetic prone to respiratory infections, and fond of wine and beer. This is clearly the crystal for me.] It has been used as an antidote to poisons. [Author's note: successfully?] Worn around the neck, emerald was believed to ward off epilepsy. Its green ray can assist healing of malignant conditions.

POSITION: Wear on the little finger, ring finger, over the heart, or on the right arm. Position as appropriate for healing. Do not wear constantly as it can trigger negative emotions. Opaque emeralds are not suitable for mental attunement.

All this from a stone. Marvellous. Emeralds really should be a lot more expensive. Two more gems – in both senses of the word – from the book, chosen from opposite ends of the alphabet:

AMETHYST: An extremely powerful and protective stone with a high spiritual vibration. It guards against psychic attack, transmuting the energy into love. A natural tranquiliser, amethyst blocks geopathic stress and negative environment energies. . . It heals diseases of the lungs and respiratory tract, skin conditions, cellular disorders, and diseases of the digestive tract. It is beneficial for the intestines, regulating flora, removing parasites. . .

ZEOLITE: Can be used to treat goiters, to dispel bloating, and to release toxins from the physical body. It has a supportive effect in overcoming addictions, especially to alcohol, and can be made into an elixir for this purpose. However, cider vinegar should be used as the preservative rather than brandy or vodka.

What evidence do I have that such books have a mainly female readership? Of 41 reviews on Amazon, 18 were from individuals whose names clearly indicated the reviewer's gender. Of these 18, 15 (83.3%) were women. But I particularly enjoyed the contribution from one of the male reviewers, Simon Walker of London, who gave the book the lowest possible rating along with the following review:

> Whoever wrote this is very clever to have written a best-selling book consisting of facts made up entirely on the spur of the moment. For the same reason, please check out 'The angel bible', 'The homeopathy bible', 'The pixies-at-the-bottom-of-my-garden bible' and the book I'm currently considering writing, 'The underpants bible', about the healing power of underpants. It's all to do with quantum vibrations. And energy and stuff.

In the UK the monthly magazine *Psychologies* is clearly aimed at a female readership; in my local store it's to be found only in the 'women's interests' section. In the summer of 2010 an edition covered the topic of astrology. The online editorial reported something alone the lines of, 'Of course we don't believe in astrology, but...' Now that's simply untrue: many women believe in astrology. Brighter women tend to say they don't believe in the daily predictions in newspapers, but they still believe in the ones specially prepared by astrologers, which – of course – they pay for. I emailed the editrix of *Psychologies* pointing out that many women believe in astrology, as she must surely have been aware, and to suggest otherwise was doing a disservice to her readers. She didn't reply.

In 2009 my daily newspaper, *The Daily Telegraph*, an unbiased deliverer of truth to the British man of a sensible right-of-centre political leaning, had an advert for phone-in psychic services. The advert sported the paper's logo and said the paper had 'vetted' the psychics to ensure they were genuine. Genuine psychics. I wrote to the editor complaining about the advert, but *he* didn't reply either. A pattern was starting to emerge.

I end with a reflection on women's use of the dreaded 's' word: 'should'. Women often use the word in a way that men rarely do. They use it in a lazy way to claim the moral high ground for their positions, regardless of perfectly reasonable counter-arguments which are being presented. A year or two ago I had a conversation with my lodger of the female persuasion, following a media report about one of the poorest countries in the world where children had been found by an undercover reporter to be manufacturing clothes for a major British retailer. She kicked off the conversation.

'I think it's appalling. It *shouldn't* be allowed.'
'But these children come from very poor families, and if they weren't working to help support their families, they wouldn't otherwise be in school.'
'Well, they *should* be in school.'
'But they live in one of the poorest countries in the world, which can't afford universal education.'
'Well, they *should* afford it.'
'Maybe if taxes were raised in this country, the money raised could go to setting up schools for these kids?'
'Good idea!'
'So, how much extra tax would *you* be willing to pay?'
'*Me?* You must be joking. I pay too much tax as it is. *You* should pay more.'

CHAPTER 4

WHAT MAKES WOMEN HAPPY?

The brutal answer to what makes women happy is 'Nothing, not for more than ten minutes at a time.' But the perfect ten minutes are worth living for, and the almost perfect hours that circle them are worth fighting for, and examining, the better to prolong them.
Fay Weldon 1931– English author and playwright: *What Makes Women Happy* (2006)

Where women find happiness in their paid employment (if at all) – women's perspectives on work/life balance – senior women executives suffering at work – would women be happier as homemakers? – a monologue on a train – clothes, shoes, paint, colours etc. – women's anxiety and entrepreneurialism – Anita Roddick and The Body Shop's gullible customers – how do very attractive women prefer to accumulate wealth: marriage to a rich man, or through work? – Tracey Emin – let's start telling women the truth about the glass ceiling

Fay Weldon, one of my favourite writers, continues the section in *What Makes Women Happy* with the following:

> Ask women what makes them happy and they think for a minute and come up with a tentative list. It tends to run like this, and in this order: sex, food, friends, family, shopping and chocolate.
>
> 'Love' tends not to get a look in. Too unfashionable, or else taken for granted. 'Being in love' sometimes makes an appearance. 'Men' seem to surface as a source of aggravation, and surveys keep throwing up the notion that most women prefer chocolate to sex. But personally I suspect this response is given to entertain the pollsters.

The omission of work from the list of what makes women happy is intriguing, given the amount of time most women in the modern era spend in paid employment. Of course it's possible that – like love? – it doesn't get a look in because it's 'too unfashionable, or else taken for granted'. But I doubt it. In my experience the degree to which women find happiness in their working lives (if they find any) is closely related to one or both of two factors: the extent to which their work is appreciated by people, and the extent to which they are able to socialise at work with colleagues and others such as patients, if they work in the medical profession.

I think it's significant that women are more likely than men to seek an improved 'work/life balance', which for women always means less (paid) work and more life. What better evidence could we seek to indicate that women don't see work as a source of happiness?

When I look back at my career and consider executives who've been overcome by the stresses and strains of their jobs – to the point of becoming depressed, having to take time off work, or abusing substances (notably alcohol) – I would have to say that a higher proportion of the women suffered than the men. Perhaps this is evidence that women are more likely than men to be promoted beyond their capabilities; but it hardly supports the cause of accelerating the progression of women into senior roles. If anything, quite the opposite.

Most of the happy women I have known in my life have been those with happy home lives; few have been senior executives. Of course there isn't necessarily a 'cause and effect' relationship here. A woman who is driven to succeed as a senior executive would probably be bored as a full-time homemaker. But by the same token, should we be pressurising women who *would* be happier as homemakers, to become senior executives?

Women's preferences in the world of work can be revealing. Women in business (even those with no children) are less inclined than men to undertake extensive travelling on their own for business purposes, staying in hotels far from home. To my mind this suggests a social dimension to women which is less commonly found among men.

Of the women I've known well in my life, none have been as confident and anxiety-free as they portray themselves publicly, a phenomenon less often encountered with men; in a sense many women are actresses in their everyday lives. In the world of work (and elsewhere, come to that) anxiety has a number of implications. Anxiety often translates into pessimism and consequently risk aversion. It follows that women should be expected to be less likely than men to become entrepreneurs, and this is what we find.

Women sometimes counter that women *are* as entrepreneurial as men and cite the case of Anita Roddick, the founder of the Body Shop empire, as an example; although she died some years ago. It must have helped her to have had customers who were so gullible as to believe they could change the world for the better through buying peppermint foot cream. Where, we have to ask, are the female entrepreneurs to rival the men who have made their fortunes through innovative product or service offerings which have changed the world around us, such as Bill Gates (Microsoft), Jeff Bezos (Amazon), Larry Page and Sergey Brin (Google), Mark Zuckerberg (Facebook)....?

Highly attractive women, given the opportunity to accumulate wealth and enjoy a high standard of living for themselves and their prospective children either through marrying a rich man or through work, always choose the easier option. Does this explain, at least in part, the drive of less attractive women to succeed in the higher echelons of business?

Women's feelings are more fragile than men's, so they have to be protected more. Women appear less able than men to accept constructive criticism. Both men and women are careful to protect women's feelings by not criticising them, and the result is predictable: the infantilisation of women. One way to discourage criticism is to discourage hierarchy, and this is predictably a central tenet of feminist ideology.

We do not pretend that women are the equals of men in the field of sports, where excellence can be objectively judged. But where judgement is subjective, it's a different matter. You'll rarely see a female art critic heaping adverse criticism on the work of a female artist; and so it is that we are asked to believe that Tracey Emin is a talented artist. If her output had been produced by a man, we'd never have heard of him.

What has this to do with women and the world of work, I hear you cry? It's possible for women to convince themselves that they're qualified for high office even when they're not, and their friends and colleagues will agree that the only reason they don't get promoted is the 'glass ceiling', although this will only leave them frustrated and angry. I propose we start being more honest with these women and telling them the truth, 'There is no glass ceiling. Get over it.'

CHAPTER 5

WHAT ARE WOMEN INTERESTED IN?

Here's how men think. Sex, work – and those are reversible, depending on age – sex, work, food, sports and lastly, begrudgingly, relationships. And here's how women think. Relationships, relationships, relationships, work, sex, shopping, weight, food.
Carrie Fisher 1956- American actress, screenwriter and novelist: *Surrender the Pink* (1990)

Women aren't interested in current affairs – a monologue on a train – clothes, shoes, colours – a study into women's interests – relationships, appearance, celebrities, soap operas – the naming of cars – women's relentless demand for advice – male and female dominance hierarchies – Katie Price – obesity – a female role model in *Mad Men*

Many years ago I remarked to a business colleague that I'd never encountered a woman with a deep interest in 'big picture' issues: politics, business and so on. He echoed my experience, commenting, 'That's why you'll never see a women on the Tube [Author's note: the London Underground train system] reading *The Economist, New Statesman* or *The Spectator.*' Those magazines have long been the leading magazines in the United Kingdom devoted to current affairs. Since that conversation over twenty years ago, whenever I've travelled on the Tube I've glanced to see what women were reading. My colleague's assertion proved to be correct. I've seen the publications being read on countless occasions, but not once by a woman.

On 6 May 2010 there was a general election in the United Kingdom, anticipated to be the most important in a generation. A dire Labour administration had been in power since 1997, and the general election was a rare opportunity to kick it into the long grass. In the end the election results were inconclusive, and a Conservative / Liberal Democrat coalition was forged.

Two days before the election I took a train to London to spend a few hours with one of my daughters, and at the start of the return journey a couple of women sat opposite me. Their ages would be around 50 and 25, I guessed, probably mother and daughter. They appeared to be of Italian extraction, probably headed for my adopted home town of Bedford, a throbbing metropolis with the country's largest population of Italian extraction outside the capital. I'll call the ladies Mrs X and Miss X. Miss X barely stopped talking for the 45 minute duration of the journey, as she flicked through a clothes catalogue. Here's a flavour of her monologue:

> 'Mmm, I'm not sure that this oyster blouse goes well with that sky blue skirt. Now if the handbag didn't have those silvery lines it would be a better match with those shoes, and I don't think the scarf…'

Forgive me if I don't relate more of what she had to say, the memory is too painful. The inane wittering continued without a break for the full 45 minutes of the journey, and as a consequence I now know more terms for 'off-white' than any heterosexual man should ever know. The point is, the young woman's brain was utterly consumed by colours and fashion. I doubt she even knew a general election was imminent.

I blame the man who invented magnolia paint. For many years paint for the interior and exterior of houses was white, then some plonker invented magnolia paint and women's brains turned to mush as a result. You can't go into the paint section of a DIY store these days without seeing a hundred variants of off-white paint on sale. Women will happily spend an hour reviewing the options before finally settling on one almost identical to magnolia. Unbelievable. In the meantime their partners, wearing haunted expressions, rest against nearby walls.

But women's interest in colours isn't limited to clothes, shoes and paints. Oh no. If you watch women looking at colour cosmetics in a store, you'll see the same rapt attention. They're in another world.

What else are women interested in? I figured that an obvious way to answer the question would be to analyse the content of 'women's interest' magazines. And so it was that I went to a supermarket in December 2009 to carry out the field research. Not without some embarrassment, due to the quizzical expressions on the faces of ladies passing by, I noted down the magazine titles and lead article titles of all 74 magazines in the 'women's interest' and 'women's lifestyle' sections. There were twelve such racks, contrasting with one rack for 'men's interest' magazines. The following table shows the results of the study.

Table 2.1: Articles in women's interest magazines

Title	Leading article title	Topics
99p	Peter Andre – I want a new girlfriend for Xmas!	Celebrities, relationships
All About Soap	Stacy and Bradley: the wedding tragedy!	Celebrities, relationships
BBC Good Food	Everyday family food – quick suppers, leftovers, side dishes	Food
Bella	The claws are out for Colleen! Jealousy behind her new show	Celebrities, relationships
Brides	Shop smart – 563 of the newest looks!	Appearance
Best	Colleen's Xmas Heartache!	Celebrities, relationships
Chat	'Please Mummy, can I ring Daddy in heaven?'	Relationships, mumbo-jumbo
Closer	The Osbornes' cracking Christmas! 'We'll hang stockings for our dogs!'	Celebrities, pets
Company	264 sexy shopping ideas!	Appearance
Cosmopolitan	Lose weight while you eat – yes, you can!	Appearance
Cross-Stitcher	[Author's note: there were so many riveting article titles, it seemed unfair to choose just one.]	Crafts, appearance
Diet and Fitness	Lose half a stone in just two weeks!	Appearance

Table 2.1: Articles in women's interest magazines (cont'd)

Title	Leading article title	Topics
Diva	Penelope Cruz – 'I knew my lesbian kiss would get a big reaction!'	Celebrities, sex
Elle	When he *doesn't* love your curves – an honest bedtime story	Appearance
Essentials	15 new beauty fixes – younger skin, easy make-up and thicker hair can be yours	Appearance
Full House!	Now our Kelsey's dancing in heaven!	Relationships, mumbo-jumbo
Glamour	No money? No problem! 482 chic looks	Appearance
Good Housekeeping	30, 40, 50, 60+? Feelgood tips to turn back the clock	Appearance
Grazia	Your horoscope for the next 10 years	Mumbo-jumbo
Hair	834 New Year style ideas!	Appearance
Hair Ideas	786 wedding ideas – real results! Exercises for brides-to-be	Appearance, relationships
Hair Now	Frizz fighting special!	Appearance
Hair Styles Only	709 new season's solutions!	Appearance
Health & Fitness	Burn fat, fast – easy moves to blitz calories	Appearance

Table 2.1: Articles in women's interest magazines (cont'd)

Title	Leading article title	Topics
Herts. and Beds. – Your Wedding	Magical locations – perfect venues for a winter wonderland	Relationships
I'm Pregnant!	How will a baby change your relationship?	Relationships
In Style	265 glam pieces + the new layering rules	Appearance
It's Fate (The Most Expert Psychic Advice and True-Life Stories)	Only a miracle could save me from the firing squad!	Mumbo-jumbo
Let's Knit!	19 stunning patterns for the New Year	Crafts, appearance
Let's Make Cards!	They'll be flocking to admire your creations! [Author's note: not all of them, possibly.]	Crafts
Love It! Real Life and Celebs	Sarah Harding – 'Cheryl thinks I'm a nutter!'	Celebrities, relationships
The IT Dresses – so-this-season rags	Boots we love!	Appearance
Marie Claire	Cameron Diaz – hot, smart, single, having it all her own way	Celebrities, appearance, relationships

Table 2.1: Articles in women's interest magazines (cont'd)

Title	Leading article title	Topics
My Weekly	Lulu's beauty secrets!	Celebrities, appearance
Natural Health	More energy plus less stress – your holistic guide to better health this year	Health
New!	Mums at Christmas! Exclusive interviews and pictures	Relationships
Now!	Posh and Becks's Christmas of War!	Celebrities, relationships
OK	Our first Xmas at home alone – Peter Andre	Celebrities, relationships
Pick Me Up!	I castrated my rapist Dad!	Relationships
Pregnancy & Birth	Look and feel fantastic – boost your bump confidence today!	Health, confidence, appearance
Prima	Kick-start your confidence!	Confidence
Psychologies	Relationships – 2 years or 20? How to grow closer over time	Relationships
Real People	Baby Jess miracle at 23 weeks	Relationships
Red	Too busy to lose weight? Your bespoke eating plan starts here	Appearance
Reveal	'Our brave little boy is home for Xmas!'	Relationships
Scarlet	Red-hot sex resolutions – your orgasmic 2010!	Sex

Table 2.1: Articles in women's interest magazines (cont'd)

Title	Leading article title	Topics
She	New Year, new you – boost your confidence, lose weight, gain energy	Confidence, appearance
Simply Knitting	Essential reading for every knitter	Crafts
Slim at Home	Two week party plan – drop a dress size!	Appearance
Slimming World	Real-life cover star Joanne – 'I lost two stones in three months!'	Appearance
Soul & Spirit (your spiritual life coach)	11-page special on Lunar Love – harness the moon to find your soul-mate!	Mumbo-jumbo
Take a Break	A headless body . . . a missing Aunt!	Crime, relationships
Tatler	Is it rude to vote Labour? . . . and other social dilemmas resolved.	Politics
That's Life!	Want to diet? Why you shouldn't	Appearance
Top Santé	Glowing skin <u>now</u>! Five-step make-up masterclass	Appearance
TV Choice	Hello Mum! Ronnie and Roxy are stunned by the arrival of their mother	Celebrities, relationships
TV Easy	Shock arrest! Archie's killer revealed!	Crime, relationships

Table 2.1: Articles in women's interest magazines (cont'd)

Title	Leading article title	Topics
TV Guide	So you think you can dance? Cat, Nigel and Arlene bring the US hit to British screens	Celebrities
Ultra Fit	Fight fat fast!	Appearance
Vogue	How to wear lace now	Appearance
Wedding Flowers	398 elegant looks – how to get perfect big day blooms	Appearance
Weight Watchers Magazine	Lose weight – and keep it off!	Appearance
What's on TV?	Killer! Sam's arrested for murder!	Crime, relationships
Woman	A Mum's goodbye – 'letters of love for my kids'	Relationships
Woman & Home	Lulu – 'Love, men, special friends . . . my new life.'	Celebrities, relationships
Woman's Own	Fern exclusive – my life-changing decision	Celebrities
Women's Fitness	Fighting fit – tone-up boxing	Appearance
Women's Health	Burn more fat! Boost your metabolism to drop a dress size fast!	Appearance
You & Your Wedding	Real brides – 359 inspired ideas for weddings and honeymoons	Appearance
Your Hair	876 stunning cuts for 2010!	Appearance

Table 2.1: Articles in women's interest magazines (cont'd)

Title	Leading article title	Topics
Yours	Fern – 'My faith gets me through'	Celebrities, religion
Zest	Skin that glows – see results in 7 days!	Appearance

Back at my office I calculated the frequency of the 12 topics of the articles. The following numbers add up to more than 74 because numerous articles covered more than one topic.

Appearance	35
Relationships	25
Celebrities	16
Mumbo-jumbo	5
Crafts	4
Crime	3
Sex	2
Confidence	2
Pets	1
Food (exc diet)	1
Religion	1
Politics	1
TOTAL	96

The only article on a political topic was in *Tatler*, and even that concerned social issues rather than politics, 'Is it rude to vote Labour?... and other social dilemmas resolved.' There wasn't a single article about business, or people in business.

Now I would contend that apart from the 'relationships' topic itself, a number of the other topics are also clearly reflected an interest in relationships, for example the interest in appearance, celebrities, sex and confidence. These 'related topics' come up 55 times. Added to the 25 mentions of 'relationships' we come to a total of 80 mentions out of a total of 96. So 83% of the article topics that interested women, in the publications they choose to buy, were relationship-related. *Why* are women obsessed with relationships? Possibly because it's often women's personal relationships – rather then the work they personally undertake – which dictate their standards of living as well as their level of happiness in life?

A number of the articles concerned storylines in television soap operas. And what are soap operas if not explorations of moral dilemmas, love, hatred, jealousy, betrayal, and all the other countless dimensions of relationships? Soap operas are watched by women, not men.

Women even manage to have emotional relationships with inanimate objects. One of my daughters, a psychologist now in her mid-twenties, is not exempt from this phenomenon. She drove a Ford Fiesta during her university course and nicknamed her car 'Raef' on account of the car's number plate ending with the letters 'RFE'. She told me it was customary for her friends of the female persuasion to name their cars, while her friends of the male persuasion didn't.

Further reflections on the articles:

- How can articles on dieting still have commercial value? What substantial new insights have there been in the past 100 years about losing weight? None.
- Which advertising genius first discovered that exclamation marks lower women's IQs and persuade them to buy their particular titles?
- What is behind women's fascination with celebrities in general and celebrity couples in particular? Possibly the heady combination of a man at the top of the male

hierarchy due to his fame and/or wealth, and a woman at the top of the female hierarchy due to her fame and/or beauty?
- Why do women need so much advice? And why do they need essentially the same advice time after time? The content of women's magazines was similar *decades* ago

Women's relationship with shoes has long fascinated me. Every season there appears a range of new styles which soon become 'must have' styles for women. Women shopping for shoes exhibit the same utter absorption that they do for colour-related matters.

Let's be honest, shall we? Women are utterly absorbed by their relationships with family, friends, and work colleagues. They are far less likely than men to be interested in the worlds of politics and business, although that doesn't stop them seeking equality in those fields.

Individual women rarely make the effort or accept the sacrifices necessary to achieve success in those fields: they expect *other* women to do so and thereby deliver equality. So it falls to a miniscule number of women to fight a large number of men for the top positions in politics and business: how could that *ever* result in gender balance?

We come to the thorny topic of physical attractiveness. British author Steve Moxon, in his book *The Woman Racket* (2008), describes the male dominance hierarchy ('DH'). In the pre-industrial world a man's position in the DH was largely dictated by physical prowess or access to men and arms, while in the developed world it is largely dictated by actual or potential financial resources. Women seek partners as high up the hierarchy as they can manage, and have their own dominance hierarchy, as Moxon explains:

So how does a female DH form if it does not involve physical contest? Mostly it's simply by inheritance – including in primates and human societies. The physical attributes of females that are attractive to males in signalling fertility of youth and beauty are predominantly genetically based, so are well conserved from one generation to the next. Attractive women will tend to have attractive daughters. The key attribute of youth is an even more pronounced 'given', in that older age cohorts are simply not 'in the game'.

In traditional societies a woman's position in the DH is largely a product of nature, as youth and beauty are the main factors. However the existence in modern societies of multi-billion dollar cosmetics, fashion and plastic surgery industries shows that beauty can be enhanced and the ravages of age can at least be postponed. The rocketing sales of celebrity and beauty magazines show that women are indeed keen to rank themselves according to a uniquely female DH; but the great difficulty involved in attempting to overcome the limitations of nature has manifested itself in the form of modern female epidemics such as anorexia nervosa and bulimia, slimming disorders being rare in males.

Perhaps the sheer difficulty of the task of climbing the female DH (males simply have to work harder or take extra risks) explains the fascination of Victoria Beckham to a female audience – her strange elfish features and cyborg-style cartoon body are more frequently found on the front covers of women's magazines than anyone else. If such an odd-looking creature is attractive to an uber-alpha male like her husband David, then women are understandably eager to re-assess their *own* DH ranking in the light of this.

Females also tend to compete by doing down other females in terms of sexual propriety – hence the common playground 'ho' and 'slag' derogations. This alerts men to a woman's propensity to indulge in extra-pair sex, and consequently might well put them off considering her as a long-term partner.

In the summer of 2009 I walked into a branch of WH Smith, a national retailer selling newspapers, books, and more besides. Something unusual was evidently about to happen: the store was full of girls and young women between the ages of 12 and

18, clearly excited to be there. The reason for the excitement turned out to be the imminent appearance of Katie Price for a signing of her third autobiography *Pushed to the Limit*. Ms Price was known as 'Jordan' during her early career as a glamour – i.e. topless – model, during which time her breasts publicly changed size a number of times with different breast implants.

During the 2001 British general election Jordan ran as a candidate in Stretford and Urmston under her real name, using the slogan 'For a Bigga and Betta Future'. As part of her comical election campaign she promised free breast implants, more nudist beaches, and a ban on parking tickets. In the end, Jordan won 713 votes, 1.8% of the votes cast.

Her personal relationships, and especially her relationship with the singer Peter Andre – who she later married – attracted extensive tabloid and celebrity magazine attention, as well as television series coverage. Her personal fortune is estimated at about £40 million. So this was the woman all the young women in the store were excited about. If the President of the Women's Engineering Society – celebrating its 90th anniversary in 2009, as you know – had been launching *her* autobiography, would the young ladies have been quite so excited?

Let's move on to a topic of relentless fascination for women: obesity. How might we explain the increase in obesity of women in the modern era? The increase has also happened with men but it simply doesn't seem to bother them to the same degree. A glance at women's magazines reveals women's obsessions with attractiveness in general and weight in particular. I don't believe that women become obsessed about these issues because of what they read, or see on television and in films. Those media are simply making money from women's pre-existing obsessions.

Has anything genuinely new been said about dieting in the past century? 'Eat a balanced diet, consume fewer calories than you expend, take some exercise. You may experience a little discomfort at times but you'll lose weight as surely as night follows day.' Let me know if there's anything more to it than is contained in those 33 words. Women don't want to face up to the reality, so they are perennial targets for dieting advice.

With the demise of the New Labour administration in May 2010 I hoped we had seen the end of Harriet Harman style pronouncements on women in the public eye: actresses, newscasters, models, and so on. Not a bit of it. From *The Daily Telegraph* of 26 July 2010, an article titled, 'We should be more like the sexiest woman alive, says minister':

> As an aspiring actress, Christina Hendricks was constantly advised to lose weight. The size-14 redhead was often told: 'We think you're an amazing actress, but you're a little too heavy for the role.' But she refused to slim down and consequently became a star of *Mad Men*, one of the most successful dramas of recent years.
>
> Now Hendricks, commonly described as 'voluptuous' in her role as the feisty secretary Joan Harris, has been hailed as an 'absolutely fabulous' physical role model for girls by Lynne Featherstone, the Equalities Minister...
>
> In May, Hendricks was voted the 'Sexiest Woman Alive' by female readers of *Esquire* magazine, eclipsing her fellow actress Megan Fox and Michelle Obama. The Liberal Democrat minister cited Hendricks as she criticised the 'overexposure' of skinny models, which she said was causing a crisis in 'body confidence' among the young. The use of models, as well as the routine use of airbrushing, meant that girls and women came under 'dreadful pressure... to conform to completely unachievable body stereotypes', she said.
>
> Mrs Featherstone said, 'Christina Hendricks is absolutely fabulous. We need more of these role models. There is such a sensation when there is a curvy role model. It shouldn't be so unusual.'

Hendricks appeared to relish the attention that her 36C breasts had generated. Asked how she felt about them, she responded, 'They are fabulous.' She also gave advice to men in the magazine on how to get women in bed. They should engage in conduct that many feminists would see as outdated, the actress said. 'Stand up, open a door, offer a jacket,' she advised. 'It makes us feel important.'

Mrs Featherstone plans to meet representatives of the fashion industry later this year and will propose that digitally enhanced images carry a warning so readers know they were altered.

Yes, Mrs Featherstone, the fashion industry will agree to do that. Give me strength. Are women really so feeble-minded as to need such interventions? The story attracted the following riposte from one of the paper's journalists, Melissa Kite:

> Someone needs to tell poor Lynne Featherstone that the world has changed. The equalities minister has just announced that she intends to hold a 'body confidence summit' to tackle the problem, as she sees it, of undersized fashion models.
>
> Ms Featherstone, a Liberal Democrat member of the Coalition who was this year voted Parliament's most attractive MP, is clearly still living in the New Labour era of pointless initiatives and, dare we say, window dressing. She also seems blithely unaware that the nanny state is on its last legs.
>
> I have a mental picture of her sitting in the Equalities Department near Buckingham Palace with her fingers in her ears muttering 'not listening, not listening' as all around her ministers slash and burn and rip up politically correct red tape. Indeed, it is testament to how much David Cameron has managed to change about Britain since May, that Ms Featherstone's proposal already looks so ridiculous.
>
> In a few months we've been spoilt with a raft of initiatives sweeping away the interfering, opinionated state, and, guess what, we like it. 'Speed cameras to be axed' was the latest dream headline at the weekend. So when the pouty Ms Featherstone declares war on skinny models and says she will call in magazine editors and fashion industry executives to address the effects of airbrushed images of physical perfection

on impressionable youngsters, I find myself saying, 'Ah, bless!'...

I'm wondering whether Ms Featherstone isn't having a spot of bother with the issue herself. I'm not so sure she doesn't stare agonisingly at herself in the mirror in the mornings trying to ape inappropriate role models and saying, 'If I squint, I do look a bit like Harriet Harman.'

CHAPTER 6

WOMEN AND LEADERSHIP

I wanna be the leader
I wanna be the leader
Can I be the leader?
Can I? Can I?
Promise? Promise?
Yippee, I'm the leader
I'm the leader
OK, what shall we do now?
Roger McGough 1937- English poet: 'The Leader'

Very few men have the qualities required for high office, but they outnumber the women who do – intellectual confidence – the estimable Margaret Thatcher – women's consensual management style – why do women require role models? – men networking on the golf course – the estimable Christina Hoff Sommers

In debates concerning the genders in the upper reaches of organisations, an obvious point tends to be missed. The qualities that make an individual suitable for high office – a directorship of a FTSE100 company, for example – are very rare even among men; those men just happen to markedly outnumber women with the qualities.

Very few people will ever have met a FTSE100 director, so they can reasonably be excused for having no idea as to what the desirable qualities for such positions are. In countries with a vaguely anti-business culture among the general population, such as the United Kingdom, people tend to under-estimate what those qualities are, which may help explain their anger at the remuneration of top executives while they don't have an issue with the often much higher incomes of celebrities and sports professionals.

One of the characteristics expected of candidates for senior appointments in business and elsewhere – in short, leaders – is a certain intellectual confidence. When faced with a challenging problem or opportunity, the person is able speedily to make up his or her mind about the matter and propose a way forward, and the person should also have a good track record of making the right 'calls'. This is very different to merely being opinionated, and such intellectual confidence is in short supply. The people who have it can expect to be well rewarded in the business world.

Women seldom have confidence of this type; when faced with a challenging problem they are typically anxious about making a mistake, and seek advice from a number of quarters. This takes time, and by the time they've made up their minds it may be too late; for example a business opportunity may have evaporated as others (generally men) have taken a risk and seized the opportunity.

Perhaps the most famous British woman in the modern era who *did* have such confidence was Margaret Thatcher, the Prime Minister of the United Kingdom over 1979-90, a woman widely regarded as Britain's finest peacetime Prime Minister of the 20th century. She's a heroine to many British people with right-of-centre convictions such as myself, and loathed by many British people with left-of-centre convictions.

Feminists are fond of arguing that women typically have a different management style to men, and are more 'consensual'. The truth, as usual, is more nuanced. Women are generally more anxious than men, and more inclined to follow than lead; which isn't exactly a desirable trait in potential leaders, is it?

Women frequently exhibit a curious (to male eyes) herd instinct. Outside the workplace this shows itself in a number of ways, including women's interest in following fashion. Inside the workplace one obvious manifestation is women's preference for appointing women rather than men, given a choice, a matter which is explored in a later chapter.

But there are other manifestations. One is the feminists' perennial assertion that women require more role models in order to be inspired to seek the highest corporate positions. This is, of course, a circular argument. We have to ask about the women who would be the role models – who will be *their* role models?

Furthermore, you have to wonder whether a woman who requires role models to inspire her is a follower or a leader. A sheep or a shepherdess? Do we simply have a lot of sheep thinking that if they and the other sheep bleat loudly enough for long enough, the farmer might appoint them as the new shepherdess?

The central problem of women's herd instinct is an obvious one. People are appointed to senior positions on the basis of their actual individual merits, not on the supposed merits of the group(s) to which they happen to belong.

Are many women following a herd instinct when they decide to undertake paid employment when they might otherwise choose to be homemakers, and possibly be happier in the latter roles? One leading businesswoman told me that if she had her time again she would have resisted the pressure of her feminist acquaintances and been a full-time homemaker, saying, 'At one time many women were bullied by men. Now they're more likely to be bullied by women. That doesn't look much like progress to me.'

Among the many myths women have about men in business is that men network effectively and 'bond' through activities such as playing golf together, and these activities play a significant role in men's decisions about corporate appointments.

Little could be further from the truth, and it shouldn't take a genius to work out why. If the assertion were true there would be a correlation between the effort men put into such activities, and their success in climbing the corporate ladder. In 33 years in corporate life I never saw any correlation. Many of the most ardent golf enthusiasts stayed in the lower echelons of corporations, where they rightly belonged. While many executives, who would have preferred to accompany their wives on shoe buying expeditions than play a round of golf, reached the boardrooms where *they* rightly belonged.

So why are some women convinced of the power of such networking? I think it's something to do with their paranoia, 'I don't play golf with the other executives, and my career isn't going as well as I think it should, so there must be a connection.'

One unfortunate result of women's herd instinct is that it makes women reluctant to denounce forcefully the militant feminists who claim to both represent and lead them. There are exceptions, such as the American writer Christina Hoff Sommers; but they are few and far between, and they appear so far to have had little impact on the tide of militant feminism which is threatening to engulf us. We can only hope that the tide will turn, for the sake of women and men alike.

CHAPTER 7

ARE WOMEN MORE EMOTIONAL AND LESS RATIONAL THAN MEN?

I mean, damn it all, one minute you're having a perfectly good time and the next, you suddenly see them there like – some old sports jacket or something – literally beginning to come apart at the seams.
  of women
Alan Ayckbourn 1939- English dramatist: *Absurd Person Singular* (1971)

Women *are* more emotional and less rational than men – why emotionality can be a problem in the workplace – emotional intelligence and workplace efficiency and effectiveness – being liked is more important to women than being respected – the futility of sending women on assertiveness courses – predominantly female workplaces are 'bitchy'

Gender-typical women are more emotional and less rational than gender-typical men due (in my view) to the gender-pattern brain issue we covered in an earlier chapter. But it would be churlish not to recognise that some people object in principle to the notion of gender-pattern brains. I find that women and those with left-of-centre political persuasions are more likely to object to the notion, when compared with men and those with right-of-centre political persuasions. We can predict without too much difficulty, then, what Harriet Harman's views on the subject would be.

So let's set aside the idea of gender-pattern brains for the moment. What is our general experience of men and women in our lives? Unless you live on a different planet to the one I live on, you will surely agree that women tend to be more emotional and less rational than men. Or you would if you were rational, anyway.

Ironically, women tend to become emotional whenever the subject of women's greater emotionality is raised in the context of the genders in the world of work, or indeed elsewhere. Why is this? Maybe they suspect the issue is one men will use to justify discrimination against women in the workplace. I would have some sympathy with that argument, if it were true. And yet I've never heard a businessman express a view on the matter; women's emotionality is something that they accept and make allowances for as and when necessary.

Perhaps something else is going on. By objecting to the issue of emotionality being raised, women are unwittingly conceding that emotionality *is* a problem in the workplace, or at least *can* be.

Having a ready answer to every possible criticism, feminists have one for the issue of female emotionality. They maintain that women are more emotionally intelligent than men – with which I agree, although I know some women with the emotional intelligence of a peanut – and that this is an asset in the workplace, with which I *cannot* agree. Emotional intelligence might make for a more harmonious working environment, but it won't necessarily make for a more efficient or effective one. If it did, women would have progressed far faster and further into the upper echelons of business than they have.

The truth is that women's emotional natures can impair their performances at work in numerous ways, but men don't appear to notice it, nor do they discriminate against women on account of it. Women struggle to work productively with colleagues they don't like, while most men have no problem doing so. To men, the idea that liking colleagues has much to do with working effectively with them, or not doing so, is an alien concept.

Because being liked is more important to women than being respected, they are often disinclined to discipline staff who are under-performing, or even to fire them if necessary. This can have a negative impact on the morale of other staff and group effectiveness. I've lost count of the number of times a female executive has maintained that all an under-performing staff member needs is further training. The classic is sending women on assertiveness courses. The women who need such courses are self-evidently in jobs unsuited to their basic temperaments, and no expenditure on training can fix that problem. The most training might achieve is to make them more convincing actresses.

I have repeatedly been struck by a word women use to describe workplaces which are predominantly female: 'bitchy'. This suggests efforts to form and sustain 'in groups' which exclude colleagues those women don't like; which can hardly be conducive to workplace effectiveness.

It's clear that women's greater inclination than men to care for elderly or unwell relatives reflects their more empathetic natures. In the context of the perennial need to celebrate women, this might reasonably be considered altruistic behaviour, and laudable. But it might also be seen as reflecting the larger emotional paybacks that women experience from caring for others, compared with men: which brings us right back to female and male pattern brains.

CHAPTER 8

THE EMPRESS'S NEW CLOTHES

We are slow to believe that which, if believed, would hurt our feelings.
Ovid 43 BC - 17 AD Roman poet

A strange scene by the River Thames – a very overweight dancer – 'The Emperor's New Clothes' – it's disrespectful to criticise women, but not to criticise men – why both men and women flatter women, and why doing so infantilises women – grossly overweight women in the United Kingdom – women's unrealistic career expectations and their 'unfairness klaxons' – depression: nature's way to persuade us to abandon unattainable goals? – when are men and women going to stop shielding women from reality? – why politicians will never admit the truth about the gender pay gap and women's 'under-representation' in the boardroom

In July 2009, on a typically balmy English summer afternoon, I was at a 'River Festival' held on the banks of the River Thames in Berkshire. A good-natured crowd was enjoying the live music and dancing on a raised stage. In line with the British custom a number of the people present – mostly teenagers or people in their 20s – were mildly or very drunk.

Onto the stage came a dance troupe consisting of young women between the ages of 16-20. Music by Abba started blaring from the loudspeakers, kicking off with *Super Trouper*. The song's chorus duly came along, and the ladies started running and leaping athletically. At this point I noted that a number of them were very overweight, another British custom. One must have weighed over three hundred pounds. When she 'leapt', her feet didn't leave the stage: she went onto the tips of her toes for a moment. The sight was a sad one, to me at least.

Such a scene would have been inconceivable when I was of a similar age to these ladies, in the mid 1970s.

But how did her fellow dancers, and indeed the crowd, react? With rapt attention and respect. She was treated as the star of the show. I expected the drunks to jeer, but they didn't. A young man of a similar weight would have been laughed off the stage. What was going on? Why was I so out of step, not only with the dancers, but the crowd too? I was reminded of a children's tale. From Wikipedia:

> 'The Emperor's New Clothes' is a short tale by Hans Christian Andersen about two weavers who promise an Emperor a new suit of clothes invisible to those unfit for their positions or incompetent. When the Emperor parades before his subjects in his new clothes, a child cries out, 'But he isn't wearing anything at all!' The tale has been translated into over a hundred languages.

I felt like the child in the tale: the only one to see things as they really were. Why would a fat woman be applauded for doing something which a fat man would be ridiculed for? It has long been considered disrespectful to criticise women, but in the modern era it has become a taboo reinforced by political correctness. It's not just that we mustn't tell a very fat woman that she will look ridiculous dancing on a stage in front of hundreds of people: we mustn't even think it. And if we all don't think it, then she *won't* look ridiculous. This is voluntary mind control on a startling scale.

Now you might think the response of the other dancers and the crowd commendable on a number of grounds, but you'd still be left with a tricky question: why would the same response not be accorded to a man of a similar size? Partly because it's more acceptable to criticise men than women, but I think there's something else. Women tend to have poorer self-confidence than men, which may contribute to their suffering higher levels of anxiety and depression too. While this might manifest itself most obviously in the matter of women's concerns about their physical appearance – has any *man* ever asked his partner, 'Does my bum look big in these trousers?' – it extends far beyond this.

Both men and women are prone to flatter women, thereby helping reduce their anxiety, but I think they do so for different reasons. Men commonly report that their womenfolk can become difficult to live with if the latter's self-esteem is not boosted on a regular basis. Most men have an innate deference and respect for women, even when it's undeserved. Women flatter other women to improve their relationships with them.

In the course of a walk in any town centre in the United Kingdom today you'll come across grossly overweight women in numbers that would have been inconceivable 30 years ago. One can only assume their female friends and relatives tell them their latest stretchy black top makes them look *terrific*. Might they not be kinder to treat them as adults and suggest they eat fewer pies and less ice cream and chocolate?

But whether it's men or women flattering women, the result is the same, and predictable. Regardless of whether we're talking about the home or the work environment, women develop exaggerated senses of their attractiveness or abilities: delusions which at least have the merit of lifting their spirits. Now this may not matter in the home, if the result is a calmer atmosphere, but in the workplace it's a different matter. Ambitious women will believe that their positions and remuneration are inconsistent with the sense they have of their abilities. This will set off their 'unfairness klaxons', resulting in frustration and anger. A few years ago I came across a highly ambitious female executive who was angry at her lack of advancement in her company. It was as painfully obvious to her senior colleagues as it was to me that she was hopelessly ill-equipped for promotion, but none of them wanted to tell her the truth for fear of hurting her feelings. So year after year she carried on, permanently aggrieved and stressed. Eventually she took a lengthy period of time off work with depression, and later resigned. An ambitious man judged as ill-equipped for promotion would have been informed of the fact and expected to accept it.

There's an intriguing link between depression and persisting with unrealistic goals. From *The Economist* of 27 July 2009:

> Clinical depression is a serious ailment, but almost everyone gets mildly depressed from time to time. Randolph Nesse, a psychologist and researcher in evolutionary medicine at the University of Michigan, likens the relationship between mild and clinical depression to the one between normal and chronic pain. He sees both pain and low mood as warning mechanisms and thinks that, just as understanding chronic pain means first understanding normal pain, so understanding clinical depression means understanding mild depression.
>
> Dr Nesse's hypothesis is that, as pain stops you doing damaging physical things, so low mood stops you doing damaging mental ones – in particular, pursuing unreachable goals. Pursuing such goals is a waste of energy and resources. Therefore, he argues, there is likely to be an evolved mechanism that identifies certain goals as unattainable and inhibits their pursuit – and he believes that low mood is at least part of that mechanism.
>
> It is a neat hypothesis, but is it true? A study published in this month's issue of the *Journal of Personality and Social Psychology* suggests it might be. Carsten Wrosch from Concordia University in Montreal and Gregory Miller of the University of British Columbia studied depression in teenage girls. They measured the 'goal adjustment capacities' of 97 girls aged 15–19 over the course of 19 months. They asked the participants questions about their ability to disengage

from unattainable goals and to re-engage with new goals. They also asked about a range of symptoms associated with depression, and tracked how these changed over the course of the study.

Their conclusion was that those who experienced mild depressive symptoms could, indeed, disengage more easily from unreachable goals. That supports Dr Nesse's hypothesis. But the new study also found a remarkable corollary: those women who could disengage from the unattainable proved less likely to suffer more serious depression in the long run.

Mild depressive symptoms can therefore be seen as a natural part of dealing with failure in young adulthood. They set in when a goal is identified as unreachable and lead to a decline in motivation. In this period of low motivation, energy is saved and new goals can be found. If this mechanism does not function properly, though, severe depression can be the consequence.

The importance of giving up inappropriate goals has already been demonstrated by Dr Wrosch. Two years ago he and his colleagues published a study in which they showed that those teenagers who were better at doing so had a lower concentration of c-reactive protein, a substance made in response to inflammation and associated with an elevated risk of diabetes and cardiovascular disease. Dr Wrosch thus concludes that it is healthy to give up overly ambitious goals. Persistence, though necessary for success and considered a virtue by many, can also have a negative impact on health.

Dr Nesse believes that persistence is a reason for the exceptional level of clinical depression in America – the country that has the highest depression rate in the world. 'Persistence is part of the American way of life,' he says. 'People here are often driven to pursue overly ambitious goals, which then can lead to depression.' He admits that this is still an unproven hypothesis, but it is one worth considering. Depression may turn out to be an inevitable price of living in a dynamic society.

The inability of women to accept the truth about themselves only serves to infantilise them, and the problem is becoming worse as the years roll by. Only a very small proportion of the senior executives in major commercial organisations, in positions making them eligible for promotion to the boardroom, are women: and the number of these executives is in decline, as we shall see in a later chapter, mainly because of choices made by women themselves.

It is so important that women are not criticised, that we must deny the realities we see before us; and so it is that in 2010 a Conservative Prime Minister appointed a Labour peer (Lord Davies of Abersoch) to lead a study into women's 'under-representation' in the boardroom. When, precisely, are women going to accept reality? Maybe when men and women stop shielding them from it? We cannot expect politicians to play any part in this, given universal suffrage. There are no votes to be secured by telling women the truth about the gender pay gap and women's 'under-representation' in the boardroom, the truth being that both are largely attributable to the choices men and women freely make in their personal and working lives.

CHAPTER 9

WHY ARE FAT WOMEN FAT?

It's a mystery,
Oh, it's a mystery.
Toyah Willcox 1958- English actress and singer: 'It's a Mystery' (song, 1981)

Fat women are different to fat men – ten large roast potatoes and a diet Coke – it may be prudent not to challenge the hormone theory of weight gain – some women's genetic predisposition to obesity – why some fat English women are orange

As an overweight man I accepted for many years the relationship between my 200-pound weight and my fondness for good food, beer and wine. Other fat men of my acquaintance were equally accepting of the relationship. Last year, at the age of 52, on my doctor's advice I embarked on a programme to lose weight and reduce my blood pressure. I cut down my calorie intake, undertook more exercise – two games of pool a week, nothing too exhausting – and after six months I'd lost 44 pounds and my blood pressure had fallen to target levels.

Women's weight problems appear to be different to men's weight problems. I never cease to be amazed at how many fat women believe there isn't a direct relationship between the calories they consume, and their weight. A fat woman recently declared to me, 'I only have to look at a chip to put on weight!' The next day I saw her in a local carvery, where customers could eat as much as they could fit onto their plates. With a plate heaving with high-calorie food items she really should have changed her plea to, 'I only have to eat ten large roast potatoes to put on weight!' Half an hour later I was at the bar when she ordered a drink: Diet Coke.

With impeccable man logic I've sometimes pointed out to overweight ladies that every atom in their bodies was either present when they were born, or had been ingested. With peccable lady logic they always beg to differ, but to date none has yet come up with a working hypothesis on womanly weight gain. Some years ago a woman told me, 'I'm overweight because of my hormones.' Quick as a flash I replied, 'Oh yes, the hormones that make you eat family-size pies!' I woke up in hospital two days later.

So it falls to me to introduce a theory which I confidently expect to land me the Nobel Prize in Physiology or Medicine. A simple observation was the key to understanding the riddle of why fat women are fat. Fat women often have fat children, and their fatness generally stays with them into adult life. The fat sons obviously eat and drink too much and exercise too little, but what of the fat daughters? Might there be a genetic dimension to their weight problem?

I haven't ironed out all the details of the theory yet, but it appears that some women are genetically predisposed to putting on weight regardless of what they eat and drink. The most obvious scientific explanation for this phenomenon is that the women are photosynthesising. Photosynthesis is the process which occurs in plants, algae, and many species of bacteria, and results from the action of light upon the green pigment chlorophyll, which enables organisms to put on mass by converting carbon dioxide from the atmosphere into organic compounds, especially sugars.

The first woman to have this genetic mutation would have been green, and we must assume that not even the most desperate men wanted green offspring. Another genetic mutation resulted in a pigment which mimics the action of chlorophyll but is colourless, so photosynthesising women are no longer green. Although it might be that the pigment isn't colourless after all, but orange. A surprising proportion of fat women – in England at least – are orange.

CHAPTER 10

FEMINISTS IN ACADEMIA

The academic community has in it the biggest concentration of alarmists, cranks, and extremists this side of the giggle house.
William F Buckley Jr 1925-2008 American conservative author and commentator: 'On the Right' 17 January 1967

Women's Ways of Knowing – excitement before a trans-Atlantic flight – Christina Hoff Sommers's criticism of militant feminists – the Feminist and Women's Studies Association – the search for a feminine perspective on atomic particles – the cunning of manginas (male feminists) – experiencing and celebrating fatness – *Professing Feminism*

Militant feminists of the American persuasion take some beating. Let's consider a book written by four of them: three are (or at least were at the time) academics, indeed professors. The book is *Women's Ways of Knowing*, first published in 1986. After reading comments on the book by the psychologist Steven Pinker I was intrigued to buy a copy, and duly bought the tenth anniversary edition. To give you a flavour of the book's content I selected a page at random. From page 54, in a section titled, 'The Emergence of Subjective Knowing':

> The kind of change that Inez experienced is the center of our discussion in this chapter: from passivity to action, from self as static to self as becoming, from silence to a protesting inner voice and infallible gut.
>
> For many of the women, the move away from silence and an externally oriented perspective on knowledge and truth eventuates in a new conception of truth as personal, private, and subjectively known or intuited; thus, we are calling this next position *subjectivism* or *subjective knowing*. Although this new view of knowledge is a revolutionary step there are remnants of dichotomous and absolutist thinking in the subjectivist's assumptions about truth. [Author's note: are you

losing the will to live yet?] In fact, subjectivism is dualistic in the sense that there is still the conviction that there are right answers; the fountain of truth simply has shifted locale. Truth now resides within the person and can negate answers that the outside world supplies.

I'd like to invite you to join the four writers of *Women's Ways of Knowing* and myself on a journey. We're strapped into our seats in a plane just before a trans-Atlantic flight from London to New York. A middle-aged actress – acting the role of a pilot – emerges from the cockpit and announces cheerily:

> Ladies and gentlemen, good morning! My name's Candy. [Author's note: she appears to be of the American persuasion] I shall be your captain on today's flight, and I'll be responsible for taking off and landing the plane. I've had little flying training but I've read *lots* of books about flying planes, and with my women's ways of knowing I'm sure we'll all be just fine. Now, let's get this baby up into the air! Stewardess, why are the four ladies over there screaming hysterically?

For a more sophisticated critique of 'women's ways of knowing' than I can muster, we turn to Christina Hoff Sommers, an American former professor of philosophy, and a self-described 'equity feminist'. Wikipedia has a good deal of interesting material on Ms Sommers including the following:

> Sommers uses the terms 'equity feminism' and 'gender feminism' to differentiate what she sees as acceptable and non-acceptable forms of feminism. She describes equity feminism as the struggle for equal legal and civil rights and many of the original goals of the early feminists, as in the first wave of the women's movement. She describes gender feminism as the action of accenting the differences of genders for the purposes of what she believes is creating privilege for women in academia, government, industry, or advancing personal agendas.

In this book I use the term 'militant feminism' in the same way that Ms Hoff Sommers uses the term 'gender feminism' above. We turn to the start of the chapter titled 'New Epistemologies' in her illuminating book *Who Stole Feminism? How Women Have Betrayed Women* (1994):

> Some gender feminists claim that because women have been oppressed they are better 'knowers'. Feeling more deeply, they see more clearly and understand reality better. They have an 'epistemic' advantage over men. Does being oppressed really make one more knowledgeable or perceptive? The idea that adversity confers special insight is familiar enough. Literary critics often ascribe creativity to suffering, including suffering racial discrimination or homophobia. But feminist philosophers have carried this idea much further. They claim that oppressed groups enjoy privileged 'epistemologies' or 'different ways of knowing' that better enable them to understand the world, not only socially but scientifically.
>
> According to 'standpoint theory', as the theory of epistemic advantage is called, the oppressed may make better biologists, physicists, and philosophers than their oppressors. Thus we find the feminist theorist Hilary Rose saying that male scientists have been handicapped by being men. A better science would be based on women's domestic experience and practice. Professor Virginia Held offers hope that 'a feminist standpoint would give us a quite different understanding of even physical reality.' Conversely, those who are most socially favored, the proverbial white, middle class males, are in the worst epistemic position.
>
> What do mainstream philosophers make of the idea of 'standpoint theories'? Professor Susan Haack of the University of Miami is one of the most respected epistemologists in the country. She is also an equity feminist. In December 1992 she participated in a symposium on feminist philosophy at meetings of the American Philosophical Association. It was a unique event. For once, someone outside the insular little world of gender feminism was asked to comment on gender feminist theories of knowledge. Watching Professor Haack critique the 'standpoint theorists' was a little like watching a chess

grandmaster defeat all opponents in a simultaneous exhibition, blindfolded.

Haack told the audience that she finds the idea of 'female ways of knowing' as puzzling as the idea of a Republican epistemology or a senior citizens' epistemology. Some of her arguments are too technical to review here. I cite only a few of her criticisms:

> I am not convinced that there *are* any distinctively female 'ways of knowing'. All *any* human being has to go on, in figuring how things are, is his or her sensory experience, and the explanatory theorizing he or she devises to accommodate it; differences in cognitive style, like differences in handwriting, seem more individual then gender-determined.

She pointed out that theories based on the idea that oppression or deprivation results in a privileged standpoint are especially implausible: if they were right, the most disadvantaged groups would produce the best scientists. In fact, the oppressed and socially marginalized often have little access to the information and education needed to excel in science, which on the whole puts them at a serious 'epistemic *dis*advantage'. Professor Haack also observed that the female theorists who argue that oppression confers an advantage are not themselves oppressed. She asks: if oppression and poverty are indeed so advantageous, why do so many highly advantaged, middle-class women consider themselves so well situated 'epistemically'?

Ms Haack identifies herself as an 'Old Feminist' who opposes the attempt of 'the New Feminists to colonize philosophy'. Her reasons for rejecting feminist epistemologies were cogent and, to most of the professional audience, clearly convincing. Unfortunately, her cool, sensible admonitions are not likely to slow down the campaign to promote 'women's ways of knowing'.

The gender feminists' conviction, more ideological than scientific, that they belong to a radically insightful vanguard that compares favourably with the Copernicuses and Darwins of the past animates their revisionist theories of intellectual and artistic excellence and inspires their program to transform the knowledge base. Their exultation contrasts with the deep reluctance of most other academics to challenge the basic assumptions underlying feminist theories of knowledge and education. The confidence of the one and the trepidation of the other combine to make transformationism a powerfully effective movement that has so far proceeded unchecked in the academy.

In an effort to learn more about militant feminism in the United Kingdom I googled the keyword 'feminism'. It resulted in 'about 114,000' website hits. I gained the firm impression after just a few website visits that militant feminism is well and truly the product of, and sustained by, academics; and therefore financed by long-suffering British taxpayers. Almost all these academics are women, it need hardly be said. From the website of the Feminist and Women's Studies Association, Fwsa.org.uk:

> The FWSA is a UK-based network promoting feminist research and teaching, and women's studies nationally and internationally. Through its elected executive committee, the FWSA is involved in developing policy on issues of central importance to feminist scholars in further and higher education, supporting postgraduate events and enabling feminist research. Committed to raising awareness of women's studies, feminist research and women-related issues in secondary and tertiary education, the FWSA liaises regularly with other gender-related research and community networks as well as with policy groups.

Two seminars promoted on the website caught my eye, the first being the following:

Celebrating the feminist within
22nd September 2010 – University of East Anglia

July 30, 2010

Feminist academics in leadership positions report difficulty pursuing feminist ideals, often preferring to leave their 'radical' feminist identities at home with some professing desires to unite their dual identities of scholar and activist. Black feminists are particularly marginalised within academia, although the increased diversity of the student population in the UK brings hope for a new generation of black feminists entering the academy. To counter the apparent attitudes in academia that are suspicious of feminists and feminism, the Centre for Diversity and Equality in Careers and Employment Research (Norwich Business School, University of East Anglia) is holding a one day free networking event for up to 40 female and male feminist academics, research staff and PhD students on the 22nd September, 2010. The day will:

- promote wider debate of what feminism can mean in academia and research;
- provide a platform for feminist academics from a range of backgrounds (age, class, gender, ethnicity, discipline) to share their experiences;
- bring discussions about feminism in universities into the open;
- provide networking opportunities to help reduce feelings of isolation and possibly lead to future collaborative projects, particularly for early career researchers, and;
- act as a pilot event for similar events in other regions in the UK.

We couldn't ask for clearer evidence that the militant feminist world is a closed one. The term 'male feminist' is enough to make any man shudder, but the FWSA had posted a message from one such person on its website, so presumably believed it had some merit:

I wonder if your research and curiosity ever brings you to look at our understanding of nuclear power and the Atomic World. Our knowledge of this subject derives entirely from a masculine way of looking and thinking about the already invisible world of the atomic particles. Our knowledge is consequently overlain with patrician and misogynist perceptions. No wonder it creates such messy issues.

I've gone some way towards developing a more balanced account. There's some surprising things to see. Nuclear fission is essentially a story of passion and romance, and finally despair. Impossible for our physicists to understand. Oh! This whole subject dearly needs feminine insight and values, to make it whole. Please don't pass it by.

Thanks and good wishes,

<name supplied>

This perspective was so reminiscent of those found in *Women's Ways of Knowing* that I felt compelled to post a reply:

I was interested to read your post about the Atomic World. I have a number of questions:

- in what sense is our knowledge of atomic particles 'overlain with patrician and misogynistic perceptions'?
- when I graduated with a science degree over 30 years ago, nuclear fission was already very well understood. Sorry to learn that is it now 'impossible' for physicists to understand. Do you happen to know how this unfortunate turn of events has come to pass?
- in what sense does the subject dearly need feminine insight and values to make it whole?

Six months after posting my questions, I'm still awaiting a reply. But maybe, just maybe, the man is smarter than we might otherwise give him credit for. For an interesting perspective on male feminists we turn to an extract from a book published in 2008, *Men are Better than Women*, penned by the American author Dick Masterson.

Manginas are my heroes

Male feminists, or 'manginas' as they prefer to be called, are so misogynistic they make Andrew Dice Clay [Author's note: a notably politically-incorrect, i.e. funny, American comedian] look like The Little Mermaid. The Little Mermaid is the seashell-on-the-boobs cartoon character from Disney.

Not all men have money, good looks, talent, wit, charm, charisma, interesting stories, cultural insights, skills, athletic abilities, political acumen, macho attitudes, an ability to eat an inhuman amount of food or other non-toxic products, a sense of style, an easygoing demeanour, video games, a sweet car, a spa, or an in-depth knowledge of everything. All men, however, are still men. That means they need to get laid and will always find a way. How do these men attract women, then? I'll tell you how – by taking charge where women have failed for the last thirty years: by being feminists.

Manginas are my heroes. They fight the fight that women declared for absolutely no reason and then completely failed at. Who else but a man could convince a woman that being a male feminist is not only possible, but also not the most chauvinistic thing anyone has ever done in the history of the world?

I'll tell you who, fucking no one! But men have done that shit. Men are like hypnosis masters when it comes to telling women what they want and what they should think about everything. Manginas are the biggest and most ingenious misogynists. It's perfectly natural and perfectly manly for a man to stoop so low as to cheapen his entire gender just to get laid. Men don't need a collective pat on the ass for everything we do in life. We're born with dicks and dignity, and neither can be taken away. We don't need a sash that counts up all our achievements and chafes our necks. That's for Girl Scouts, and the only thing I want to know about Girl Scouts is when they sell their cookies.

On a personal note, I have nothing against misogynism, or whatever it's called. I wouldn't call myself a misogynist, but that's a little like not calling a square a rectangle. Manginas are some of the manliest men on earth, because they know deep down within their stomachs that women can't stand up for themselves without a firm hand firmly supporting them by the ass. It's a throwback to chivalry that says, 'Sweetheart, if you want anyone to take your rights seriously, shut up and let a man do the talking.'

Onto the second seminar advertised on the FWSA website:

Experiencing and Celebrating Fatness
Bigness Beyond Obesity: Seminar 3

ESRC seminar series: Fat Studies and HAES

18th-19th November 2010, London (The Hopkins Room,
Stratford Library, 3 The Grove, Stratford, London E15 1EL).

This seminar will address the intersection between Fat
Studies, Health At Every Size and fat activism. It will explore
individuals' experiences of activism, sites for intervention, and
the possibilities for fat activism in relation to health and
beyond. There will be a combination of presentations and
workshop activities.

Beneath the details of the seminar were a number of apt
Google Ads. My eye was caught by one with the title, 'Lose
7lbs of ugly body fat every week!' Another was for gastric
bands.

The seminar was sponsored by the ESRC, the Economic and
Social Research Council, which derives most of its funding
from the Department for Business, Innovation and Skills,
which in turn derives its funding from long-suffering British
taxpayers. What seminars might logically follow on from
'Experiencing and Celebrating Fatness'? Obvious contenders
are 'Experiencing and Celebrating Ugliness' and 'Experiencing
and Celebrating Stupidity'.

I don't know of a book critiquing Women's Studies / Gender
Studies courses in the UK. But anyone seeking insights into the
chilling realities of the movement in the United States should
read the second edition (2003) of a book written by two
American academics, Daphne Patai and Noretta Koertge:
Professing Feminism. Why American taxpayers continue to fund

such unremittingly left-wing and destructive courses in their institutions of higher learning, without protesting loudly, is a mystery. As is, to be fair, why the taxpayers of other countries – including those of us in the United Kingdom – do so too.

CHAPTER 11

MILITANT FEMINISM
(GENDER MARXISM)

The opinions that are held with passion are always those for which no good ground exists; indeed the passion is the measure of the holder's lack of rational conviction.

Sceptical Essays (1928)

Lord Bertrand Russell 1872-1970 Nobel Prize-winning British philosopher, logician, mathematician, historian, free trade champion, pacifist and social critic

Feminism is a very recent and very radical philosophy – different variants of feminism – the evolution of the human brain – feminism is unnatural for both men and women – feminism is a variant of Marxism – feminists' use of false logic – the late Anita Roddick – gender biases among engineering and psychology students – executive directors of FTSE100 companies – cognitive dissonance – The Seekers and the end of the world – why Harriet Harman will never change – feminist fantasy women – emotional intelligence – Margaret Thatcher – the happiness of women – 'stay-at-home Moms' – co-operation and competition – ladies and gentlemen – do militant feminists hate men? – only discrimination against men is now acceptable – misogyny and misandry – Mary Daly gets a bit excitable

It's all too easy to forget in the developed world in the modern era just how startlingly radical a philosophy feminism is, when we compare it with age-old ideas on the natures of men and women and how they should relate to each other. Widespread support for feminism is limited to possibly the last half century (let's be generous) and the developed world. That's 50 years out of the 100,000+ years of the existence of 'modern man': just 0.05 per cent of the timescale. And limited to less than half of mankind.

What are the chances that such a profoundly radical view about the nature of men and women and how they should relate to each other will still have widespread support over the years and decades to come? Only time will tell.

Like all philosophies and faiths feminism has a tendency to splinter into different forms. One variant is termed 'choice feminism', reflecting the view that women should be free to choose whether they work for a living, or stay at home and be supported by their partners, who are invariably men. The irony is lost on these particular feminists, you have to assume.

Men, it hardly needs saying, don't enjoy the same choice. Very occasionally a woman will support her partner in a role as 'house husband', looking after the children and home, as she pursues her career. I've never come across such an arrangement personally, but I'm told they exist. What women *never* do is offer to support their male partners if there are no children involved. Men never have the choice which so many women blithely exercise.

My objection is not to equity feminists as described by Christina Hoff Sommers, but to gender feminists, who I term 'militant feminists'. The former seek equality of opportunity for women with men – who could possibly object to that? – while the latter seek equality of *outcome* with men, for example in the senior executive levels in business. And they seek equality of outcome although very few women want to do what is necessary to attain and retain those positions. So they are seeking not equality, but special treatment. They present women as victims suffering discrimination – discrimination against men is never objectionable, indeed it's to be exercised whenever possible – to deliver what should be 'rightfully' theirs.

This brings us on to the topic of the evolution of the human brain. There is no evidence to suggest that the human brain has evolved over the course of the past 100,000 years. Unless you're a creationist you'll probably be convinced by the strong and growing evidence supporting the 'Out of Africa' hypothesis of the spread of humans around the world. Barrett, Dunbar, and Lycett in their book *Human Evolutionary Psychology* (2002) cover the topic, and its implications, at length. Research since the book's publication has further supported the 'Out of Africa' hypothesis. The authors write:

> This hypothesis argues that all living humans share a recent common ancestor (or a very small number of ancestors) that lived in Africa some time between 100,000 and 200,000 years ago. After occupying virtually the whole of sub-Saharan Africa, one population crossed the Levant land bridge around 70,000 years ago and, over the next 30,000 years, spread rapidly across Eurasia and into Australia, finally breaching the Bering Strait to cross into the New World by around 15,000 years ago.

Working on the assumption that modern ideas about how society should be run differ from views in Africa between 100,000 and 200,000 years ago, what might we anticipate about the adaptiveness of the human brain to cope with modern ideas such as feminism? The authors of *Human Evolutionary Psychology* report two schools of thought about the adaptiveness of the human brain:

APPROACHES TO THE STUDY OF HUMAN BEHAVIOUR
The broad field of study that we characterise as human evolutionary psychology (that is, the evolutionary-oriented study of human behaviour and cognition) is currently divided into two quite distinct camps which disagree fundamentally on some key issues. In this section, we summarise their basic positions. . .

Human Behavioural Ecology

On one side of the fence, there are those individuals who take a functional perspective and consider a trait to be biologically adapted if it increases the fitness (the number of genes passed to future generations) of those who bear the trait relative to those who do not. Individuals working in this field adopt an approach that is virtually identical to that taken by behavioural ecologists who study non-human animals. That is, human behavioural ecology (HBE) focuses on measuring differences in reproductive success between individuals in relation to differences in the behavioural strategies that they follow. Because many of those who adopt this perspective were originally trained in anthropology, they are sometimes referred to as 'Darwinian anthropologists'. . .

Evolutionary Psychology

On the other side of the fence from the human behavioural ecologists – and facing in an entirely different direction – are those who consider themselves to be practising evolutionary (or Darwinian) psychology (EP). As might be expected, workers in this area study human adaptation from a largely psychological perspective and their parent discipline is not behavioural ecology but cognitive psychology. The aim of EP is to identify the selection pressures that have shaped the human psyche over the course of evolutionary time, and then test whether our psychological mechanisms actually show the features one would expect if they were designed to solve these particular adaptive problems (for example, choosing mates or detecting cheats). . .

Environment of Evolutionary Adaptedness

One important source of disagreement between the two approaches centres around the concept of the Environment of Evolutionary Adaptedness (EEA). This issue arises out of the fact that EP and HBE disagree about the extent to which we can expect humans to be adapted to current environments due to a capacity for rapid shifts in phenotype as a consequence of increases in brain size and a capacity for flexible 'off-line' planning of action. EP on the other hand takes the view that the massive cultural changes that have taken place in the last 100,000 years have occurred *at a pace that is simply too fast to allow human brains (and hence behaviour) to adapt* [Author's italics]. The psychological adaptations we possess today were selected for in our past environment of evolutionary adaptedness (EEA) and are not geared for the modern world. Consequently EP argues that, a priori, there is no reason to expect any modern behaviour to be adaptive since present environments are so different from those in which the behaviour evolved.

If the EP school of thought is correct, it follows that the modern human mind cannot have evolved to be comfortable with modern expectations of how society should be run, such as those held by feminists. Feminism in this sense is deeply *unnatural* for both men and women. We see this reality manifest itself in numerous ways in the workplace, not least in the consistent finding that women don't like working for women, a topic we'll be covering in a later chapter.

Feminism originated from the same school of thinking as Marxism. Feminists share the sense with others of a left-wing persuasion that the world is unfair to them, and that a bright future awaits them if they fight long and hard enough. For feminists, the world of their dreams will be one run along lines more attuned to how women think and feel. We are fortunate in the modern era to know that Marxism, when tested extensively, failed as a philosophy: and failed badly. Why should feminism too not fail in time?

I cannot think of a group of people so addicted to the use of false logic as militant feminists. Whenever I hear them speak, or read their writings, I am struck by their incessant use of false logic. The logic often runs along the lines of, 'x is demonstrably true, so it follows that y must also be true.'

This is most often seen in arguments about women in the workplace. For example, if women can point to a single example of a successful female entrepreneur – Anita Roddick is their frequent choice although she died some years ago – it follows that women are as entrepreneurial as men. And if 50% of successful entrepreneurs aren't women, then there must be an external reason for that, unconnected with women themselves. Oppression or discrimination by men, in all likelihood.

Militant feminists go unchallenged so much of the time because what they claim as 'truth' isn't readily and demonstrably false. But if the same logic were applied in the physical realm its absurdity would be clear to see: 'Men's average height is 5'9", Anne is 6'1" tall, so women are on average 4" taller than men.' Right.

The same false logic applies to any field in which women are not represented sufficiently highly in the eyes of militant feminists. In the world of work, this of course applies to high-profile professions (e.g. politics), well rewarded professions (e.g. law), and the like. Militant feminists never consider the near absence of women in unpleasant or dangerous lines of work as 'under representation'.

It is never a problem when women dominate professions. Only a small proportion of engineers are women – in the United Kingdom fewer than 10% of mechanical engineering graduates in 2009 were women – and this is apparently a 'problem' to be addressed. In the same year over 90% of psychology graduates were women, but this is *not* a problem to be addressed.

Can we agree that 99.997 is close to 99.999? OK. Well, 99.997% of British men of working age aren't executive directors of FTSE100 companies, the equivalent figure for women being 99.999%. But this *is* a problem to militant feminists: like children in a playground, militant feminists want what others have as a matter of 'right'.

It's not so much that militant feminists won't consider the validity of evidence that flies in the face of their convictions: it's more that they *can't* do so. For an explanation of this we need to have some understanding of the phenomenon of cognitive dissonance.

Cognitive dissonance is a theory first put forward by the American social scientist Leon Festinger in 1957. In his book *Cognitive Dissonance: Fifty Years of a Classic Theory* (2007), Joel Cooper, Professor of Psychology at Princeton University, charts the progress of dissonance theory. He writes:

> Leon Festinger, whose work on social comparison theory had already made him an influential figure in social psychology, made a very basic observation about the social lives of human beings: we do not like inconsistency. It upsets us and it drives us to action to reduce our inconsistency. The greater the inconsistency we face, the more agitated we will be and the more motivated we will be to reduce it.
>
> Before formalising the definition of dissonance, let us imagine some inconsistencies that can happen in social life. Imagine that you prepared at great length for a dinner party at your home. You constructed the guest list, sent out the invitations, and prepared the menu. Nothing was too much effort for your party: you went to the store, prepared the ingredients, and cooked for hours, all in anticipation of how pleasant the conversation and the people would be. Except it wasn't. The guests arrived late, the conversations were forced, and the food was slightly overcooked by the time all of the guests arrived. The anticipation and expectation of the great time you were going to have are discordant with your observation of the evening. The pieces do not fit. You're upset, partly because the evening did not go well, but also because of the inconsistency between your expectation and your experience. You are suffering from the uncomfortable, unpleasant state of cognitive dissonance...
>
> Festinger was adamant about one point. People do not just *prefer* consistency over inconsistency... The party host does not just wish the party had gone better; he must deal with the inconsistency between the hopes, aspirations, and effort that

he put in prior to the party and the observation that the party did not go well. How can that be done? Surely, if the host changes his opinion about how well the party went, then there is no longer an inconsistency. Perhaps the guests loved a slightly blackened lamb and their quietness at the table reflected their enjoyment of the meal.

Festinger's insistence that cognitive dissonance was like a drive that needed to be reduced implied that people were going to have to find some way of resolving their inconsistencies. People do not just *prefer* eating over starving; we are *driven* to eat. Similarly, people who are in the throes of inconsistency in their social life are *driven* to resolve that inconsistency. How we go about dealing with our inconsistency can be rather ingenious. But, in Festinger's view, there is little question that it *will* be done.

An article which appeared in a Minneapolis newspaper gave Festinger and his students an ideal opportunity to study inconsistency in a real-world setting. Cooper's account of this remarkable example of cognitive dissonance is reproduced below:

An article that appeared in a Minneapolis newspaper gave Festinger and his students an ideal opportunity to study inconsistency in a real-world setting. The article reported on a group of west coast residents who were united in a belief about a significant event: the belief that the Earth was going to be annihilated by a cataclysmic flood on December 21, 1955. All of the people would perish in the cataclysm except for those who believed in the prophecies emanating from the planet Clarion; they alone would be saved from the flood.

Festinger reasoned that if Earth survived December 21, then the people in the little group, dubbed The Seekers by Festinger, Riecken, and Schachter (1956), would face a considerable amount of inconsistency on the next morning. While the rest of the world awoke to just another day, The Seekers would face a calamitous amount of inconsistency. The world's very existence would be inconsistent with their belief that the world as we know it was to have ended on the previous evening.

The Seekers was a serious group: this was not a collection of individuals who had a mild premonition of the world's demise. Their beliefs were specific and strong. As the December day approached, Seekers members sold their possessions and quit their jobs. Some, whose spouses did not share their beliefs, divorced. The Seekers members were united in their support of their leader, Mrs Marion Keech, who believed she was the medium through whom the unearthly beings on the planet Clarion communicated their wishes. She received her messages through automatic writing – a paranormal belief that a person's hand is seized by the spirits in another world and is used to communicate messages from the Great Beyond.

Clarion was specific. The group was to gather at Mrs Keech's home on the evening of December 20. They were to await the arrival of a spaceship that would come to Earth and whisk the group away from danger.

The Seekers were not publicity hounds. They sought no attention for their beliefs or their prophecy. When the reporter whose story appeared in the Minneapolis newspaper attempted to interview them, they grudgingly gave only the briefest interview. Publicity was not their goal; protecting themselves from the cataclysmic end of the Earth was.

As a social psychologist, Festinger saw the immediate relevance to the theory he was generating. If people are driven to deal with inconsistency, how would Marion Keech and her followers react to the morning of December 21 when the sun rose, the sky brightened, and the spaceship from Clarion failed to appear? The clear and specific anticipation of the world's demise, the elaborate preparations for the group to be saved, the broken marriages and other personal sacrifices, all would stand in stark contrast to the world's having made just another turn around its axis. Festinger and his colleagues predicted that the dramatic inconsistency would create the state of cognitive dissonance and the group would be driven to find some way to reduce it. They would need to find some way of restoring consistency to their mental maps of the cosmic events.

One of the researchers, Stanley Schachter, infiltrated the group. He carefully observed the group's preparations and specifically observed the events as they unfolded just after midnight on December 20. The group gathered near midnight, waiting for the arrival of the spacecraft. Tension and excitement were high. They had followed the Clarions' instructions meticulously. Mrs Keech's grandfather clock ticked the final seconds to midnight. No spacecraft.

Someone in the group checked his watch and saw that his watch still read only 11:55. All watches were reset. At 12:05, even by the ticking of the newly set watches, there was still no spacecraft. Another member of the group suddenly realized that he had not fulfilled all of the instructions given by the Clarions. They had insisted that all metal objects be removed from the human space travellers. Thus, they came with no zippers, belt buckles, or bra straps. But now a Seeker realized that he had a metal filling in a tooth. He removed it. [Author: I imagine that at this point some of the other Seekers 'forgot' they too had metal fillings.] Still, no spacecraft.

There followed a terrible few hours following the midnight disconfirmation of the prophecy. People sobbed and wept. Had they been abandoned by the Clarions? Had they been wrong all along, just like their more cynical spouses and former friends had told them? Shortly past 4:00 am, Mrs Keech received her final message from Clarion. The message provided the answer to their questions, and also provided the opportunity to restore consistency between their doomsday beliefs and their observation that the spaceship had not come and there had been no Earth-destroying cataclysm.

The Clarions' final message was brilliant. Through Mrs Keech's trembling hand, it said:

> This little group, sitting all night long, has spread so much goodness and light that the God of the Universe spared the Earth from destruction.

So that was it. The beliefs had not been wrong after all. God had been planning to destroy the Earth. All of the preparations for the cataclysm had not been in vain. In fact, it was precisely and only because of the preparations, sacrifices, and faith of the group that the Earth still existed on the morning of December 21. The sun still shone because of them; people went to work because of them; people still had homes to return to and families to love them . . . all because of the determination of the small group of Seekers.

Before December 21, Festinger et al (1956) had made a prediction. They hypothesised that The Seekers, who shunned publicity and notoriety, would take their cause to the public following the disconfirmation. And The Seekers did that with gusto. As soon as their new belief was in place – as soon as they had generated the story that their actions had saved the world – they took their case to the public. They looked for social support for their story. They desperately wanted others to see that their actions had not been in vain, that their prophecy had not been disconfirmed, that there was no inconsistency between their belief in the cataclysm and the bright sunny day that had dawned on December 21.

The premise of dissonance theory is that people do not tolerate inconsistency very well. The Seekers had found a way, post hoc, to make their actions feel consistent to themselves and they now sought validation in having the world believe them. They printed flyers, called newspapers and magazines, offered to talk on radio programs, all in an effort to bolster their new found consistency.

There are probably many factors that influenced the group of Seekers in their actions. Who can guess what had initially influenced these individuals to believe in the prophecy and the automatic writing? Who can guess what motives each individual may have had in the wake of the disconfirmed prophecy? But one thing seems certain. Caught in a major inconsistency among their beliefs, behaviours, and observations of reality, The Seekers did just what Festinger and his colleagues predicted they would do: they were driven to find a way to restore their consistency – driven to find a new belief that would make sense of what they had done and driven to convince a sceptical world of the truth of their new position.

Let's not expect Harriet Harman to admit she's been wrong about so many things for so many years any time soon. The world proves her right – to her own satisfaction, and those like her – every day of the week.

If far more men than women seek to become directors of major organisations – and they do – there has to be an explanation. For militant feminists the explanation is always the same: a lack of role models for women. It is trotted out *decades* after those role models first existed. But the explanation begs one big question: do leaders look for role models to emulate? Of course they don't.

Militant feminists portray women collectively as superior to men in numerous regards, regardless of the reality that there is as much diversity among women as among men. I call the women the 'feminist fantasy women'. Compared with men they are said to be:

- harder working
- more perceptive
- more emotionally intelligent
- more co-operative and 'collegiate'

The first assertion is simply untrue, and we shall see that at all ages between leaving education and retirement, women are far more likely then men either not to work (in the paid employment field, anyway) or to work part-time. Are women more perceptive than men? Some are, some aren't. The same goes for emotional intelligence. Some men have considerable emotional intelligence, while some women have poor emotional intelligence.

Emotional intelligence is relevant to a subject that consumes women: their interpersonal relationships. Because women would rather manipulate these relationships – especially with men, both in the home and in the workplace – than work hard for their prosperity, it's important to them to spend a good deal of time thinking about how to employ emotions. Women may be more co-operative than men, but it's the very reason they are seldom effective as leaders: it's not in the nature of women to be leaders. With rare exceptions, such as Margaret Thatcher.

The women I have known throughout my life are nothing like feminist fantasy women, and they have not become more like them during the 35 or so years of my adult life, from about 1975. I know few women in paid employment who would not work fewer hours if they could, whether to spend more time with their family members and friends or engaged in other unpaid activities.

The happiness of women I know is inversely proportional to the stress levels engendered by their jobs: the more stressful the job, the less happy the woman. Compared with male executives, it seems to me, female executives are more stressed by their jobs. And they respond with higher levels of anxiety, depression, and substance abuse, particularly with alcohol.

The idea that women share common characteristics and interests – an idea which underpins the notion of feminist fantasy women – is an interesting one. On one level it is a denial of individualism. Feminists hate the idea that women might exercise choice and not be engaged in the struggle against men, especially when their choice is to be supported by men – even when this enables them to better care for the couple's children. In the United States there is enormous hostility among some working women towards 'stay-at-home Moms', a phenomenon which exists in the United Kingdom but appears less bad-tempered.

Individuals advance in their workplaces through delivering more value than their colleagues, displaying greater leadership skills, working harder etc. It results, in short, from competition. But because co-operation comes more naturally than competitiveness to women it follows that for women to advance, their inclination will be to do so by co-operating. And that is exactly what they have been doing for many years, through overt and covert efforts to deliver 'gender balance'. These efforts are frequently illegal but in the absence of an effective response from men they simply carry on. Men continue to show their customary deference towards women – they continue, in other words, to be gentlemen. Well, not all of them, possibly…

What drives militant feminists? Do they simply hate men, and if they do, does it follow that they will *never* be happy with women's lot in the world? To many people these questions may be comparable with, 'Is the Pope a Catholic?' and 'Do bears crap in woods?', but they're worth exploring. Because if the answers to both questions is 'yes', then we can expect only one thing from militant feminists: relentless discrimination against men, disguised as support for women. Discrimination against men – and ideally against white middle-aged, middle-class men – is the only discrimination which is considered acceptable, even laudable, in the modern era.

All my adult life – I'm now 53, so let's say from the mid 1970s – I've been familiar with the term 'misogyny', the hatred of women. In any discussion between men and women about gender issues, the men will be swiftly and bitterly denounced by the women as 'sexist', and probably 'misogynistic' too. The effect is to quash debate, nuanced or otherwise, because there cannot be a point to debating with such a vile person.

But what about the hatred of men, or 'misandry'? I wasn't even aware of the term until I started my researches for this book. Misogyny has been a much-studied phenomenon for decades, partly down to the 'women's studies' industry. For some insights into misandry we turn to a notable book co-written by Professor Katherine K Young and Paul Nathanson – both at McGill University in Canada – and published in 2001, *Misandry (The Teaching of Contempt for Men in Popular Culture)*:

Central to all ideologies is *dualism*. Like Marxists, ideological feminists identify a 'class' that is inherently hostile, one that has forged a universal conspiracy to dominate, exploit, and oppress. The class of men is privileged and, virtually by definition, evil. The class of women, on the other hand, is underprivileged and, virtually by definition, good. Justice, therefore, is the triumph of women over men. The old sexual hierarchy has been stood on its proverbial head, not transformed. Not all feminists are dualistic, and thus ideological, but some of the most brilliant, innovative, and influential ones are.

Consider the following dualistic passage from Mary Daly, among the most fashionable feminist critics of Christian theology: 'The weapons of Wonderlusting women are the Labryses/double axes of our own Wild wisdom and wit, which cut through the mazes of man-made mystification, breaking the mindbindings of master-minded double-think... Recognizing that deep damage has been inflicted upon consciousness under phallocracy's myths and institutions, we continue to Name patriarchy as the perverted paradigm and source of other social evils. [Author's note: Mary dear, calm down and make yourself a nice cup of tea, there's a good girl.]

Naomi Goldberg, among many others, has made dualism more accessible to rank and file feminists: 'I only hope that a feminist rhetoric based in the body inspires theories that value life more than has a patriarchal rhetoric based in the mind.' This is just an upside-down version of the classic body-mind or matter-spirit dualism that is endemic in Western thought, only now it is the mind or spirit associated with maleness that is evil, not the body or matter associated with femaleness. It is profoundly anti-intellectual too, even though Goldberg herself teaches at a university...

All too often, the rhetoric of difference turns into that of *hierarchy*. Why has hierarchy been so pervasive in discussions of gender since the 1980s? One answer is found in the historical lineage of feminist ideology, which, as we have noted, is a variant of Marxism. Instead of transcending the old class hierarchy, Marxism merely reversed it. Instead of being ruled by a bourgeoisie, the new 'classless society' would consist only of 'workers'. But in the meantime, before the revolution, members of the proletariat may consider themselves morally superior to the bourgeoisie. Likewise, the new genderless society will consist only of women and male converts to feminism. In the meantime, women can consider themselves morally superior to men...

Ideological feminists promote a *utopian* vision of society. Like the Marxist version, it is defined in purely secular terms as a classless society attainable on earth and within history. And in both cases, the advent of this classless society coincides with a radical transformation of human nature.

Some ideological feminists like to describe this visionary society in terms of sexual equality – social, economic, legal, and political – to be brought about by reforming the patriarchal order. To institute that kind of world would take more than the reform of patriarchy, however, which is by (their) definition utterly devoid of value. Patriarchy would have to be destroyed through revolution before any new society could be built on the ruins.

The new order would have room for every conceivable perspective, in short, *except* that of men. What place men might have – or even want to have – in a world based explicitly on ideological feminism (or 'feminine values' or 'women's spirituality') is another matter. The fact is that this new order would be anything other than egalitarian. It would merely substitute some form of matriarchy, though possibly one based on an attitude of *noblesse oblige* towards men, for patriarchy. Women seek 'power for', Marilyn French and others have claimed, not 'power over'. They reject, presumably, anything to do with systems of control or domination. Ironically, their own program involves precisely that. The world they describe is one in which citizens, at least male citizens, are carefully controlled and duly punished for deviation from the norm prescribed by ideological feminists. This is a world that can be achieved only by social engineering on a colossal scale.

Other ideological feminists describe utopia in frankly religious terms – neo-pagan ones for the most part, occasionally with a thin veneer of Christian or Jewish imagery to legitimate them. These women hope to restore a lost golden age under the aegis of a Great Goddess, a paradise that was destroyed by evil patriarchal gods and their male supporters. It does not take much imagination to see that this myth is merely the reversal of an ancient one. In short, Original Sin is blamed on Adam (and men, his 'followers'), not Eve (and women, her 'followers'). Salvation is to come through a new Eve, therefore, not a new Adam such as

Christ. The new Eden would be a paradise for women – but would it be a paradise for the entire community, for men as well as women? Probably not. Some women might say that the new order would benefit men whether they like it or not, that it would be 'for their own good'. But they could do so only by relying on the same condescending and patronising mentality – *noblesse oblige* – that they themselves have come to resent from men...

We turn now to feminist *consequentialism*. Like Marxists and nationalists, ideological feminists believe that the end of creating a new order justifies whatever means that might involve. Feminists, as we say, seldom resort to violence as a justifiable means. They refer instead to law reform. That certainly does not sound morally problematic, not when you consider the alternative of violence, but it can be highly problematic on closer examination. The laws proposed are intended to serve the needs of women, for one thing, not those of men. Whether these new laws can effectively and appropriately serve the needs of society as a whole, therefore, is a moot point. Besides, changing public consciousness is not necessarily as innocent as getting people to discard their old prejudices. Very often, it involves getting them to replace the old prejudices with new ones. In this case, that often means presenting men as worthy of nothing but ridicule and contempt. That this often boils down to prejudice, not merely disapproval of this or that individual man, can be seen almost any day of the week on television, at the movies, in newspapers and magazines...

Like both religious fundamentalism and Marxism, feminist ideology seems to have an answer for every challenge. At no point after conversion are women forced or even encouraged by ideological feminists to question their presuppositions or analysis. Nor do they force women to question their own behaviour or take responsibility for it.

Because feminist ideology has created a closed system of meaning, it resembles religion in yet another way. Like sectarian churches, which are often characterized by both fundamentalism and dualism, it relies on a profound distinction between insiders (the elect, who have seen the light) and outsiders, (the 'world', with its heathens, which must be either converted or shunned). This applies not only to men but also, ironically, to some women as well.

So, back to the earlier questions: do militant feminists hate men, and if they do, does it follow they will *never* be satisfied with women's lot in the world? A resounding 'yes' to both questions, I think you'll agree.

CHAPTER 12

POLITICAL CORRECTNESS
(CULTURAL MARXISM)

Being politically correct means always having to say you're sorry.
Charles Osgood 1933- American radio and television commentator

The antipathy of political correctness towards Western values – emotion trumps reason – political correctness as the 'solution' to patriarchal hegemony – the 'unacceptable' gender pay gap – the 'acceptable' gap between the retirement ages of men and women – discrimination, now one of the most unforgivable sins – why criticism of women is not permitted – Harriet Harman's suspicion of ageism on *Strictly Come Dancing* – Harriet Harman and a 'ginger rodent'

For an understanding of the origins of political correctness, and how it manifests itself in the modern era, we turn to a book written by Anthony Browne, the snappily-titled *The Retreat of Reason: Political Correctness and the Corruption of Public Debate in Modern Britain* (2006). It was published by Civitas, The Institute for the Study of Civil Society. From the first chapter, 'What is Political Correctness?':

> The phrase 'political correctness' conjures up images of left-wing councils banning black bin-bags, nativity scenes being banned by the Red Cross and handicapped people being called 'otherwise-abled'. Some of these cases, such as renaming firemen as firefighters, merely reflect a changing reality. Others are just the most overt symptoms of political correctness, and easily ridiculed: he's not dead, he's metabolically challenged.
>
> But political correctness is more than a joke or updating of historic language usage. It is a system of beliefs and pattern of thoughts that permeates many aspects of modern life, holding a vice-like grip over public debate, deciding what can be debated and what the terms of debate are, and which

government policies are acceptable and which aren't. It has grown in influence over the last few decades to the extent that it has now become one of the most dominant features of public discourse, not just in Britain, but across the Western – and particularly the Anglophone – world.

PC is also surprisingly unexamined as a phenomenon, the subject of few academic treatises and few books, at least outside the US. Criticism of it has rarely graduated from ridicule to analysis. Part of the problem is that there is no standard definition of political correctness. Peter Coleman, a former Australian government minister from the Liberal Party, wrote:

> Political Correctness is a heresy of liberalism. It emerges where liberalism and leftism intersect. What began as a liberal assault on injustice has come to denote, not for the first time, a new form of injustice.

He said that it was liberalism that has been taken over by dogmatism, that it is 'intolerant', 'self-righteous' and 'quasi-religious'. The Politically Correct are more intolerant of dissent than traditional liberals or even conservatives. Liberals of earlier generations accepted unorthodoxy as normal. Indeed the right to differ was a datum of classical liberalism. The Politically Correct do not give that right a high priority. It distresses their programmed minds. Those who do not conform should be ignored, silenced or vilified. There is a kind of soft totalitarianism about Political Correctness.

The US conservative commentator Paul Weyrich, the President of the Free Congress Foundation, is also exercised by the intolerance of political correctness, although his main concern is its antipathy to Western values:

> The United States is very close to becoming a state totally dominated by an alien ideology, an ideology bitterly hostile to Western culture. Even now, for the first time in their lives, people have to be afraid of what they say. This has never been true in the history of our country. Yet today, if you say the 'wrong thing', you suddenly have legal problems, political problems, you might even lose your job or be expelled from college. Certain topics are forbidden. You can't approach the truth about a lot of different subjects. If you do, you are immediately branded as 'racist', 'sexist', 'homophobic', 'insensitive', or 'judgmental.'

The US commentator William Lind, director of the Center for Cultural Conservatism, is among those who have described PC as 'cultural Marxism', declaring that it is 'Marxism translated from economic into cultural terms'. [Author's note: Marxism. Is this why political correctness makes us see red?] He wrote:

> The cultural Marxism of Political Correctness, like economic Marxism, has a single factor explanation of history. Economic Marxism says that all of history is determined by ownership of means of production. Cultural Marxism, or Political Correctness, says that all history is determined by power, by which groups defined in terms of race, sex, etc, have power over which other groups. Nothing else matters.

The *New York Times'* culture correspondent, Richard Bernstein, who came out against multiculturalism in his book *The Dictatorship of Virtue*, was also concerned about how PC tried to overturn the dominant culture and power structures. In a landmark 1990 article which sparked debate about PC in the US, he wrote:

> Central to pc-ness, which has its roots in 1960s radicalism, is the view that Western society has for centuries been dominated by what is often called 'the white male power structure' or 'Patriarchal hegemony.' A related belief is that everybody but white heterosexual males has suffered some form of repression and been denied a cultural voice.

Across much of Britain's public discourse, a reliance on reason has been replaced with a reliance on the emotional appeal of an argument. Parallel to the once-trusted world of empiricism and deductive reasoning, an often overwhelmingly powerful emotional landscape has been created, rewarding people with feelings of virtue for some beliefs, punishing with feelings of guilt for others. It is a belief system that echoes religion in providing ready, emotionally satisfying answers for a world too complex to understand fully, and providing a gratifying sense of righteousness absent in our otherwise secular society. . .

Because the politically correct believe they are not just on the side of right, but of virtue, it follows that those they are opposed to are not just wrong, but malign. In the PC mind, the pursuit of virtue entitles them to curtail the malign views of those they disagree with. Rather than say, 'I would like to hear your side', the politically correct insist: 'you can't say that'.

Believing that their opponents are not just wrong but bad, the politically correct feel free to resort to personal attacks on them. If there is no explicit bad motive, then the PC can accuse their opponents of a sinister ulterior motive – the unanswerable accusations of 'isms'. It is this self-righteous sense of virtue that makes the PC believe they are justified in suppressing freedom of speech. Political correctness is the dictatorship of virtue. . .

But what is the point of political correctness? Why are some things politically correct, and others not? At its most fundamental, political correctness seeks to redistribute power from the powerful to the powerless. At its most crude, it opposes power for the sake of opposing power, making no moral distinction between whether the power is malign or benign, or whether the powerful exercise their power in a way that can be rationally and reasonably justified. . .

America, as the world's most powerful country, can never do any good, even though it is the world's most powerful liberal democracy, the largest donor of overseas aid, and it defeated both Nazism and Communism.

The West, as the world's most powerful cultural and economic group, can safely be blamed for all the world's ills, even though it is largely responsible for the worldwide spread of prosperity, democracy and scientific advance.

Multinational corporations are condemned as the oppressors of the world's poor, rather than seen as engines of global economic growth with vast job-creating investments in the world's poorest countries, pushing up wages and transferring knowledge.

Conversely, political correctness automatically supports the weak and vulnerable, classifying them as nearly untouchable victims, irrespective of whether they merit such support or not. . .

In the battle between emotion and reason, emotion wins most of the time for most people: the heart trumps the head because it is more difficult to live with bad feelings than bad logic. Few are the souls tortured by bad reasoning; many are those tortured by guilt. However overwhelming the evidence, people believe what they want to believe, and find it very difficult to believe what they don't want to.

The easiest way to overcome the dissonance between what you want to believe and the evidence is not to change what you believe, but to shut out the evidence and silence those who try to highlight it…

People tend to believe that which makes them feel virtuous, not that which makes them feel bad. Most people have a profound need to believe they are on the side of virtue, and can do that by espousing beliefs publicly acknowledged as virtuous. Nothing makes multimillionaire Hollywood actors who live in Beverly Hills feel better about themselves than campaigning against world poverty by demanding more aid from the West (rather than holding African leaders responsible for the plight of their people by demanding better governance).

From the chapter 'How Political Correctness Affects Policies':

One of the rallying cries of the politically correct is the 'unacceptable' gender pay gap between men and women: women's full-time hourly pay is on average just 80% of that of men. Unions and the Equal Opportunities Commission regularly launch campaigns on the issue, insisting it shows just how prevalent sex discrimination still is in the workplace. Few ask whether the gender pay gap may be due to other factors, because that would be to appear to justify the pay gap and thus sex discrimination.

It is clear that, other factors being the same, equal pay for equal work is not just fundamentally fair and just, but also an essential basis for an efficient economy taking optimal advantage of the skills of all workers. If women are paid less for equal work than men just because of their gender, then that is irrational, prejudicial and unjust.

But even in a workforce with a total absence of sex discrimination, there could still be a gender pay gap. The presumption that any pay gap is only explicable by sex discrimination is a presumption that men and women are identical in all their lifestyle choices and legal rights, when they are not.

Men's legal retirement age is five years later than women's, encouraging them to work longer careers, which uplifts their average earnings. Women get far more extensive parental leave than men, encouraging career breaks and limiting their lifetime work experience, thus depressing their average wages. On average, each week, men work nearly twice as many hours in paid employment as women, building up considerably more experience in their careers, which in a meritocracy would be reflected in greater pay. In addition, surveys suggest that women opt for more socially rewarding or emotionally fulfilling jobs, while men put a higher priority on high wages at whatever cost.

The danger is that if the only accepted explanation for income differentials is discrimination, then a range of policies will be adopted that may either be counterproductive, or actually introduce discrimination. Policies that specifically favour women at the expense of men are not only unfair, but by undermining meritocracy they undermine the efficiency of the labour market.

From the chapter 'The Trouble with Discrimination':

Once upon a time, 'discrimination' – which is so central to much of political correctness it is worth special consideration – was seen as a positive attribute, which enabled people to discriminate between good and bad. People of discernment actually tried to educate themselves to become 'discriminating', a by-word for having good judgement.

Now 'discrimination' – an ill-defined, catch-all term – has become one of the most unforgivable sins, something that no respectable person would seek to justify under any circumstances. Anything that is portrayed as 'discriminatory' in any way is automatically deemed intolerable.

The fight against discrimination is one of the foundation stones of political correctness, underpinning and motivating much of it. Shami Chakrabarti, on becoming director of the left-wing pressure group Liberty, declared she believed in 'zero tolerance of any form of discrimination'. The European Charter of Fundamental Rights promises to outlaw all discrimination, turning politically correct sloganeering into Europe-wide law upheld by a court in Luxembourg:

> Any discrimination based on any ground such as sex, race, colour, ethnic or social origin, genetic features, language, religion or belief, political or any other opinion, membership of a national minority, property, birth, disability, age or sexual orientation shall be prohibited.

There are noble intentions behind these declarations that few civilised people would disagree with, and making these declarations rewards the declarers by making them feel virtuous (as one government lawyer said to me). The fight against discrimination has righted many hideous wrongs, such as denial of services to ethnic minorities and women's disenfranchisement. But having won the most obvious and justifiable battles, the intentions are often rendered meaningless by the flawed, often hypocritical and usually intolerant thinking behind them. . .

There are widespread double standards on various forms of discrimination. In general, discrimination – even irrational, prejudicial discrimination – is either tolerated or promoted so long as it is against the powerful, while discrimination against those deemed vulnerable is deemed indefensible. 'Gender profiling' by police forces that targets men is perfectly acceptable, while 'racial profiling' which targets blacks is not.

Those who wage war on 'all forms of discrimination' often promote so-called 'positive discrimination', which is nonetheless discrimination which should thus supposedly be worthy of 'zero tolerance'.

The difference in retirement age between men and women is irrational prejudicial discrimination, the continuation of which (at least until 2020) is only explicable because it is men (otherwise perceived to be privileged) who are discriminated against. It is inconceivable that if it were women who were discriminated against that it would not have ended by now, even though it would be slightly more justifiable because women actually live longer.

There are no longer any male-only colleges in Oxford and Cambridge, having come under great pressure to change. But women-only colleges, which are just as blatantly sexist, continue to justify their existence on the grounds that they benefit women – despite the fact that women greatly outperform men at all levels of the education system, up to and including the attainment of first-class university degrees.

Men are become increasingly angry at the yawning gap between how some women in the developed world continue to portray themselves – as *still* disadvantaged – and the reality they see all around them in their working and personal lives. But they seem to be doing almost nothing about it. The disinclination of men to be critical of women in areas related to their noble struggle for equality and fairness is only strengthened by the prevailing culture of political correctness.

Steve Moxon's 2008 book *The Woman Racket* is 'a serious scientific investigation into one of the key myths of our age – that women are oppressed by the patriarchal traditions of Western societies'. Drawing on the latest developments in evolutionary psychology, Moxon convincingly demonstrates that men – or at least the majority of men, who are low-status – have always been the victims of deep-rooted prejudice, and have been manipulated by women, because women have power over men through being the 'limiting factor' in reproduction. That is, they have power because they control which men can, and which men cannot, have children. Moxon explains why the idea that men exercise 'power' over women is nonsense, biologically speaking. He shows that domestic violence – even of the most violent nature – is more often committed by women against men than vice versa. And he overturns numerous other gender-related myths. It hardly needs saying, but Harriet Harman makes a number of appearances in the book.

I couldn't resist including in this chapter another newspaper article about Ms Harman. It was written by Anita Singh for *The Daily Telegraph* of 17 July 2009, and titled ' "Ageist" BBC must reinstate Arlene, says Harman':

Arlene Phillips, the *Strictly Come Dancing* judge who was dropped from the show in favour of a younger star, was the victim of age discrimination, according to Harriet Harman. In a surprising government intervention [Author's note: Hardly 'surprising' given that it involved Ms Harman; the woman has the stamina of ten ordinary mortals] Labour's deputy leader and the Equalities Minister described the BBC's decision to replace Phillips as 'absolutely shocking' and called for her to be reinstated.

The veteran choreographer, 66, has been replaced by Alesha Dixon, 30, a pop star who won the ballroom competition in 2007. The male judges, who range in age from 44 to 65, and the show's 81-year-old host, Bruce Forsyth, have been retained, while the ballet dancer, Darcey Bussell, 40, will also join the show.

Miss Harman told the Commons yesterday, 'It's shocking that Arlene Phillips is not going to be a judge on *Strictly Come Dancing*. As Equalities Minister I am suspicious that there is age discrimination there. So I'd like to take the opportunity of saying to the BBC: if it is not too late, we want Arlene Phillips in the next edition of *Strictly Come Dancing*.'

Ironically, on the rare occasions Harriet Harman is politically incorrect in public, she displays a real talent for it. From *The Independent* of 31 October 2010:

The former equalities minister Harriet Harman was forced to apologise last night for branding the Chief Secretary to the Treasury, Danny Alexander, a 'ginger rodent'. Ms Harman, Labour's deputy leader, admitted she had been 'wrong' to use the description during a speech at the Scottish Labour conference in Oban. She also called the Liberal Democrat 'the front-man for the Tory cuts'.

Her remarks were attacked for being anti-Scottish, given that 13 per cent of Scots have red hair compared with just 2 per cent of the population globally. For his part, Mr Alexander insisted he was not ashamed of his colouring. 'I am proud to be ginger and rodents do valuable work cleaning up mess others leave behind,' he said via Twitter.

CHAPTER 13

WHY DOES FAIRTRADE COFFEE ALWAYS TASTE LIKE MUD?

There are three intolerable things in life – cold coffee, lukewarm champagne, and overexcited women.
Orson Welles 1915-85 American filmmaker, actor, theatre director, screenwriter, producer

Among the depressing phenomena of the modern era we must include the Fairtrade industry. The central premise of the industry is that consumers pay more for their products and services than they would otherwise have to, with some of the premium helping to raise the incomes of poor farmers etc.

Anyone with even an elementary grasp of economics could predict the result of this disconnect between price and quality. Buyers of Fairtrade products must cover a cost beyond the premium paid to farmers: the cost of the Fairtrade organisation itself. Either product prices have to rise so much that they greatly dampen demand, or Fairtrade buyers source poorer quality and cheaper product so consumers pay a lower price premium. Fairtrade buyers invariably choose the latter option, and that's why Fairtrade coffee (and tea etc.) *always* tastes poor.

So widespread is the demand for Fairtrade products, regrettably, that we even find them in restaurants. And so it was that I recently found myself drinking an appalling cup of coffee – obviously Fairtrade coffee, I didn't need to look at the menu for confirmation – in one of Bedford's finest Italian restaurants. I called the waitress over and complained that the coffee tasted like mud. 'Of course it does, sir,' she replied, 'it was ground only five minutes ago.'

CHAPTER 14

WOMEN AND POLITICS

The vote, I think, means nothing to women. We should be armed.
Edna O'Brien 1932– Irish novelist and short story writer

On what grounds do women cast their votes? – why the UK has the transport infrastructure of a banana republic – the strategic defence initiative will give Britain aircraft carriers without aircraft – lady voters' aversion to bald leaders of political parties – how the suffragettes delayed universal suffrage – a ladies' discussion in a public house – why my lady lodger would *never* vote for the Conservatives – Harriet Harman's introduction of all-women shortlists for prospective parliamentary candidates – why I cancelled my Conservative party membership – both the major political parties' leaders support all-women shortlists – Harriet Harman fights for northerners – Harriet Harman wields a .44 Magnum revolver – what men must do, apparently – when will British men strap a pair on?

What persuades women to cast their votes for one party rather than another in general elections? The evidence suggests they do so with an eye to just three areas: healthcare, childcare and education. This isn't surprising, given that these are the areas most obviously of importance to women and their families on a day-to-day basis. They're important areas *but they're not the only important areas*. Women have not the slightest interest in areas such as the nation's defences, the size and role of the public sector, the justice system, the transport infrastructure, and countless other issues of interest – in a voting intention sense – only to men.

Women – including female politicians – are proficient at campaigning for public funds to be spent on their behalf; while men (and male politicians) do not display the same parochialism. Hence – to take but one example – the enormous public expenditure on detecting breast cancer, compared with the derisory expenditure on detecting prostate cancer.

Women's lack of interest in issues beyond 'women's issues' clearly poses a risk for the country. Politicians in the modern era have become increasingly proficient at exploiting women's lack of interest in politics, and accordingly we hear them endlessly invoking notions of 'fairness' and 'equality' which resonate more with women than men. Over time ever more money has to be spent on areas which appeal to women, and ever less money on areas with little emotional resonance and therefore little interest to women. Which might explain why the United Kingdom has the transport infrastructure of a banana republic, and why defence expenditure is facing the most severe cuts in 30 years while expenditure on the National Health Service has been ring-fenced. From the BBC's online news service on 19 October 2010:

> David Cameron has confirmed defence spending is to be cut by 8% in real terms over four years, as he unveils the strategic defence review. He said RAF and Navy numbers would be reduced by 5,000 each, Army numbers by 7,000 and the Ministry of Defence would lose 25,000 civilian staff by 2015.
> Nimrod reconnaissance planes would be axed and there will be fewer frigates and destroyers, he said. Labour's Ed Miliband said the review had been 'hastily prepared'.
> Mr Cameron opened his Commons statement by denying the review was simply a 'cost saving exercise', saying it was a 'step change in the way we protect this country's security interests'. He said the defence budget would fall by 8% over four years but will meet the NATO target of spending 2% of GDP on defence and would still leave Britain with the fourth largest military in the world.
>
> KEY POINTS
> Harrier jump jet retired
> Nimrod spy plane cancelled
> 5,000 RAF personnel axed over five years

5,000 Navy personnel cut
7,000 army personnel cut
25,000 civilian MoD staff axed
Trident replaced but £750m savings from fewer warheads
Two aircraft carriers saved, but one will not enter service

There would be no cuts to support for troops in Afghanistan – which is funded separately from the Treasury's special reserve, he told MPs. Mr Cameron vowed to push ahead with replacing Britain's Trident nuclear missile system but said their replacement would be scaled back, with the number of warheads per boat cut from 58 to 40, as part of a £750m package of savings. The life of the current Trident submarines would also be extended, with the final spending decision on their replacement delayed until 2016 – after the next general election...

He also said naval manpower would fall to 30,000 by 2015 and the total number of frigates and destroyers would drop from 23 to 19 by 2020. BBC defence correspondent Caroline Wyatt said the decision to decommission the Ark Royal and axe the UK's force of Harrier jump jets meant that, until at least 2019, no planes would be able to fly from the new aircraft carriers. Shadow defence secretary Jim Murphy described the arrangement as 'peculiar' and 'driven by finance'. He told the BBC: 'What's the purpose of an aircraft carrier if not to carry aircraft? And I think to leave our country without a single fixed-wing aircraft able to fly off our aircraft carriers for a decade is a very worrying decision. It can't be driven by security needs or strategic needs. No-one considering the security needs of our country would come to the decision that a decade without an aeroplane on an aircraft carrier is the right decision.'...

The last strategic defence review in 1998 took more than a year, while this one has been carried out in five months, leading to accusations that the government has rushed the process.

Journalists know that women have no interest in politics beyond the 'human interest' side; hence the relentless stream of stories for female readers which have nothing to do with politics, but concern politicians' and politicians' spouses' attire, marital indiscretions etc.

It's well known that women's voting tendencies are influenced by the party leaders' appearances, and they are particularly averse to parties led by bald men; which may explain, at least in part, the electoral failures of parties led by Winston Churchill (1945), Neil Kinnock (1992), and William Hague (2001). Iain Duncan Smith, the leader of the Conservative party over 2001-3, didn't survive long enough to fight a general election, such was his perceived unelectability.

When did the pretence that women have any interest in politics begin? Political movement towards women's suffrage in the United Kingdom began before the First World War, and in 1918 Parliament passed an act (the Representation of the People Act) granting the vote to women over the age of 30 who were householders, the wives of householders, occupiers of property with an annual rent of £5 or more, and graduates of British universities. Women in the United Kingdom finally achieved suffrage on the same terms as men in 1928.

Among the great icons of feminism are the suffragettes, so I was grateful to learn something of the reality of the movement in *The Woman Racket*:

> The cry of 'votes for women', in great contrast to the brutal suppression of various movements through history which could be characterised as 'votes for ordinary men' (notably the Chartists, little more than half a century before), was a push at an open door. Parliament had been long persuaded of the case, despite the lack of popular demand for female suffrage. The tactic of the suffragettes was counter-productively to try to kick the door in. What is not appreciated today is that it was directly as a result of suffragette militancy that legislation for universal suffrage was not hastened but *delayed*, and introduced not in full but in two stages.

The female suffragist cause was an extremely well-to-do affair generally: not middle- but *upper*-class. The only places in the country where there was any significant involvement by working-class women were some of the Lancashire textile towns. Everywhere else it was characterised by the absence of a working-class or of even a middle-class element, in contrast to other political movements at the time. Very well politically-connected, wealthy, and titled women made up the Women's Social & Political Union. Far from being the case that ordinary women were clamouring for the vote, there was general indifference, as Gladstone, prime minister at the time, remarked.

Militancy confirmed the one fear the general population had about the female franchise – irresponsible behaviour by those who would be newly enfranchised. The twin concerns that the movement needed to address – being unrepresentative and irresponsible – were exactly the concerns that the suffragettes haplessly highlighted and confirmed.

This was of little if any consequence to the suffragettes, because through their connections they well knew they were nonetheless secure in that parliamentary opinion was substantially in favour of women getting the vote, despite MPs knowing that there was little support in the country. They were simply playing at politics, and managed to turn newspapers from offering almost uniform open support to being obliged to attack their methods.

The onset of militancy in 1908 spawned The Ladies League for Opposing Women's Suffrage, which by 1914 boasted 42,000 members. They appealed over the heads of the politicians by canvassing female local government electors, whom they found *consistently opposed to female suffrage by a factor of four to one* [Author's italics], but this had no impact on MPs.

As women, and even more so as well-to-do women, the suffragettes knew full well that they were immune from physical harm, regardless of what they did. The sole fatality in the campaign, Emily Davison, was a well-to-do woman too out of touch with the real world to know that the King's racehorse would not be made to stop simply by jumping out from the rail and standing in front of it. Suicide it was not, it is now known. Suffragettes, unlike Chartists and their ilk, never needed to be brave. They never needed even to fear loss of any reputation. A night or more in the cells was generally seen as a badge of honour, as suffragettes had *carte blanche* to be shameless.

Unabashed by the fact that men were dying in huge numbers in a war over which half of all men had been denied the expression of any opinion whatsoever; throughout World War I, Sylvia Pankhurst campaigned undaunted, along with The Women's Freedom League. Pankhurst set up a 'League of Rights for Soldiers' and Sailors' Wives and Relatives'. This focus away from those who were the real sufferers, is exemplified in an absurd statement by Isabella Ford, writing in 1915: 'Women have more to lose in the horrible business than some men have; for they often lose more than life itself when their men are killed.'

Two leading suffragette organisations did agree to suspend their window breaking, arson, policemen-hitting and the like, right from the start of WWI, when they realised that their campaign would be seen to be a disgrace. The leader of the whole movement, Emmeline Pankhurst, with her daughter Christabel, toured the country speaking at meetings to recruit young men into the army. Christabel wrote of her mother: 'She called for wartime conscription for men, believing that this was democratic and equitable'.

Did she also think it democratic that her supporters handed white feathers to every young man they encountered wearing civilian dress? These would be those reserved for essential heavy industrial work, government employees, those too unfit for service, boys too young to enlist, and convalescents from physical or psychological wounding, as well as those very few men who had indeed taken the sure route to total social ostracism and punishment beatings by declaring themselves conscientious objectors.

These last would not include Emmeline's daughter, Sylvia, because being a woman she was free to actively campaign against the war effort with impunity. But her mother's white feather brigade contributed to so many children lying about their age in order to enlist, making them even more likely to be killed than the average soldier, on account of the extra vulnerability of their impetuous youth.

It cannot have been unknown to Emmeline, the foremost and most well-known suffragette of all, that even by 1914 and the start of World War One, half of adult men were still not entitled to vote; and that therefore they had no say in the political process that brought about Britain's involvement in the war.

For the first part of the war, soldiers were not called up but volunteered, albeit under massive social pressure. Conscription would mean that all men below a certain age could be forced into a situation where they could be ordered to take part in attacks in which they faced a very good chance of being killed or seriously wounded, in a war which overall they stood a high chance of not surviving, and an even better chance of being maimed and so unable to live a normal life afterwards. This would apply disproportionately to those men without the vote, because conscription had an upper age limit of forty-five.

The subset of younger men aged 21 – 45 was made up of those within the electorate less likely to have established themselves in terms of tenancy, property ownership or residence – the very criteria by which many would have failed to be enfranchised. How could Emmeline Pankhurst of all people have had the hypocrisy to actively campaign for conscription at a time when the majority of those who would be conscripted did not have the vote?

Militancy was not the women suffragists' worst blunder. This was that they saw themselves as quite separate from, and unhelped or even hindered by, progressive male enfranchisement. They repeatedly demanded that the next step should be purely in regard to women. The root of their difficulties was a false belief that there was no clamour amongst the working classes for extending the male vote.

They could not have been more wrong. Presumably, they must have falsely extrapolated from the indifference of working-class women for votes for themselves to imagine that enfranchisement was generally not an issue for the whole working class. In fact, the male franchise was a big issue for working men, and their women supported them. This delusion was motivated by something worse than that the women suffragists simply did not care about the extent of adult male suffrage.

A common theme in the movement, on both sides of the Atlantic, was that the vote initially should be extended to women through an education qualification. The converse of this was also argued, and quite openly: that *uneducated men should be denied the vote.*

The suffragettes wanted first and foremost an elitist enfranchisement of themselves to join the men of their own upper- and upper-middle classes, and only argued for universal *female* suffrage because it was more politically expedient. Their second preferred option was to give way and allow the vote for the entire 'sisterhood', but only if there was qualified voting for men. The sentiment was here perhaps a little less elitist but decidedly separatist, betraying the common attitude of women of being not only anti-male per se, but just against the majority of lower-status men. This is why women prominent in the Labour movement at the time were not persuaded by the suffragettes and stuck to campaigning for adult suffrage and not for a separate bill for women.

The wider perception was that the suffragettes created a needless divide between the sexes, and in the years before politicians were fully persuaded the tactic of an initial partial extension of franchise for women backfired. It alerted politicians that gallantry could be aroused to concede the vote to a section of the female population, and this would then act as a Trojan horse for a complete capitulation to democratic rule by the masses.

The elitism of the suffragettes' demands is even more apparent when you consider that these privileged women were married to men who often already provided *two* votes for the household in having a business as well as a residence qualification. Upper-class or upper-middle-class women felt aggrieved not so much that their husbands or the husbands of friends (if they were in business or academia) could command two votes to their none, but that the vote had been accorded to other men beneath their social milieu. This is the reason for campaigning for a male educational qualification. Ladies of leisure received an education (falsely) regarded as superior to the technical education of upper-working-class men, so this was a ticket with which to maintain social differentials.

After 1918 the observation was made by one politician that full male suffrage had taken 600 years to achieve, so why should female suffrage take only ten? But the overriding male deference to women as ever ruled the day. Influential men joined in the women's campaign, and the wider 'chivalrous' principle was allowed to overcome what in any other matter considered by government would have been continuing inertia. Yet this issue concerned the very survival of the elected members of political parties themselves. Any proposed changes to the electoral system make political parties extremely wary. Albeit that the Rubicon had been crossed in

1918; with politics in some turmoil the unpredictable effect of the entire mass of young women suddenly joining the electoral roll must have given politicians of all parties some worry. The underlying reason for the short delay, was to see what the great change in the franchise of 1918 would lead to. After being sure that the destabilisation was containable, only then could MPs responsibly proceed further. Ten years, and just a couple of elections, would have been a minimum period to assess this.

Women's lack of interest in politics is widespread, but now and again we come across startling examples of the phenomenon. Which brings me to my tale of a visit to a public house in the early evening of Wednesday, May 5, 2010. The day before a general election widely regarded as the most critical for 20-30 years, an opportunity to re-elect or reject the appalling left-wing administration which had run the country since 1997.

I sat down with a Guinness at a table in a quiet spot near a group of four ladies who I guessed, from their facial resemblances, represented four generations of the same family. Give or take a few years, I'd say they were about 20, 40, 60 and 80 years old. The youngest had a young son, just able to walk, who was being looked after by his inebriated father nearby.

The ladies were cheerful, chatty, and a little loud after a few drinks. And so it was that I was privileged to unwittingly overhear their animated conversation over the course of an hour. This mainly consisted of discussions about the boy whose first two names were Rio Ferdinand, I was later to learn from the barmaid. A celebrity English soccer player.

The ladies appeared riveted by discussions about the boy's hair, facial expressions, attempts to walk and talk, and his similarities to family members both living and deceased. The breaks from discussions on the God-child consisted of exchanges about the previous evening's television soap operas, the hair styles of various female friends and acquaintances, and titbits of celebrity gossip gleaned from the pages of the celebrity magazines that were clearly the ladies' main reading material. I listened in vain for anything with the slightest intellectual content, or signs that the four women had ever received an education, watched a documentary on television, had the slightest interest in current affairs, or read a book.

I shall denote the ladies by their ages: W20, W40, W60 and W80. Just as W20 was taking her leave, I overheard the following conversation. Readers might like to imagine the words spoken in the accent adopted by the divine Audrey Hepburn in her role as Eliza Doolittle, the flower seller in the film *My Fair Lady* (1964), *before* her elocution lessons:

W40:   'Ere Cheryl, you votin' tomorrer?
W20:   Wodger mean?
W40:   In vee election.
W20:   Izzat tomorrer? I fort it were next week.
W40:   Nah, tomorrer. I'm gonner vote fer Cameron, 'e seems nice. Always smartly dressed, inny?
W20:   Well I fink he's a posh twat. I don't like 'im. I'm gonner vote for someone else. *Anyone* else. Don't know 'oo.
W60:   I'm gonner vote Labour. Always 'ave, always will.
W80:   I'm gonner vote Tory. Always 'ave, always will.

Each of these women had the same voting power in the following day's general election as people who had made the effort to be well informed about current affairs. How *could* that be right?

Returning home in low spirits, I asked my lady lodger – in her late thirties – which party *she* was planning to vote for. She said she wasn't sure, 'but it won't be Conservative because my Mum didn't like Margaret Thatcher back in the 1980s.' I pointed out that the Conservatives were now putting forward policies which I knew she would support. But she was adamant that she would remain with her position *regardless of the policies that the Conservatives were putting forward.* How can democracy function properly when so many voters vote emotionally rather then rationally? It can't.

The prime motivation of women in politics appears to be to further women's interests at the expense of men. When you look for it, it's not difficult to find examples of the mindset. We turn to the ultimate example of campaigning militant feminist politicians: the dreaded and dreadful Harriet Harman, Member of Parliament for Camberwell and Peckham, whose titles before the 2010 general election included Deputy Leader of the Labour Party, Labour Party Chair, Minister for Women and Equality, Leader of the House of Commons, and The Lord Privy Seal. She must have had the largest business card on the planet.

In the foreword of the paper 'Women's Changing Lives: Priorities for the Ministers for Women – One Year On Progress Report', presented to Parliament in July 2008, Harriet Harman wrote the following:

> A modern democracy must be fair and equal. The government has fought for equal representation and it's because of this that we have record levels of women MPs, as well as more black and Asian MPs and councillors than ever before. But we need more women and more black, Asian and minority ethnic MPs and councillors to make our democracy truly representative.
>
> That's why in March I announced that political parties will be able to use all-women shortlists for the next five elections.

Wow. Because of the action of a militant feminist politician, until about 2030 I – and every other man in the United

Kingdom – could be stopped from becoming a prospective MP *solely on the ground of gender*, regardless of our fitness for office. While an utterly incompetent female candidate would *automatically* be deemed more worthy of public office than the most competent male candidate.

To ban *either* of the sexes merely on the grounds of gender would surely and inevitably reduce the pool of competent people willing to stand for public office,which can only lead over time to Parliament having even fewer competent MPs and ministers. Still, in Hattie World that would be a small price to pay for more equal gender representation. To Ms Harman equality is always more important than quality.

The possibility of women-only prospective parliamentary candidate shortlists is so extraordinary that even the Labour Party must surely have mentioned the matter in its 2005 General Election manifesto? No. Ms Harman and her like have nothing but contempt for democratic processes.

I've long been a Conservative voter. I was a member of the party for a time, and I worked for it in its campaign headquarters over 2006-2008. In October 2009, when it became known that the party was planning to employ all-women prospective parliamentary candidate shortlists – using Harriet Harman's legislation – to select candidates for the next general election, I cancelled my membership of the party.

Ed Miliband, a self-confessed socialist MP whose late father was a Marxist theorist, beat his politically more moderate brother David to the leadership of the Labour Party. His first job in politics was as an aide to Harriet Harman, which might explain his permanently haunted expression. He wrote speeches for her and in his first speech as leader to the Labour conference in October 2010 he found time to declare himself a supporter of all-women prospective parliamentary candidate shortlists. So the leaders of *both* the British major political parties now support the militant feminist agenda.

Harriet Harman has been an opposition MP since the 2010 general election, and over time we will hear less of her often comical but always determined focus on equality issues. So please indulge me as I wallow in nostalgia for the times when 'Mad Hattie' was at her most influential. From *The Daily Telegraph* of 13 July 2009:

> Discrimination against northerners by public bodies could be banned under plans being considered by Harriet Harman, the Equalities Minister. Her office is looking at how it can ensure that the boards of national organisations are not dominated by Londoners and other southerners, her deputy disclosed. The remarks were made by Michael Foster, an equalities minister, in a parliamentary debate on 'diversity in public appointments' when replying to Meg Munn, a Labour MP.

Marvellous. Another clipping for my file *Harriet Harman (stuff you couldn't make up)*. Now I've noticed myself that short fat ugly people with beards – both men and women, I'm not making a sexist point here – are under-represented as bar staff in upmarket wine bars. I should have alerted Ms Harman to this shocking inequality when she had the power to do something about it.

Where *did* the woman get her energy from? Was she plugged into an electrical supply while she slept? And did I become a little obsessed with her? Possibly, but I wasn't alone. A friend told me he once had a dream in which he was a Cabinet minister, and Harriet Harman was chairing a Cabinet meeting, the first in her new role as Prime Minister. The meeting took place in the context of a national emergency, and the atmosphere was tense. As the meeting was about to begin, in an effort to lighten the mood, a fellow minister remarked out loud to Ms Harman, 'Harriet, may I kick off proceedings by remarking on how very *pretty* you're looking this morning?' Whereupon she frowned and drew a .44 Magnum revolver [Author's note: The gun used by Clint Eastwood in *Dirty Harry*] from her handbag, slowly took aim, and shot his right arm off at the shoulder. She then glared around the table at the other ministers and growled, 'Does anyone *else* think I'm looking pretty this morning?' They all stared glumly at their papers and mumbled, 'No, Prime Minister.'

Whilst working on my book *The Fraud of the Rings* I wrote to Harriet Harman in the hope of securing a meeting (appendix 5) but unfortunately she was too busy to meet with me. It was only later that it came to my attention that she'd written a book published in 1993, *The Century Gap (20th Century Man, 21st Century Woman)*. I looked for the book on Amazon and found 22 used copies available for £0.01 (plus postage and packaging). At that price, I couldn't resist ordering a copy. From the back cover:

> Women have arrived ahead of time in the 21st century – then, as now, they will have an important role in the workforce as well as at home. But this revolution in women's lives has not yet been matched by men, who remain firmly stuck in the 20th century. That is the Century Gap.

The following extract is taken from just three successive paragraphs in a section titled 'Men Contributing More':

> What must men do . . . They will have to . . . They will have to . . . Then they will feel able to . . . They must begin to . . . They must dramatically increase . . . They must . . . Men must . . . They must . . . They must . . . they must . . .

On behalf of men everywhere, might I respond feebly with, 'But *why* must we, Mistress Harriet? What will happen to us if we don't?' When, one might ask, will British men finally strap a pair on and demand of their politicians that the dire influence of such women be curtailed in the national interest?

CHAPTER 15

POLITICIANS AND
THE FAIRNESS QUESTION

A fair society is one in which some people fail – and they may fail in
something other than precise, demographically representative
proportions.
William A Henry III 1950-1994 American cultural critic and author: *In Defence of Elitism*
(1994)

Against fairness – *le fair-play* – the two opposing meanings of 'fairness' –
preferential protection against redundancy for women in the public
sector

If a single word could be said to represent the acceptable face
of militant feminism, it would surely be 'fairness'. What
reasonable person wouldn't want more fairness in society?
Politicians use the term all the time, and infantilise voters in the
process. From *The Economist* of 3 July 2010, an article titled,
'Against fairness: what's wrong with the British coalition
government's favourite word':

> How could anyone dislike the notion of fairness? Everything
> is better when it is fair: a share, a fight, a maiden, a game and
> (for those who think blondes have more fun) hair. Even
> defeat sounds more attractive when it is fair and square.
>
> A sense of fairness, as any parent knows, develops
> irritatingly early. A wail of, 'It's not fair!' is usually the first
> normative statement to come out of the mouths of babes and
> sucklings. People seem to be hard-wired to demand fairness.
> Studies in which people are offered deals that they regard as
> fair and unfair show that the former stimulate the reward
> centres in the brain; the latter stimulate areas associated with
> disgust.
>
> For the British, fair play is especially important; without it,
> life isn't cricket (especially when you score a perfectly good

goal against the Germans and it is unfairly disallowed). Their country becomes quite pleasant when the weather is fair, though unfortunately it rarely is. And these days fair-trade goods crowd their supermarket shelves.

Fairness is not only good, but also moderate, which is another characteristic that the British approve of. It does not claim too much for itself. Those who, on inquiry, admit that their health and fortunes are fair-to-middling navigate carefully between the twin dangers of boastfulness and curmudgeonliness, while gesturing in a chin-up sort of way towards the possibility of future improvement.

The French have taken to using *le fair-play* in sport, presumably because (as their coach's refusal to shake hands with his opposite number after losing to South Africa suggested) their own culture finds the concept rather difficult. When talking politics, however, the French, like the Americans, tend to go for the more formal notion of justice. But fairness appeals to the British political class, for it has a common sense down-to-earthiness which avoids the grandiosity of American and continental European political discourse while aspiring to do its best for all men – and of course for all maidens too, fair and otherwise, for one of its virtues is that it does not discriminate on grounds of either gender or skin colour.

Not surprising, then, that Britain's government should grab hold of the word and cling to it in the buffeting the coalition has had since the budget on 22 June proposed higher taxes and even sharper spending cuts. 'Tough but fair' is what George Osborne, the Conservative chancellor of the exchequer, called the cuts he announced. 'It is going to be tough, but it is also very fair,' said Vince Cable, the Liberal Democrat business secretary. At last, something they could agree on.

Yet the fact that everyone believes in fairness is a clue to what's wrong with the notion. Like that other warm-blanket word, 'community', it signals limp thinking. What exactly is 'fair' about restricting trade, for example? Or 'unfair' about letting successful people in business or other fields enjoy the fruits of their enterprise without punitive taxes?

'Fairness' suits Britain's coalition government so well not just because its meanings are all positive, but also because – like views within the coalition – they are wide-ranging. To one lot of people, fairness means establishing the same rules for everyone, playing by them, and letting the best man win and the winner take all. To another, it means making sure that everybody gets equal shares.

These two meanings are not just different: they are opposites. They represent a choice that has to be made between freedom and equality. Yet so slippery – and thus convenient to politicians – is the English language that a single word encompasses both, and in doing so loses any claim to meaning.

Fairness is fudge. This newspaper will have none of it. We reject the wide, woolly notion of fairness in favour of sharper, narrower words that mean what they say, like just or cruel. Sadly, British politicians are unlikely to follow our lead. They will continue to paper over their cracks with fairness. Which, given how handy the word is, is probably fair enough.

I've been a subscriber to *The Economist* for many years and you can't beat it for extensive and insightful coverage of current affairs. You'll never see a woman reading it but that's only because women have no interest in current affairs, to be fair.

I opened *The Daily Telegraph* of 27 September 2010 and read an article which might have been more appropriate in the paper's April Fool's Day edition. It was titled, 'Women will challenge unfair cuts, say unions':

> The impact of public-sector cuts on female workers could lead to a 'landslide' of claims against employers, unions warned yesterday. Women could endure a disproportionate amount of pain from cuts because they make up the majority of the public-sector workforce and a large proportion of clerical, caring, catering and temporary workers. Figures from the Office for National Statistics show that almost two-thirds of public-sector workers are female.
>
> Officials from Unison, the public sector trade union, warned that they would mount legal action against any employer found to have discriminated against women and not carried out impact assessments before cutting jobs and cutting services. Dave Prentis, the union's general secretary, said officials would not watch equality improvements being

undone by organisations which cut jobs indiscriminately. 'It is easy to see that women are literally in the firing line when it comes to public sector job cuts and that is not acceptable,' he said. 'The Government must take account of the impact of public spending cuts on women and rethink their strategy.'

The Equality and Human Rights Commission is to meet Treasury officials today to discuss how cuts will be invoked on 'vulnerable' groups of workers. 'The commission recognises that the Government needs to take difficult decisions as part of its deficit reduction programme,' said a spokesman. 'However, we also want to ensure that equality issues are taken into account when decisions are made.'

Julie Mellor, a partner from PriceWaterhouseCoopers, the accountancy firm, said: 'It's definitely an issue that needs to be looked at as there is a strong chance the spending cuts will have a disproportionate effect on women.'

A Treasury spokesman said: 'The Government takes its equalities responsibilities very seriously, and has made clear that it will look closely at the impact of Spending Review decisions on different groups.'

Let me see if I have this right. Almost two-thirds of public sector workers are women, but they are seeking preferential protection from being fired. A Conservative-led coalition is sympathetic to this viewpoint and is supported by public sector trade unions and a partner at a major accountancy firm. You couldn't make it up, could you?

The absurdity of the feminist position in this area is such that even female columnists writing for left-leaning newspapers have commented on it. Catherine Bennett wrote an article titled, 'Women should stop whingeing about the coalition cuts' for *The Observer* on 31 October 2010:

> What exactly is a gender equality impact assessment? Thanks to the government's recent, assessment-lite budget, which has prompted a legal challenge from The Fawcett Society, more and more of us should soon be confident in answering this frequently asked question. Before the Fawcett intervention,

even experts on equality could appear perplexed. For instance, Yvette Cooper, now foremost among politicians routinely demanding to know if government departments have subjected their budgetary plans to gender equality assessments, is not known to have tackled her previous Labour line managers about their own duties in this respect. Indeed, just recently, she admitted that it took her a while to comprehend that the coalition's emergency budget was, in fact, a concerted attack on a whole sex's life-chances. 'For the first time,' she told Beatrix Campbell, 'I started to worry – what does this mean for my daughters?'

Good question. Just how dependent are the prospects of the Cooper-Balls girls on their anxious mother's child benefit? Are we talking cuts in tap-dancing lessons here, or somewhat cooler bedrooms, or actual danger of starvation? Can we rule out a forced move from Stoke Newington to, say, Clapton or, yet more chillingly, Wood Green? As economists continue to work on the possible implications of the government's cuts on an educated professional household living, like the Cooper-Balls, on a combined income of more than £130,000 in a house where, following some judicious flipping, the mortgage must surely be at a manageable level, there is no doubt that, as The Fawcett Society has shown, the forthcoming cuts are likely to damage the interests of poorer women, not to mention those of their poor partners and their poor children, male and female.

It also appears that with lamentable negligence the Treasury did not carry out an equalities impact assessment of its budget in accordance with the Equality Act of 2006, which requires public authorities to give 'due regard' to the impact of their decisions upon women. Does the act apply to the Labour party? No, or we can be sure someone would have demanded a gender equality assessment of a leadership contest that featured four men and a specially conscripted buffoon.

The Fawcett Society, a pressure group that agitates for equality between the sexes, has appointed specialist lawyers and applied for a judicial review of the government's conduct. Meanwhile, in the absence of an official gender assessment, it is having great success in publicising its own conclusion – that women will suffer disproportionately from the government's cuts. For example, forthcoming cuts to public services will unfairly affect women because almost 65% of the workers in those services are women. Also, women are less well paid than men and more of them receive state benefits, such as those earmarked for children.

Women are especially vulnerable to the government cuts, the society says, because of 'their sizable caring responsibilities' in the family. This means that 'many women with caring responsibilities for children and elderly relatives will find it harder to manage as the help they've thus far relied on dries up'. All of which amounts to a 'disastrous blow for women's equality' which will 'dismay women across the UK'.

I wonder. Although we cannot be sure that everyone from Coleen Rooney to the Dowager Duchess of Devonshire has not put on her dismayed face at the prospect of this disastrous blow to women's equality, there must be a suspicion that a number of women feel quite differently since, much like men, *they do not constitute a homogeneous group* [Author's italics] or political party. Even affluent female whingers about child benefit might shrink from describing this collective setback, as some protesters do, as part of an ideologically inspired campaign to re-domesticate women; a coalition remake of *Rosie the Riveter*.

Even women who have children might consider the Fawcett's designation of women as the officially caring sex to be quite as offensive and old-fashioned as the recent comments from Jill Kirby, director of the Centre for Policy Studies, who told the BBC that, when the cuts bite: 'It may be better news for women not to spend money on childcare any more and to look after their own children and fit jobs into the child's day.'

Of course, the employees of The Fawcett Society have a job to do and if this exaltation of a woman's reproductive destiny attracts a legion of new, Conservative members, all well and good. Less likely to inspire general sympathy, perhaps, is the claim that women have been unfairly targeted in these cuts because they are so heavily represented in the public services.

In the absence of clear options, it is not obvious that Labour's deficit-cutting plans would have ultimately been much kinder. Moreover, to the male and heartless, who are already blogging to this effect, emphasis on this huge gender disparity only confirms that the women must previously have been especially favoured by the public sector. Renewed female complaints about the increase in retirement age, which will now afflict both sexes identically, similarly remind angry men how fortunate some women have been. If there is justice in a gender-based approach, then champions of women workers should concede that they survived the recession in better shape than did men because of the hit to manufacturing and manual work. If talk of a 'mancession' was overstated after 2007, and as nothing compared to the earlier fate of British miners and steelworkers, men did lose jobs at twice the rate of women in that downturn and their pay suffered more because fewer men work in the public sector.

What is gained by identifying victims of the next round of economic punishment as overwhelmingly female, rather than overwhelmingly poor? Even if it didn't mean defining all women as mothers and all men as indifferent to childcare? It is surely overstating the influence of *Made in Dagenham* to think that, in families which face female redundancy, we can expect more indignation about flouted gender equality assessments than a shared fury about much broader unfairness.

As for solidarity: there could not be a clearer invitation, where non-women are concerned, not to give a toss. If, as looks increasingly probable, these massive cuts go through without one decent collective protest, even on Twitter, perhaps some of this passivity can be attributed to the competition between rival identity groups to own the bloodiest place under the axe: women v men, young v old, north v south, public v private, students v non-students, science students v arts students, dogs v cats. When it could so easily be everyone v banks. Even the Countryside Alliance had the sense to get ramblers marching beside their sworn enemies, the landowners.

None of which is to diminish, in any way, the importance of gender equality assessments. One only wishes that Ms Cooper would ask for them more often, starting with troop deployment in Afghanistan.

CHAPTER 16

HOW FAIR IS BRITAIN?
MEN AND WOMEN AT WORK
AND THE GLASS CEILING DELUSION

A society that puts equality – in the sense of equality of outcome – ahead of freedom will end up with neither equality nor freedom.
Milton Friedman 1912-2006 American economist and statistician: *Free to Choose* (1980)

The glass ceiling delusion – gender discrimination favours women, not men – what Elvis may be doing these days – female executives often exercise a choice not available to male executives – does a higher proportion of female executives enhance a company's profitability? – a proposal to run a company along 'female lines' – the competing struggles of middle-class women and low status men – women aren't interested in business – Holly Branson – the report from the Equality and Human Rights Commission: 'How Fair is Britain?' – The Fawcett Society and their comments on the 2010 Equality Bill – occupational segregation – employment status by age and gender – occupational choices of men and women – we should *expect* a gender pay gap – male v female suicides, and deaths at work – systemising v empathising natures in the workplace – internal v external focus – the realities of the commercial world – women are risk averse – women's impact on the language of business – interpersonal skills – a passion for fruit and vegetables – a passionate idiot – an honest banker – the number of women just below board level is in decline – only a minority of women are work-centred – the gender pay gap isn't the result of discrimination

In a 33 year long business career, mainly working at a senior level in major corporations, I never came across an example of discrimination against women, the 'glass ceiling' of feminist myth. On the contrary. The gender discrimination I came across was invariably in favour of women. On occasion companies would – in a desperate effort to 'improve' gender balance – promote women whose experience and expertise was simply not up to the mark. A man with the same experience and expertise wouldn't have been promoted.

Why are some women so wedded to the idea of the glass ceiling? Well, it's an appealing conspiracy theory, and like many conspiracy theories it can't be disproved. A man might be convinced that Elvis Presley was abducted by aliens on 16 August 1977 and transported in their spaceship to the planet Xlodić 217k where he is currently performing twice nightly, and I couldn't prove him wrong. But the burden of proof would lie with him rather than with me, and I would live with the assumption that he was wrong. Wrong, and barking mad.

Female executives often exercise a choice which is open to very few male executives, to resign and be supported by their partners. Knowing this risk, companies could quite reasonably discriminate against women, but they don't. There are other grounds, too, for potentially discriminating against women, notably the possibility that they will take extended leaves of absence for bearing and bringing up children. Given the choice between a male and a female executive for promotion, companies' self-interest would lie in promoting the man.

A good deal of nonsense has been written about companies with higher proportions of female executives being more profitable than companies with lower proportions. The writers are confusing cause and effect. Women are drawn to the pleasant working environments and generous remuneration packages offered by employers who are highly profitable. If women did have qualities which made organisations more profitable they'd have taken over the boardrooms by now.

Here's an idea. Why don't we test the hypothesis that women enhance the profitability of companies by asking a number to pool their resources, buy an existing successful company, and then run it along 'female lines'. Sadly, women would never risk their own money in this way – they're smart enough to know that the company would in time go bankrupt. You can be sure the first thing such a company would do, would be to seek preferential treatment from companies ordering the goods or services they provided.

For many years feminists presented their struggle for 'equality in the workplace' as one aspect of a wider struggle for egalitarianism, which included low status men. But how would they respond if their struggle *conflicted* with that of low status men? In April 2011 we got the answer to that question. From an article in *The Daily Telegraph* of 1 April, 2011, concerning the Universities Minister David 'Two Brains' Willetts:

> The Government's social mobility strategy, which will conclude that movement between the classes had 'stagnated' over the past 40 years, will be published next week and Mr Willetts blamed the entry of women into the workplace and universities for the lack of progress for men.
>
> 'Feminism trumped egalitarianism,' he said, adding that women who would otherwise have been housewives had taken university places and well-paid jobs that could have gone to ambitious working-class men.
>
> The minister set out his views during a briefing with journalists on the social mobility strategy, which will include a plan to test the population at seven ages, from birth until the age of 30, to measure whether life chances were improving for children from different backgrounds.
>
> Figures to be published are expected to paint a grim picture of the prospects for advancement for children from the poorest backgrounds dating back to the 1960s. Asked what was to blame for the lack of social mobility, Mr Willetts said: 'The feminist revolution in its first round effects was probably the key factor. Feminism trumped egalitarianism. It is not that I am against feminism, it's just that it is probably the single biggest factor.'
>
> Mr Willetts, who set out his views on feminism in his recent book, *The Pinch*, said that, as a result of better education for

women, households now contained two people who were either both financially successful or struggling to get on.

'One of the things that happened over that period was that the entirely admirable transformation of opportunities for women meant that with a lot of the expansion of education in the 1960s, 70s and 80s, the first beneficiaries were the daughters of middle-class families who had previously been excluded from educational opportunities,' he said.

'And if you put that with what is called "assortative mating" – that well-educated women marry well-educated men – this transformation of opportunities for women ended up magnifying social divides. It is delicate territory because it is not a bad thing that women had these opportunities, but it widened the gap in household incomes because you suddenly had two-earner couples, both of whom were well-educated, compared with often workless households where nobody was educated.'

Figures released by the Office for National Statistics yesterday showed a 23 per cent rise in mothers working full-time between 1996 and 2010. Two thirds of women were now in employment, compared with fewer than three quarters of men. Last month, there were nearly a million men out of work, compared with fewer than 500,000 women.

As we would expect, responses from feminists were universally contemptuous of David Willett's arguments. They found it laughable that poor social mobility might be laid at the door of middle-class women in well-paid jobs.

Women may have been taking up many of the jobs that might otherwise have gone to working-class men, but they aren't interested in business *per se*. Their interest in the workplace is largely confined to their relationships within it. I've noted this on a number of occasions when travelling on trains. Two or more businesswomen may start a conversation about a business issue they're facing, but before long they will return to familiar territory: relationships, fashion and so on:

'Isn't Mary an awful boss? She's always been so mean to me.'

'Isn't the new Business Development Director from Miggins Inc sexy? *I* would!'

'I've got to give a presentation to the sales team on Friday. Should I wear my Dolce & Gabbana suit and my lucky Manolo Blahniks again?'

Women are particular disinterested in the 'big picture' aspects of business which are of importance in the boardroom, such as strategy: analysing the firm in relation to its threats and opportunities, and taking the decisions that will enhance the firm's prospects of success in the long term. Being prepared to take risks, knowing that some will end in failure; but knowing equally that not taking risks will *certainly* lead to failure.

Women are risk averse, a matter we shall explore in a later chapter, and this militates against their advancement in business. A leading businesswoman told me, 'I hate to say this, but having a board consisting only of women would be like having a board consisting only of chartered accountants. A sporting analogy would be a soccer team with ten goalkeepers and one striker. You could never win; the best you could hope for would be to lose slowly.'

Women aren't interested in business even when they're going to be handed major businesses on a plate. From the 'Mandrake' column in the 15 October 2010 edition of *The Daily Telegraph*:

> Mandrake disclosed last year that Holly Branson was being groomed to take over from her father, Sir Richard Branson, as the head of the Virgin business empire.
> The medical graduate is clearly not finding all aspects of the learning process a barrel of laughs, though. 'I'm doing a business course at the moment,' she said at the launch of the Virgin Red Room website. 'It's really hard. I'm usually quite good at learning things, but I just don't find the business stuff that interesting, so it makes it harder to get my head around.'

The Equality and Human Rights Commission, formed in 2007, is required by law to report to parliament every three years on how far Britain has progressed towards being a fair society, and how far the country still has to go. Its first triennial report, extending to some 750 pages and downloadable online, was 'How Fair is Britain? Equality, Human Rights and Good Relations in 2010', and it was published on 11 October 2010.

For the purpose of this book, let's focus on the report's conclusions with regards to men and women at work. One of six organisations which 'provided invaluable assistance as we developed our research' was The Fawcett Society. From their website Fawcettsociety.org.uk:

> Fawcett is the UK's leading campaign for equality between women and men. Where there's an inequality gap between women and men we're working to close it.

No mention there, you'll notice, of the possibility that women (and men, for that matter) might make life choices which lead to 'inequality gaps' in the first place. No, gaps are unfair, and all of them must be closed. The Fawcett Society is, of course, only interested in inequality gaps which they believe disadvantage women, not those that disadvantage men. You don't have to spend too long scanning their website to have your intelligence insulted:

> Women working full-time are paid on average 17.1% less an hour than men for doing work of equivalent value.

I emailed The Fawcett Society to enquire what 'equivalent value' meant in the above context. In the absence of a response a month later I could only conclude that 'equivalent value' was a wholly subjective value judgment, not reflecting supply and demand of suitably qualified workers in the workplace. I wasn't surprised at the lack of response to my email; I had written a letter to Ceri Goddard, the Chief Executive of the Society, on 1 September 2010 (appendix 8), and hadn't received a response to that either.

The Fawcett Society is a militant feminist campaigning organisation. The fact that the Conservative / Liberal Democrat coalition have introduced 90% of Labour's 2010 Equality Bill – the remaining 10% being under consideration – isn't enough for these strident ladies. From an article on their website, 'Coalition plans around Equality Act "Endorse Pay Gap" ':

> Rendering the Equality Act virtually toothless undermines every speech Coalition ministers ever gave endorsing the notion of a fairer Britain. The Fawcett Society has today warned that the Coalition's failure to implement the Equalities Act 2010 in full risks not just endorsing but widening the gender pay gap in the current and foreseeable economic climate.
>
> The government has stated that it is now 'reviewing' several sections of the Act that was passed by parliament in April 2010. All of the sections under review were opposed by the Conservatives in opposition but supported by the Liberal Democrats. Among these are the provisions that would give government the power to require big business – private sector companies with over 250 employees – to establish whether they have a pay gap between men and women, and publish their findings if they do not make enough voluntary progress in the next three years. Ceri Goddard, Chief Executive of The Fawcett Society, said:

> 40 years after the Dagenham machinists first striked for equal pay, women working in Dagenham earn an average 30 per cent less than men and nationally the gap between the average man and women's pay is a staggering 16.4 per cent [Author's note: militant feminists are an excitable lot, aren't they? A surprisingly large number of things appear to be staggering, shocking, utterly nonsensical...]

It's ironic that the film charting their struggle hit cinemas the same day that the key equal pay measures in the Equality Act 2010 are being held back by government. Rowing back on the requirement for big business to publish and take action on any differences in pay between men and women employees – so to conduct gender pay audits – is tantamount to endorsing the shocking gender pay gap.

All our research and experience shows that gender pay audits are key to shrinking the persistent gap in pay between women and men – it's utterly nonsensical to suggest we can tackle pay differences between men and women if we can't see where they are – more transparency is key. While banning secrecy clauses will go some way to creating a more transparent discussion around pay, it's not nearly enough to ensure real progress. Done right, conducting a pay audit is a simple and inexpensive process that can happen alongside annual accounts...

The Equalities Act 2010 is a litmus test of the government's commitment to fairness. Failing to implement it in full sends out a clear signal that creating a more equal society is a low priority for the Coalition.

Alongside concerns around measures to combat the pay gap, we are also worried that government plans to review the mechanism that allows those who may face 'double discrimination' – black women for example – to bring just the one claim means making it harder for some of those most at risk of discrimination to defend themselves.

Scrapping the Positive Action clause that would allow organisations to better address under-representation of people with protected characteristics would also be a backwards step – especially at a time of rising unemployment.

People at risk of discrimination face even tougher times than the rest during periods of financial unrest; watering down equality law during a recession weakens what little protection some of the most marginalised in our society have.

Rendering the Equality Act virtually toothless undermines every speech Coalition ministers ever gave endorsing the notion of a fairer Britain. The Act isn't perfect, but the government seems determined to implement it in name only.

Following an emergency budget that is seeing over 70 per cent of public spending cuts being borne by women this adds insult to injury, and joins the increasing battery of anti equality measures emanating from the coalition that is far outweighing its positive actions.

The foreword of the EHRC report 'How Fair is Britain?' starts with the following:

> Britain[1] is a country where we despise prejudice, embrace equality and believe in the fundamental right of the individual to make the most of his or her talents in a free society. We are increasingly at ease with diversity of all kinds, and intolerant of discrimination of any kind.
>
> Yet all too many of us remain trapped by the accident of our births, our destinies far too likely to be determined by our sex or race; or opportunities far too often conditioned by the fact that our age, or disability, or sexual preferences, or deeply held religion or belief make us lesser beings in the eyes of others. And far too many of us are still born into families without the material or social capital to give us the right start in life.
>
> In short, we twenty-first century Britons are a largely fair-minded people. But we are not yet a fair society. And we know that no individual can be truly free to realise their potential, or to exercise their inalienable human rights as long as they are imprisoned by the invisible, many-stranded web of prejudice, inertia and unfairness that holds so many back.

[1] Author's note: the report is politically correct from the very first word, Britain no longer being 'Great', it would seem.

Phew. All that is missing is any recognition that individual outcomes in life could be even remotely related to individual ambition, effort, or choices made in the areas of education or employment. No, most of the population – including women – are victims. In the area of 'pay gaps' the report defines the term 'occupational segregation' (p.382):

> Occupational segregation means the fact that different groups of people tend to do different types of jobs. We use two specific measures to look at this. The first is 'vertical' segregation, which shows the proportion of people in different levels of seniority and types of occupation. The second measure is 'horizontal' segregation, which shows the

proportions of the workforce who are drawn from a particular group in different sectors (for example, the numbers of men and women who work in engineering).

In a section titled, 'Certain inequalities remain persistent', (p.385), we find this gem:

> Mothers of children under the age of 16 are four times more likely than fathers to be economically inactive: being a parent exacerbates the gender gap.

In the immortal words of one of my daughters when she was a teenager, 'No shit, Sherlock!' What is to be done about this particular shocking gender gap? Perhaps vast numbers of women will start to work full-time to support their husbands and children? That will happen some time soon, I'm sure. The report (p.389) offers an interesting analysis:

Table 10.1: Employment status by gender in Britain, 2006/2008 (%)

	Men	Women
Full-time employment rate	59	39
Part-time employment rate	6	26
Self-employment rate	14	5

If we add the full-time employment numbers to the self-employment numbers we conclude that 73% of men fall in these two categories, and just 44% of women. Men could feel legitimately aggrieved about the relative economic inactivity of women, but being men, it wouldn't *occur* to them to complain.

The report (p.390) analyses employment further by age and gender, see Tables 10.2 and 10.3.

Table 10.2: Employment rates by age and gender in Britain, 2006/08 (%)

Male workers

	Overall	16-19	20-24	25-29	30-34	35-39	40-44	45-49	50-54	55-59	60-64	65-69	70+
Full-time	59	20	56	73	73	71	70	67	64	53	33	5	1
Part-time	6	20	11	4	3	3	2	3	3	5	8	8	2
Self-employed	14	1	5	9	13	16	17	18	18	17	16	8	2
Totals	79	41	72	86	89	90	89	88	85	75	57	21	5

Table 10.3: Employment rates by age and gender in Britain, 2006/08 (%)

Female workers

	Overall	16-19	20-24	25-29	30-34	35-39	40-44	45-49	50-54	55-59	60-64	65-69	70+
Full-time	39	14	45	53	42	36	39	44	42	31	10	2	0
Part-time	26	30	18	17	25	30	31	29	27	26	19	8	1
Self-employed	5	0	2	3	5	6	7	7	7	6	4	2	1
Totals	70	44	65	73	72	72	77	80	76	63	33	12	2

The data show clearly that *in all age bands* women are markedly more likely than men to work part-time than full-time. So much for the notion that women's preference for part-time work solely reflects a need to look after young children before they start school and in the early school years. Some of women's relative preference for part-time work in later years may be attributable to their taking care of family members, including elderly parents or grandparents. But it doesn't follow necessarily that they would *prefer* full-time work to such caring duties, if given a choice.

The data also shows clearly that in all age bands women are markedly less likely to be self-employed than men. My explanation for this is that women are risk-averse by nature, and self-employment has never been the preferred option for the risk-averse. Women are not queuing up to become self-employed plumbers and electricians; instances of their doing so are still so uncommon as to attract media attention.

Pages 411-414 of the report include the following:

> The gender pay gap (as measured by median hourly pay excluding overtime) narrowed between 2008 and 2009... The full-time gender pay gap fell from 12.6% in 2008 to 12.2% in 2009...
>
> Recent analysis found that men and women with similar qualifications face substantial pay differences. However, it is hard to separate out the effect of career breaks. Importantly, the influence of motherhood on the gender pay gap is apparent well before women become mothers. A study of graduates three years post graduation found that gender differences in career expectations explained 12% of the gender pay gap, with women much more likely to expect to take a break for family reasons than men (and men expecting their partners to do this). This highlights how childcare issues may impinge on pay even prior to motherhood, given the expected household division of caring responsibilities.

Shouldn't we *expect* that anticipated future childcare responsibilities will make women less competitive in the workplace, and thereby reduce their income prospects? Or should we expect them to fight tooth and nail for that next promotion, only to exit the workplace – possibly temporarily, possibly not – when they have children? Would that be fair either to their female colleagues, or to their male colleagues who would have been passed over for promotion and who won't enjoy the option of being supported by a woman while he cares full-time for their children?

The report covers the issue of occupational segregation with regards to gender on pages 421-425. Two measures of occupational segregation are provided:

> Vertical segregation – proportions of each gender employed in each of the nine main occupational groups.
>
> Horizontal segregation – proportions of each gender in each occupation, summed across all occupations.

Data for this part of the report are drawn from the Labour Force Survey 2006/2008. We encounter a left-wing perspective almost immediately, in the first chapter on vertical segregation:

> The Labour Force Survey identifies nine occupational categories which indicate the level at which people are working, from managerial and professional posts to elementary occupations. Vertical segregation is the extent to which different groups are employed at different levels in organisations, so highlights *the extent to which promotional opportunities are unequally distributed* [Author's italics.]

There's a glaring deceit at the end of that paragraph: the levels of vertical segregation indicate outcomes, not opportunities. There's no mention of obvious alternative explanations, including the one that more men than women might seek senior positions with higher incomes.

The report presents separate age-related data for men and women on their occupational groups, not the most user-friendly way of presenting the data. But if we combine the data to compare men and women by occupational group we find the following:

Table 10.4: Major occupational groups of men
and women in Britain, 2007/09 (%)

	Men	Women
Managerial	19	12
Professional	14	13
Associate professional	14	16
Admin/secretarial	5	19
Skilled trades	19	2
Personal services	2	15
Sales	5	10
Process plant and machinery	12	2
Elementary	11	10
Sample size	71,000	63,000

The most basic knowledge of remuneration in different lines of work tells us that – given the above – we must *expect* men, on average, to earn more than women. The 'gender pay gap' has nothing to do with discrimination: it is the result of men being more motivated than women to pursue higher-paid lines of work than women, and then being more willing than women to do what it takes to be promoted and earn more money. The only wonder is that the gender pay gap is not larger than it is. The report continues:

> Boys are more likely than girls to expect to work in engineering, architecture or as mechanics. Girls are more likely to expect to work in teaching, hairdressing, beauty therapy, childcare, nursing and midwifery. These career choices have major implications for employment trajectories and income levels...
>
> Horizontal segregation appears to be highly entrenched... Overall, women account for:
>
> - 77% of administrative and secretarial posts
> - 83% of personal services posts
> - 65% of sales posts
>
> While there are signs of improvement in women's presence in the professions, this varies widely across professional groups; the proportion of women in engineering, information technology and working as architects, planners and surveyors remaining stubbornly low, with women making up:
>
> - 6% of engineering posts
> - 13% of information technology posts
> - 14% of architects, planners and surveyors

Here, as throughout the report, there is an unstated but surely inferred belief in the 'blank slate' theory of human nature, and a refusal to accept the legitimate right of women to make the life choices they wish to make, when those choices don't accord with feminists' wishes.

Let's finish this commentary on the report with two statistics from page 639. Three times as many men as women commit suicide, and almost all people killed at work are men: only four fatalities (out of 129) at work in 2008/09 were women. So women are far less likely than men to commit suicide, or to be killed at work: isn't that great news?

Let's move on to consider how systemising natures (more common in men than women) and empathising natures (vice versa) might be expected to play out in the workplace. The following equation is the fundamental economic reality for all commercial organisations:

$$\text{Revenues} - \text{costs} = \text{profits (or losses)}$$

Each of the elements is represented by hard numbers. You can only increase profits, or reduce losses, through doing one or both of two things: increasing revenues, reducing costs. You can't increase profits through empathising. Your staff may be strong empathisers, but all else being equal you'd lose market share to a competitor staffed by strong systemisers. The focus of empathisers will be on their relationships with their immediate colleagues, but this *internal focus* does little or nothing to improve the efficiency or effectiveness of the organisation. At best it makes for a more harmonious working environment.

Strong systemisers, on the other hand, are hard-wired to improve both efficiency and effectiveness, and this requires both an internal focus – on the efficiency of operations, for example – as well as an *external focus* on customers, competitors, and vendors. This doesn't mean that relationships with customers, vendors etc. aren't important. They are. But in the harsh competitive worlds in which commercial organisations operate, those relationships are only part of the story.

I worked for 25 years in the procurement of goods and services for major organisations, and while I and my colleagues sometimes enjoyed cordial relationships with local vendors, competitive pressures meant that if a good or service was available at a lower cost from foreign vendors – sufficiently low to compensate for associated risks such as currency fluctuations, longer leadtimes etc. – we had little choice but to stop buying locally and start buying from abroad. If we hadn't, our employers would have been placed at a competitive disadvantage to our competitors who *did* buy from abroad. Buying goods and services from the most competitive sources lies at the heart of capitalism, a system which works just fine when left alone by politicians. It has to be said the global banking crisis shook many people's faith in capitalism, but it shouldn't have. The crisis could never have occurred if politicians hadn't allowed a reckless expansion of the money supply, so the blame for the crisis should have been laid squarely at politicians' doors.

The most successful firms conduct relentless searches for greater efficiencies, which sometimes means replacing people with machines, or outsourcing all or part of what departments do. A systemising mind is clearly more prepared to do these things than the empathising mind, which will tend to rail against the tough decisions required in business: 'But Jean is a single mother with two young children to support, she'll be devastated if she loses this job…'

In all I spent over 30 years working at a senior level in commercial organisations before taking early retirement in 2010, at the age of 52. The most effective business people I encountered over these 30 years – including the successful entrepreneurs – were almost all men, and highly talented systemisers. They saw how systems worked and devised ways of making them work better, often in radically different ways. Women, by comparison, tended to suggest minor, low risk improvements, usually changes with little or no negative impact on people.

Appendix 3 contains the questionnaire on the Systemising Quotient ('SQ'), the maximum score for which is 80. It's drawn from Professor Baron-Cohen's *The Essential Difference* (2003). In his guidance on how to interpret SQ scores, the professor states:

> 51-80: very high (three times as many people with Asperger Syndrome score in this range, compared to typical men, and almost no women score in this range).

'Almost no women score in this range.' That's not misogyny, that's maths. Almost no women score highly for systemising, a trait we would expect to be advantageous in the top echelons of business.

The next attributes we would expect to result in far more men than women in the boardroom are men's competitive streaks. It hardly needs saying that for an individual to become an executive director of a major company requires not only experience and capabilities, but also fierce competitiveness. The ability to deliver superior tangible results than colleagues for the company over an extended period. Where does empathy come into this? It doesn't. If anything, it militates *against* personal competitiveness.

There's another issue we should expect to result in far more men than women being highly successful in business in general, and successful entrepreneurs in particular: women's aversion to risk taking. Success in business comes not from doing what your competitors are doing, but in taking different approaches. By the time a risk averse business person decides to invest in a particular direction, his or her competitors have the market sewn up. It was one of the important lessons learnt by major corporations in the 1970s: the larger their teams analysing possible future options in detail, the lower their long-term profits. The phenomenon was termed 'paralysis through analysis'. Flair and an acceptance of risk are important in business. An MBA won't give you flair, and will probably make you more risk averse than when you started the course. Very few top entrepreneurs have MBAs.

But there's a downside for men. For every successful entrepreneur there are many failed ones, some of whom go bankrupt. Becoming an entrepreneur is a gamble far more men than women are prepared to take. So we should expect the vast majority of both successful and unsuccessful entrepreneurs to be male: and that's exactly what we find. And it's not going to change anytime soon.

Onto the language of business, where women have had a curious impact. Seeing everything through the lens of interpersonal relationships, women conclude that strong interpersonal skills are vital for a business person's success. And so it is that for many years, in many disciplines, strong interpersonal skills have been stated as necessary in the vast majority of job descriptions for executive roles, although few executives actually have the skills. So they have to pretend to have them, during the interview and selection processes. Sometimes they even go through the humiliation of role playing exercises for the titillation of those of the female persuasion, notably people working in Human Resources – a function known as 'Human Remains' throughout my business career – almost all of whom are women.

Business also now suffers from the curious phenomenon of overblown prose, so beloved by women. I recently came across a consultancy assignment brief which started as follows:

> Are you truly passionate about controlling stocks of fresh fruit and vegetables? If so, then this could be the opportunity of a lifetime!!!

Surely only a woman could have written those words, I thought, a suspicion confirmed by the multiple exclamation marks. It's no longer sufficient to be interested in a line of work, or competent at it. No, you have to be passionate or, better, *truly* passionate. I was once turned down for a consulting assignment on the sole grounds (according to the agency) that I hadn't appeared to the lady interviewer sufficiently passionate about the role. As it happened, I had once worked alongside the person who finally landed the assignment. He was an incompetent fool but, crucially, a *passionate* one.

What is known about women's preferences in relation to paid employment in general? For insights into this we return to Steve Moxon's *The Woman Racket*. The remainder of this chapter is drawn from the book with the author's kind permission, from the chapter titled, 'Sex at Work: why women are not in love with work, yet the pay gap is so small':

> The opportunity for men to compete with each other for status is universally provided by work, for which men receive as reward the proxy for status: money. Status acquisition is the only option for men if they are to have any 'mate value' and obtain sexual partners; either long-term or fleeting. From a biological perspective, women neither need nor have any use at all for status (that is rank as measured in male terms), because they already have 'mate value' inherent in the degree to which they have a combination of youth and beauty. Some

people are just more honest about this than others: witness this recent posting on the classifieds website *Craiglist*:

> I'm tired of beating around the bush. I'm a beautiful (spectacularly beautiful) 25-year-old. I'm articulate and classy. I'm not from New York. I'm looking to get married to a guy who makes at least half a million a year. I know how that sounds, but keep in mind that a million a year is middle-class in New York, so I don't think I'm overreaching at all.

This led to an equally candid response from a (male) merchant banker:

> In economic terms, you are a depreciating asset and I am an appreciating asset. Your looks will fade and my money will likely continue into perpetuity. You're 25 now and will likely stay pretty hot for the next 5 years, but less so each year. Then the fade begins in earnest. By 35, stick a fork in you!

Men never choose women on the basis of status; such male criteria being, biologically speaking, a meaningless way to view women. Work is consequently very much on the male side of life's equation, and it must be expected that men will tend to want much more of it than do women – both for the monetary reward and to 'climb the greasy pole', for which they will be prepared to put in more effort regarding the task, and to enter into more competition. Inevitably then, for this reason (even before we consider various others) men will always, on average, outdo women – in top jobs especially – but also across the board, in terms of pay and promotion. This is reflected in what is found when looking in the most general terms at the difference between men and women…

Women in going backwards can't be 'catching up'. Even with perfect equality of opportunity, it should be expected that for a top job like director of a leading company, men will easily be beating women into the boardroom. And so they are. Not only is the proportion of women directors of the top hundred UK companies just one in ten, but almost all of them are non-executive. Even across the top 250 UK companies, at the time of writing (2007), there were less than a couple of dozen women who have any executive responsibility. Yet government ministers, quangocrats and activists continue to claim that it's merely a question of time before women catch up with men at the top. This social inertia notion might have more credence if the number of women in positions that are a springboard to the directorial board was increasing. They're not. They're *declining*.

Of the senior management posts in the 350 largest UK companies, only 12% were held by women in 2007, compared to 40% in 2002. That's an enormous drop in just five years. The exodus is still greater if you look at the less high-powered 'head of function' roles (that is, positions where there is anyone reporting to you) in the 250 largest UK companies, where women declined from one in five in 2002 to just over one in ten in 2007 .

Senior and 'head of function' managers are the pools of women from which future board members could be drawn, so we can expect corresponding falls in the numbers of women on the board, even though it's from a very low base. This is already happening. Of the top 100 UK companies, there were just twelve executive directors in 2006, which is almost a halving of the number from the previous year. It's been happening for some time: the same story of decline in women on the board and as executive directors had been apparent at the onset of the new millennium.

The news had appeared to be advancement, when in the decade up to the millennium the proportion of all companies boasting a woman on their board had climbed from just two per cent to ten per cent. This is illusory, however. Many of these are minuscule businesses, directed by the owners themselves. Most business growth has been of such concerns, and a significant proportion of this has been by women. There are now a million self-employed women in Britain. In business, women tend to be present as decision-makers in inverse proportion to the degree of hierarchy. In big companies, not to have a token woman board member is bad PR, and there is no commercial risk if an appointee is non-executive; and this accounts for most of the relatively small numbers of women there are at this level...

All this is astonishing in the face of the constant media exhortations and government pressure to get more women into senior positions. It takes time to climb the corporate ladder, but the aspirations of women at least to get into the lower echelons of senior management should have been fully realised many years ago now. Social inertia explanations have been replaced with a resurrection of the old rhetoric about discrimination; though now supposed to be in ever subtler form. There is refusal to face up to the simple fact that women do not cut this particularly competitive kind of mustard in the way that men do. Instead of going into business, women have concentrated further in areas where they have always been established: the public sector in general, but particularly in education and health. Anywhere where real competition, risk and innovation are less important. Even then, near the top of an organisation in a 'female' employment niche/sector, the sheer hassle puts women off... Managing a company at the top is all about dealing with irreconcilables in a moneyed world. Conflict, in other words. This is not what women are looking for at work...

Women have woken up to not just the stress and thorough lack of empowerment that work actually provides, but what is for women the pointlessness of it. Their message will be more and more warmly received, though working-class women have always known the harsh reality of work. The push towards women treating work in a similar way to how men do, though clearly still persisting amongst a small minority of women, will seem in retrospect a short-lived bubble, with women who do remain in full-time work doing so only through a perceived necessity. This not least because house prices have risen owing to the rise of the dual-earning couple, so women are to an important extent now locked into work...

Hakim [Author's note: LSE sociologist Catherine Hakim, referenced elsewhere in this chapter in Moxon's book] cites further research showing that secondary earners forced to work full-time are the most dissatisfied of all workers. So again, the social inertia theory to try and explain disparity between the sexes is a hopeless fit to figures which show precisely the opposite of what it predicted. This is all the more remarkable because it comes in spite of the relative collapse of the female archetype of home-maker and mother, which has had a profound impact on women and as a psychological 'projection', is the source of the bizarre notion that the male is redundant...

Underlying all this is what Catherine Hakim has identified as a persistent set of alternative lifestyle preferences that women make. Only a minority of women (between ten and fifteen per cent) are 'work-centred' and so work continuously in permanent full-time jobs, whilst a rather larger proportion (a fifth) are 'home-centred', giving priority to children and home-making, and don't want to work at all. That leaves the bulk of women making up the balance in the 'adaptive' group, who fit employment around family responsibilities, either working part-time or moving in and out of full-time jobs. The women of the 'work-centred' sub-group are the least representative of their sex, because the attitudes of women in the 'adaptive' group are very similar to those of the 'home-centred'. They see work as not primarily about bread-winning or having a career, or of developing an ability or skill; but more as a social activity providing supplementary income. They also have the same attitude as 'home-makers' regarding the sexual division of couples into a wage-earning male and a home-making female. Only about a *quarter* of women who hold full-time jobs view their working life as a career...

The difference that makes the 'work-centred' women stand out is that they have elected to progress up a career ladder. For some this will be through intra-sexual competition (with other women), or because the job had become an end in itself; but these motivations are usually far weaker than they are in men. Ultimately women's 'climbing the greasy pole' is not for the reasons that men have to, but – as evolutionary psychology would suggest – so that they place themselves in the milieu of higher-status men. They may have careers but their working is anything other than an end in itself, in common with most women who work. Some women carry on forever trying to climb; forgetting to jump off as their working life becomes an unintended end in itself. These women *appear* to be very like men, but they are not.

Long-term data show that women's preferences (rather than circumstantial constraints) are increasingly important in their decisions about work, especially for younger women (Blossfeld, 1987). Furthermore, this is so regardless of their level of education, social class, and whether or not they have children. Contrary to what most would imagine, research demonstrates that women are not constrained from working by childcare and home-making. This further underlines the homogeneity of the three preference groups, and points up that there is a fundamental divide between men and women in a systematic and uniform difference in attitude to work or, more precisely, to status-seeking. The upshot is that no steady increase of women in work can be expected. The opposite is likely, as in France where the 'home-centred' group has swollen to a third of all women.

There is no reason why those women who feel cut out for it should not opt for a work life as a 'pseudo-male', as it were; as increasingly they have been encouraged to do. It's just that the majority of those women who want to work full-time have ample scope to choose a different, less overtly competitive sector or niche. Something that has a more social front end; more to do with care; perhaps more creative, rather than, say, ruthlessly deciding between irreconcilable options in the boardroom. This is one reason why employment sectors and niches have always tended to polarise the sexes, and why we should expect not less but more of this. That most women still continue to shun the male work model confounds social trends predictions and undermines the tediously regular claims of discrimination by the late and unlamented Equal Opportunities Commission.

Conversely, the convoluted and flimsy excuses used to explain women's lack of progress is evidence itself of a root deeper than social norms – evidence which gets stronger with every year that passes. And all this is despite the collapse in female roles – housewife, mother, even exclusive sex-provider – which has left women feeling they have less scope, and so further encouraging them to fill male roles...

Why is there a pay gap, and why is it so small? With the failure to understand the sex differences in attitude to work, the pay gap supposedly results from sex discrimination. And just as with the failure of women to get anywhere near parity with men in getting into top jobs, the stubbornness of the pay gap to close is put down to social inertia or ever more subtle forms of sex discrimination. I'm not dealing here with the historical pay gap that certainly did exist, but which was actually not in any way against women's interests in the context of a view of social justice that focused on the family household. Here I will confine myself to the contemporary pay gap – with women on average earning four-fifths of what men earn.

That the pay gap has nothing at all to do with discrimination was confirmed in the 2006 report by the Women and Work Commission, which instead blamed the culture in schools and the workplace (but which was an indirect way of saying that actually it's down to women's choices). It remains anathema to say this, because it reveals that women have not and will not change – that is, they will not change the basis of their preferences, though they will react contingently. Not only is the pay gap not due to discrimination, but that it's as low as it is indicates sex discrimination *against men*...

The pay gap is easily explained by men tending to have harder jobs, putting in longer hours, taking more responsibility, etc; which in turn is easily explained by multiplying together the impact of the sex difference in how performance generally is distributed, and the radically polarised attitude to work of the sexes. Then there is the drawback women have in moving up any employment scale in having and raising children. Breaks in employment or reducing full-time work to part-time, inevitably hold women back, and there is nothing corresponding in men's lives that systematically produces anything similar.

There are still other reasons behind the disparity in average income between the sexes, to do with the predilection of women for work that is more in keeping with their natural tendency towards social networking, as opposed to the natural male inclination towards goal-directed competition. Jobs that are at the social front end, such as receptionists; and caring roles, such as nurses; are overwhelmingly female staffed. Most of the sex-typical female kinds of employment – even when full-time – tend to be low paying, for simple supply/demand reasons: they are pleasant and socially rewarding positions that are easy for employers to fill. It's certainly true that female sex-typical work *sectors* are very much reduced as a proportion of the economy than they once were – going 'into service' was by far the most usual female job prior to the First World War – but female sex-typical work *niches* within the full range of work sectors are abundant, and 'gender neutral' jobs in administration that are at least conducive to women have grown substantially. With thoroughgoing equal-opportunity initiatives, most of the population is considered eligible for recruitment, so pay levels can be pitiful, which puts men off. Women have made up most of these new recruits, so again average female pay across the whole economy will be further reduced.

CHAPTER 17

GENDER BALANCE IN THE BOARDROOM: AN ASSAULT ON THE FOUNDATIONS OF A FREE SOCIETY

Few trends could so thoroughly undermine the very foundations of our free society as the acceptance by corporate officials of a social responsibility other than to make as much money for their stockholders as possible.
Milton Friedman 1912-2006 American economist and statistician: *Capitalism and Freedom* (1962)

Executive and non-executive directors – far fewer women than men want to be executive directors – the circular argument at the heart of the 'female role model' proposition – positive discrimination for women – equal opportunities don't necessarily lead to equal outcomes – degrees awarded to women in male-typical fields, 1973/2003 – women working in fields formerly identified as male, 1973/2003 – top 20 reasons why female executives are uncommon in the most senior levels of major businesses – the CBI's shameful position on gender balance in the boardroom – an assault on the foundations of a free society

For militant feminists the two major inequalities in the workplace are the gender pay gap and the gender imbalance in Britain's boardrooms. We covered the first inequality in the last chapter, and we come on to the second. When militant feminists talk of gender imbalance in Britain's boardrooms they are talking of gender imbalance among the executive directors of major organisations, usually the top 100 by market capitalisation (the 'FTSE100') or the top 250 (the 'FTSE250') – the country's biggest employers. We need to distinguish at the outset between executive and non-executive directors. From Wikipedia:

The role of the Executive Director is to design, develop and implement strategic plans for their organization in a cost-effective and time-efficient manner. The Executive Director is also responsible for the day-to-day operation of the organization, including managing committees and staff and developing business plans in collaboration with the board for the future of the organization. In essence, the board grants the executive director the authority to run the organization.

A non-executive director ('NED') or outside director is a member of the board of directors of a company who does not form part of the executive management team. He or she is not an employee of the company or affiliated with it in any other way. They are differentiated from inside directors, who are members of the board who also serve or previously served as executive managers of the company (most often as corporate officers).

NEDs have responsibilities in the following areas, according to the Higgs Report, commissioned by the British Government and published in 2003:

> Strategy: Non-executive directors should constructively challenge and contribute to the development of strategy.

Performance: Non-executive directors should scrutinise the performance of management in meeting agreed goals and objectives and monitoring, and where necessary removing, senior management and in succession planning.

Risk: Non-executive directors should satisfy themselves that financial information is accurate and that financial controls and systems of risk management are robust and defensible.

People: Non-executive directors are responsible for determining appropriate levels of remuneration of executive directors and have a prime role in appointing, and where necessary removing, senior management and in succession planning.

NEDs should also provide independent views on:

- Resources
- Appointments

- Standards of conduct

Non-executive directors are the custodians of the governance process. They are not involved in the day-to-day running of the business but monitor the executive activity and contribute to the development of strategy.

We can expect executive directors to be highly experienced and successful business people, while non-executive directors need not be, and often aren't. Non-executive directorships need not be onerous; a number of women manage to hold down several simultaneously.

Most appointments of women to the boards of FTSE100 and FTSE250 firms have been NEDs. Feminists have criticised these appointments as 'window dressing', and for once I agree with them. But seeking an equal balance of men and women as *executive* directors is perverse if we are prepared to recognise an interesting phenomenon: the number of women who *want* to become executive directors of major firms is greatly outweighed by the number of men who wish to. So, even without consideration of the relative numbers of able and experienced men and women *eligible* for such roles, we should expect women to be greatly outnumbered in boardrooms.

Feminists have a perennial response to the tricky issue of women not wanting such roles: more role models are required. This is a circular argument, of course; if women will only seek executive directorships when there is a pre-existing 'critical mass' of female directors, how will the critical mass be achieved in the first place? Who will be the role models' role models?

The critical mass has not been achieved through women exercising opportunities, so militant feminists are pursuing a course with determination: positive discrimination for women to improve their representation in the senior levels of organisations. The introduction of 'positive action' in public sector organisations in the Equality Act 2010 is in reality the introduction of positive discrimination for women under another name.

For gender balance in boardrooms to be achieved on the basis of merit rather than through positive discrimination there would have to be gender balance in the senior ranks just beneath the boardroom. But that has never existed and it never will; at least not without positive discrimination in favour of women. And what would positive discrimination result in? A large number of women who have no wish to be directors, or who do not have the necessary abilities, being forced by overt or covert pressures to become directors. Is this the victory of which militant feminists dream? It would be a hollow one; but maybe that matters little to them.

Canadian psychologist Professor Susan Pinker wrote a highly illuminating book about men and women and their relationship to the world of work, *The Sexual Paradox: troubled boys, gifted girls and the real difference between the sexes* (2008). Pinker on the advancement of women in the workplace in recent decades:

> Gender equity legislation and the thinking behind second-wave feminism, so formative for the baby-boom generation, had unintended effects. Together they created the impression that *all* differences between men and women were created by unjust practices and therefore could be eased by changing same. With new laws and policies in place and women making up almost half of the workforce, there was a leap of faith that it was only a matter of time before all occupations would be split 50-50. Equal numbers of men and women working side by side, doing exactly the same work for exactly the same number of hours and pay, seemed a logical extension of the sixties-based egalitarian ideal.
>
> So when 50-50 didn't happen in all jobs by the year 2000, there was a vast feeling of letdown. 'Full equality is still a

distant promise,' wrote British journalist Natasha Walters in 2005, about the fact that women's salaries when averaged are 85 per cent of the average male salary...

The assumption seemed to be that if the social order had *really* changed, women would be exactly like men by now. They'd make the same choices, opting in equal proportions for chief executive positions, careers in theoretical physics, or political office. Even among women who haven't chosen such fields themselves, the wider the discrepancy from 50 per cent, the greater the sense of chagrin. That's because *it is largely taken for granted that gender discrimination is what is behind these numbers* [Author's italics].

Though discrimination still exists – both Wall Street and Wal-Mart have faced recent class action suits by women who feel their advancement has been blocked – as I talked to high-achieving women and started to look at the data, it became clear that women's and men's interests and preferences are also skewing the picture. *Equal opportunity doesn't necessarily lead to equal results* [Author's italics]. In fact, women's preferences stand out in higher relief precisely because they *do* have options. By looking at what has changed dramatically in thirty-odd years, and what has changed just a little, we can get a feeling for the pursuits women choose once doors are opened to them.

One of the most remarkable transformations over this period has taken place on the university campus. In 1960, 39 per cent of undergraduate students were female. Now 58 per cent of American university students are; indeed, women outnumber men on college campuses throughout the developed world. Their strong academic profiles – in everything from debating to building houses for Habitat for Humanity – have meant that high-achieving women have their pick of schools and disciplines. Professional degree programs in law, medicine, pharmacy, and biology, all fields formerly dominated by men, are now evenly divided or admit more women. Two highly competitive fields – clinical psychology and veterinary medicine – are now between 70 and 80 per cent female.

Clearly, girls and women are excelling in the classroom and making significant inroads outside it, so efforts to narrow the gender gap have succeeded in Western countries. 56 per cent of all high-paying professional jobs are now held by women, and women hold more than half of all professional and managerial positions in Canada and Britain. [Author's note: these data have to be taken with a pinch of salt, because the relative proportion of women to men in executive positions declines as we look at higher and higher levels in business. The inference in the line 'women hold more than half of all professional and managerial positions in Canada and Britain' appears to infer some degree of equivalence. But a person responsible for, say, three people is *not* equivalent to a person responsible for, say, 300.] Even at the top echelons of business, where female executives have been notoriously absent in the part, a 2006 study of Fortune 500 companies has uncovered an interesting phenomenon. While almost half the companies have no women at the helm [Author's note: I assume the term 'at the helm' means 'on the executive board'] the other half promote more women to executive officer positions, and they move them up faster – when they're younger and have less experience than men in comparable positions (the women are promoted after an average of 2.6 years on the job while in their forties, the men after 3.5 years and in their fifties). Currently, any gender gaps in pay are narrower than they have ever been.

One reason for the continued hand-wringing is that though women have flooded certain disciplines where they had been rare a few decades ago, there are still noticeable discrepancies in others. More women are studying engineering, physics, and computer science than ever before, but they are not exactly falling over themselves to enter those fields the way they have in medicine and law. Even with dozens of task forces and millions consecrated to increasing gender diversity, female enrolment in engineering in most schools hasn't budged past 20 per cent. Men have entered teaching, nursing, and social work – but these, too, remain predominantly female enclaves. Even with more choices, women still cluster in certain occupations, just as men continue to hang together in others.

Table 11.1: The percentage of degrees granted to women
in male-typical fields

	1973	2003
Veterinary medicine: Canada	12	78
US	10	71
Pharmacy: US	21	65
Law: UK	…	63
US	8	49
Medicine: Canada	17	58
US	9	45
Business: US	10	50
Architecture: US	13	41
Physics: US	7	22
Engineering: US	1	18

Table 11.2: The percentage of women working in fields
formerly identified as male

	1973	2003
Orchestra musicians	10	35
Lawyers: Canada	5*	34*
US	5	27
Physicians: Canada	…	31
US	8	26
Federal judges: Canada	1	26
US	…	23
Employed in science and engineering	8	26
Legislators: Canada	7	17
UN countries	…	16
US	3	14
Foresters and conservationists	4	13
Aerospace engineers	1	11
Telephone and computer line installers and repairers	1	6
Firefighters	0	3
Manufacturers' agents	<1	3
Electricians	0.6	2
Plumbers and pipe-fitters	0	1

… means no data available

* Data were only available for the years 1971 and 2001

From my own experience of working in the private sector for 33 years before taking early retirement in 2010 I believe there are numerous reasons why so few women are in evidence as we look at the senior reaches of companies, and this manifests itself most strikingly – as we might expect – in the boardrooms. I have seen the same reasons both when I started my career, and in more recent years. Most are attributable to women's basic natures, so they cannot be expected to change. My 'top 20' reasons are outlined in Table 11.3. I consulted widely with senior executives of both genders, and they were in broad agreement with the list.

Table 11.3: Top 20 reasons why female executives are uncommon in the most senior levels of major businesses

1. Many women have alternative options to work for attaining a high standard of living
2. Women seek a satisfying work/life balance
3. Women are not interested in business
4. Women are more motivated than men by the social engineering potential of business
5. A private sector worker is 43.3% more likely to be a man than a woman
6. Women take educational choices unlikely to lead to senior executive positions
7. Women are more likely than men to 'step off the executive treadmill'
8. Women don't like to make decisions for which they might be criticised
9. Women are more likely to have empathising natures than systemising natures
10. Women have to take career breaks if they decide to care for their young children full-time

11. Women are less independently-minded, confident, innovative and entrepreneurial than men, and more risk-averse and gullible
12. Women value happiness over power
13. Women prefer to ascend the corporate hierarchy on the coat-tails of men rather than through their own merits
14. Women treat the working environment as a social club
15. Women visibly suffer in the workplace when under stress
16. Women don't like working for women
17. Women lack the ruthlessness required to lead large teams
18. Women who require role models to inspire them are followers, not leaders
19. Women prefer to promote women rather than men
20. Women perceive the battle for senior positions in gender terms, not individual terms

Taking each of the reasons in turn:

1. Many women have alternative options to work for attaining a high standard of living

Many women and – let's be honest – very attractive women in particular, especially if well-educated, can attain high standards of living through relationships with prosperous men. How much more pleasant and less onerous that must be compared with working hard for many years in the (possibly futile) hope of ascending a corporate hierarchy. If and when these women marry and subsequently divorce, their financial positions may *still* be attractive. The appealing option of having a prosperous partner finance a high standard of living is rarely available to men, given that women don't like supporting men financially.

2. Women seek a satisfying work/life balance

People are generally free to pursue whatever work/life balance they wish. But pursuing a more satisfying balance usually means doing less work and having more life: in short, being less valuable to the firm. In the competitive worlds we are considering, this *must* result in a competitive disadvantage for the individual in question. If you're a director of a major company, and two senior employees of equal abilities respectively work 40 hours and 60 hours per week, who is going to be contributing more and therefore be a more likely candidate for promotion? An insistence on work/life balance *must* become increasingly disadvantageous as we ascend the corporate ladder.

Certain aspects of life in the senior levels of businesses seem particularly objectionable to women: such jobs commonly require that the executive travels widely and frequently, often alone, staying away from home for extended periods. Relocation is frequently required. Male executives are more prepared than female executives to make these sacrifices.

3. Women are not interested in business

Because women have no interests that compare in intensity with their interest in relationships, it follows – as night follows day – that they're less interested in business *per se* than in their relationships with work colleagues. They're not interested in the 'big picture' changes in markets and business options, knowledge of which is vital to making and keeping major organisations competitive.

Women are intrinsically less businesslike than men, and I've came across curious examples of this phenomenon when I've considered publishing talented but previously unpublished authors. In the past year I've been approached by two male authors and two female authors wishing me to publish their first books. One of the male authors' books was totally uncommercial in my view, and while he didn't agree with my assessment, he accepted my position with good grace. The other male author's book was of more interest but we couldn't agree on commercial terms, and our discussions came to an amicable end.

My experience with the aspiring female authors was very different. Female author #1 had written an interesting light-hearted book about her life on the French Riviera, and she accepted my quotation for transforming her manuscript from a very sorry state into something approaching readiness for publication. I spent two weeks working on the book then sent her the revised files, only to be informed that she'd changed her mind, and would now be publishing the book herself. She hoped I hadn't spent *too* long working on it, and ended with 'Kind regards, Anne xxx'.

Female author #2 told me she had almost given up hope of seeing her (cookery) book in print. She'd spent almost a year trying to work out how to self-publish the book, and had made little progress. I had the benefit of two years' experience of publishing five books at that point, and she soon realised I was the key to her realising her book publishing dream. In the light of my experience with female author #1, I explained to her that I would only proceed with the project upon her written agreement to contract terms, which included the financial aspects of the deal. She readily agreed and I sent the contract to her along with a letter recommending she take legal advice on any terms which weren't perfectly clear. Three or four days later the contract was returned, signed, so I set to work. The contract stipulated that I would receive no payment for the work but would receive a proportion of the profits from the sales of the book, if there were any.

The manuscript was in a very sorry state, the formatting was dire, and errors of spelling and grammar littered every page. Through working hard for a month – during which time she changed her mind on every aspect of the book, necessitating a good deal of extra work on my part – I managed to get the book's content into a fit state for publication, and sent her (as email attachments) the final files for proofing.

Within an hour of receipt of the files she called me to say she was thrilled with the book, thanked me for all my work, but she'd looked again at the contract terms and decided that she couldn't accept term 5.2(ii). This term happened to be the one which would result in my receiving income, as the publisher, from any sales of the book. She kept bleating that it wasn't 'fair', whereupon I explained it was *perfectly* fair; apart from which, the right time to query it would have been *before* I worked on the book for a month. I enquired whether any comment had been made about the term when she sought legal advice, to be met with, 'Oh, I can't afford legal advice, I just thought we'd chat about any areas I wasn't happy with. Anyway, it's a woman's prerogative to change her mind.'

I was so incensed that I lost my customary cool and tore up the contract while we were still talking on the telephone. The woman had benefited from my two years' experience of book publishing and my month's hard work developing a publishable manuscript, whilst paying me nothing upfront and wishing to deny me income post-publication.

A few weeks later she published the book herself. I emailed her to ask whether, in the light of my efforts (without which her book would never have seen the light of day) she might be kind enough to send me a complimentary copy. She sent one, and it had clearly been carefully selected: it had a torn page. I won't be offering to work for other female authors any time soon.

4. Women are more motivated than men by the social engineering potential of business

This motivation is evident in how women operate within their firms, and how they work with parties which come into contact with them. Within the firm, women's ingrained desire for equality, fairness, justice, blah, blah, blah, results in a range of actions which make the firm less efficient and effective. One obvious area is the promotion of individuals deemed to be in 'oppressed minorities' – women, ethnic minority groups etc. Often the conceit of 'all else being equal' is used: if a man and a woman, say, are deemed equally worthy of promotion, the woman should be promoted: low-level positive discrimination.

In all my years of interviewing hundreds of applicants for jobs, or existing staff for promotion, I never once faced the problem of two candidates of equal merit. Positive discrimination results in individuals being promoted in preference to colleagues where their lesser capabilities are not so glaring as to invite outright scorn. And so the balance of gender, race, or whatever is 'improved', but at an invisible cost to the organisation.

Women's social agendas extends outside the firm too, and they are happy to compromise the interests of the firm in pursuing the agendas. I worked in procurement for most of my career, buying goods and services for major organisations. More and more women have been entering the field of procurement in recent years, and the result has been predictable. They are manipulating their firms to buy goods and services from women-owned or minority-owned businesses, they're enthusiastic supporters of corporate responsibility programmes, and so on. It seems to me that most of these women don't understand what makes capitalism works; and if they do, they're hostile to it.

5. A private sector worker is 43.3% more likely to be a man than a woman

Women represent 65.2% of public sector workers and 41.1% of private sector workers (source: Unison). So men represent 58.9% of private sector workers. Roughly speaking, for every two private sector workers who are women, three are men. This alone would be expected to lead to a marked gender imbalance in the senior reaches of companies.

6. Women take educational choices unlikely to lead to senior executive positions

The optimal educational choice for a person wishing to reach the senior levels in business is a business degree from a leading institution, such as The London Business School. From Steve Moxon's *The Woman Racket* :

> The London Business School's female intake is only one in five of the total [Author's note: the proportion is higher in American business schools] and this is mirrored in business schools nationwide. There is subsequent heavy attrition in numbers of females, not just owing to their family commitments, but also, compared to men, through their having less focus and more other interests that conflict with both the desire and the effort necessary to climb the hierarchy. And this does not take into account the high proportion of men who will get there through other, less direct or riskier routes, who never went to business school. Business is the field of the entrepreneur after all, who is born with the attitude and the drive. He's not a product of a college course. Just ask Sir Richard Branson or Sir Alan Sugar.

We'll be considering the subject of entrepreneurship later in this chapter.

7. Women are more likely than men to step off the executive treadmill
We'll be returning shortly to Susan Pinker's *The Sexual Paradox*, which provides insights into the world of the female senior executive. But for now let me just state something I've seen in many major organisations: women are far more likely than men to simply abandon their careers when it suits them. Companies invest heavily in their senior executives' development and it follows that positive discrimination for women – who are more likely than men to abandon their careers – flies in the face of the economic interests of the firm, and in turn the interests of the firm's owners, its shareholders.

8. Women don't like to make decisions for which they might be criticised
This is a curious one, but I came across it all the time in my business career. I would ask a female executive with an impressive-sounding job title for a decision on something – possibly something trivial – and would be met with, 'I'll have to speak to Bob and get back to you on this.' Now this may be partly attributable to the scourge of job title inflation – when did *you* last meet a secretary? – but I think there's more to it. Over many years I came to the conclusion that women are happier than men to do jobs where they don't have to use their discretion in making decisions; they prefer to work within a clearly defined framework of policies and guidance. And I suspect the reason is that so long as they stay within that framework, they are largely immune from criticism. Men seem more prepared than women to use their judgement and accept criticism when they make poor decisions.

9. Women are more likely to have empathising natures than systemising natures

The matter of empathising and systemising natures was covered at length in chapter 2. The reason for raising it in this context is to state what I see as a blindingly obvious truth: the higher in a hierarchy a person works, the greater will be the need to use systemising capabilities, and the lesser will be the need to use empathising capabilities. It follows that an increasingly higher proportion of men than women should be expected as we ascend corporate hierarchies, and of course this is exactly what we see.

10. Women have to take career breaks if they decide to care for their young children full-time

The sheer frequency with which women debate the issue of mothers with young children working or not working is a clear indication of the angst that the question creates in the mind of women lucky enough to enjoy the choice. But of course there's no easy answer. Taking years off from their careers may well hamper women's prospects of advancement. It would be the same for men, if they took such breaks: but they don't. The option to take lengthy career breaks, or not to take them, is limited to women alone.

11. Women are less independently-minded, confident, innovative and entrepreneurial than men, and more risk-averse and gullible

Women are often highly opinionated about the smaller matters in life, but rarely as opinionated about the larger matters. Their instinct is to seek other people's opinions when presented with challenging problems, even in circumstances where their own experience and expertise should enable them to make up their own minds quickly. Women tend to have less confidence than men on the same organisational level as themselves. One practical consequence of women's need to consult widely is, hardly surprisingly, a lack of decisiveness. It may be increased by women's fears of making mistakes.

When problems or opportunities present themselves, women's instincts are to consider what has worked in similar circumstances before, and simply repeat it. They're less likely than men to formulate innovative solutions. An ability to innovate in business is merely an expression of creativity; and in all fields where creativity is important, men make up the majority of leading practitioners. Why should business be any different in this respect than, say, the visual arts, music etc.?

An aptitude for innovation is linked, I think, to a relish for taking risks. In the corporate levels just below boardroom level, executives with a track record of making poor decisions about risk will have been eliminated, leaving those with a good track record. Innovativeness is linked to independence of thought; and men are more independent-minded than women.

Outside the world of conventional large businesses, men's lesser aversion to risk and greater aptitude for innovation are evident in the field of entrepreneurship: men being overwhelmingly more likely than women to be entrepreneurs, whether successful or not.

Onto another topic which militates against women attaining high office: gullibility, which is partly evidence of a lack of independence of thought. As is often the case we need to consider how women *act* and not at what they *say*. The producers of commercials aimed at women conduct much research into what persuades women to buy products. And what seems to work with women is some sort of curious transference process. When a woman is exposed to an advert for face creams, she looks at the model on the screen, poster, or whatever, and thinks, 'You're incredibly beautiful, you have the flawless skin which I'd like, and although you look about 17 years old and I'm 52, you attribute your alabaster skin to Gloreal Pro-Jeunesse 217K Face Sculpting Serum. So if I use the product, my skin will look the same. What's that? 73 out of 98 women agreed it improved the appearance of facial lines? Scientific proof! I must have it… after all, I'm worth it!!!'

How could a mind capable of such mind-numbing gullibility be trusted to make the rational decisions which are required in the most senior positions in business? It couldn't.

12. *Women value happiness over power*

We return to Canadian psychologist Susan Pinker's *The Sexual Paradox* (2008). She makes it clear that women are 'under-represented' at senior levels in organisations only because they are exercising choice. I wrote to Harriet Harman (appendix 6) enclosing a copy of the book but, surprisingly, I didn't receive a reply. An illuminating excerpt from the book:

> The personal story on the newspaper's back page was headlined, 'My Glass Ceiling Is Self-Imposed', and it pinged my eyes open faster than the black coffee I had just poured down my throat. A female executive on the fast track (to the Chief Executive Officer's position) had refused a promotion to vice president in a multinational company earning billions and felt she needed to explain why, though she was writing under a pseudonym. Methodically, systematically, she detailed how her company provided every possible perk to promote women's success, including networked home offices so they could telecommute, flex hours, no pressure to put in face time, an in-house dry cleaner and gym, an income supplement for a nanny, and on-site care for sick children. Her company was rated one of the top hundred companies to work for in

the United States, and one of the top hundred in Europe. Still this executive had stalled her own advancement just when she was expected to rise like a helium balloon. Her promotion would have put her third from the top in a company of 12,000 employees with offices in more than 60 countries, and on the short list to become the company's CEO within a few years.

Pinker tracked the women down and met up with her. She continues:

> She was a business person who got straight to the point, telling me within five minutes that aside from a job she loved, she also had two small children, a husband, and parents, all of whom were central to her happiness and to one another's. A promotion would require moving to another city, and while it would boost her status and salary, it would destabilize her family. If she enjoyed her work, was respected for it, and had a well-rounded personal life, why jinx things by climbing yet a rung higher? Still a director of her company, she didn't regret turning down the opportunity to become vice president for a minute, she said. 'My husband loves his work, my children are very happy and settled, and I love my job. My long-term future is not as strong as it might have been, but I derive my happiness and sense of self-worth from much more than just my career.'
>
> Her explicit message: work is essential, but so are the needs of her family. The subtext? Saying so is somehow shameful – hence the pseudonym, both for the newspaper and for this book. It's not a wise gambit to turn down a promotion, much less ascribe one's reasons to the time-warped notion that the feelings of loved ones matter to you as much as achievement at work.

Pinker wondered if the woman in question could be representative of other highly placed women, and we shouldn't be too surprised by what she writes on the subject:

> There's plenty of evidence that many more women than men refuse promotions out of considerations for family, including

women at the top of their game. In 2006, when investment analyst Carolyn Buck Luce and economist Sylvia Ann Hewlett tried to get to the bottom of the 'hidden brain drain' of female talent by surveying 2,443 women with graduate or professional degrees, they discovered that one in three women with MBAs chose not to work full-time – compared with one in 20 men with the same degree – and that 38 per cent of high-achieving women had turned down a promotion or had deliberately taken a position with lower pay. Instead of being forcibly barred from top positions, *these women were avoiding them.* [Author's italics].

When the researchers looked at women's motivations to work, they discovered that *having a powerful position was the lowest-ranked career goal of highly qualified women in every sector* [Author's italics]. For 85 per cent of the women, other values came first: the ability to work with people they respect, to 'be themselves' at work, and to have flexible schedules.

The most talented senior businesswoman I came across in 33 years in business resigned from her company in her mid forties and bought and subsequently managed a small upmarket lingerie shop. She tells me she's never been happier.

13. Women prefer to ascend the corporate hierarchy on the coat-tails of men rather than through their own merits

A sizeable proportion of senior female executives owe their positions to close relationships with one or more senior male executives, and this can be a source of resentment among the women's male and female colleagues. A problem arises when the male executive(s) in question leave(s) the organisation, because the female executives have not built up the credibility to continue working at a high level without strong executive sponsorship.

14. Women treat the working environment as a social club

Women are not, of course, alone in treating the working environment as a social club. Many men do so too, but on a far lesser scale.

About ten years ago I was working on an assignment with a medium-sized retailer. One day I was using a desk in the Human Resources department, and spent the afternoon working on my laptop. Two women, maybe in their late forties or early fifties, were at their adjoining desks in the department. One of them was the deputy Human Resources Director.

From lunchtime until 5p.m., with only a few short telephone interruptions, the two women gossiped non-stop about their partners, children, friends, shopping, television programmes, celebrity news, and other matters of no relevance to their work. At precisely 5p.m., as they were preparing to leave, I was privileged to overhear the following:

> 'Anne, are you planning to apply for the HR director vacancy when Mr D leaves?'
> 'No, I want to move to part-time working so I can spend more time with the grandkids and potter about the garden. My roses are a *picture* this year!'
> 'OK. Still, with the glass ceiling being what it is, you might not have got the job anyway!'
> 'Too right. It's still a man's world, isn't it?'

I once had a lodger of the female persuasion, who in her mid-thirties had a new (female) boss appointed. For some months the two of them had Friday afternoons set aside so that the latter could mentor the former with respect to management skills. Some months into the arrangement I asked my lodger how the arrangement was progressing. 'Brilliant!', she said with relish. 'She's the best boss ever – we spend Friday afternoons shopping!'

15. *Women visibly suffer in the workplace when under stress*

A few years ago I carried out a consulting assignment in the London headquarters of a major service company. The deputy Finance Director was a single woman in her mid-thirties with no children, well versed in all the accounting skills required for her job. Both she and I reported to the Finance Director, an overbearing man disliked both inside and outside his department and (being short in stature) nicknamed 'Napoleon'.

To say that working for Napoleon was stressful would be an understatement; his penchant for demanding endless revised versions of complex spreadsheets, so as to improve their accuracy by a fraction of a percentage point, would have made even a nun kick a sickly puppy into a fast-flowing river. But the pay was good, and I tried to take the stress in my stride. I found that a large measure of Talisker or Lagavulin Scotch Whisky in the evenings soon put Napoleon out of my mind. Alcohol has long been the self-medication of choice for men seeking to cope with stress, and it's increasingly the self-medication of choice for women coping with stress too.

Working in the corner of an open plan office, with her staff in close proximity, my female colleague was frequently and visibly highly stressed, often to the point of being tearful; and occasionally she *did* burst into tears. On one of these occasions I took her for a coffee and asked her why she put herself through the stress rather than confronting her boss or resigning. She replied along the following lines:

> I recently bought a flat and a new car, the costs of which requires me to earn a good salary, and that only comes with jobs like this, which are highly stressful. But I really hate this job. I'd give it up tomorrow to be a mother and housewife, if the option presented itself.

To militant feminists, this woman – by virtue of holding down a well-paid, pressurised job – would be viewed as a success. But the woman knew otherwise, every working day of the week. A man who was so visibly stressed during his working day would be relieved of his duties, but some misplaced sense persuades us to allow women to carry on, if they're prepared to. It's no wonder that so many female executives are absent from work on stress- or depression-related grounds.

Apart from the impact on the individual, what is the impact on the firm of allowing a person insufficiently robust for their work to continue working? Colleagues will not want to add to their stress and will shy away from dealing with them in a businesslike manner, which can only damage the efficiency and effectiveness of the firm.

16. Women don't like working for women

I've often come across this phenomenon, but I was in two minds about including it in my 'top 20'. My own experience is that women like working for women when they enjoy a good personal relationship; but when they don't, they dislike working for them for one or more of three reasons: they find women bosses dour, ungrateful, and spiteful. One said to me, 'Bad female bosses are like elephants: if they don't like you, and you make a mistake, they'll never let you forget it, even *years* later. Male bosses tend to be more generous. They'll point out you've made a mistake, ensure you've learned from it, and that will be that. Case closed, never to be reopened.'

From a section titled, 'Women tend to revile women bosses', in *The Woman Racket*:

It might be expected that, with the separate social organisation of the sexes, having a boss of the opposite sex might be problematic, and that with women sticking together the most benign arrangement is women working for a woman boss. Paradoxical though it seems, nothing could be further from the truth. Organisations function best where bosses are male – whether their underlings are male or female – and worst when bosses are female. They function worst of all when a woman manages women.

Research reveals that women overwhelmingly prefer not to work under another female. This is a profoundly negative feeling about women as line managers and not a positive feeling about men in the role. A useless male boss is preferred to a competent female one. It's not just an issue of women not liking working for women superiors, but that they don't want to co-operate with or even acknowledge them (Molm, 1986). Some female secretaries actually walk out of recruitment when they find that their prospective boss is a woman. (The squabbling on *The Apprentice* came to a head when Miranda Rose got the boot for disloyalty after being appointed P.A. by the power-hungry Adele Lock. The job appeared to have no purpose other than to improve Ms. Lock's level of self-esteem and had disastrous consequences for the female social network as well as for the 'enterprise'.)

A survey for the Royal Mail in 2000 reported that only seven per cent of women preferred a female superior. In a 1991 survey, of women who had worked through the Alfred Marks agency under both men and women, less than a fifth said they would want a woman line manager in future, and two-thirds said they would never work under a woman again and wanted their boss to be male. Almost the same proportion (three in five) expressed just the same to researchers for *Harper's Bazaar* magazine in 2007 – and these were professional women in top jobs.

Women's unwillingness to work for a woman line manager is greater compared to *men's* (Mavin, Sandra & Lockwood, 2004; Mavin, Sharon & Bryans, 2003). Women can positively welcome work beyond their job description when it's for a male boss. However hidden, it appears that a sexual frisson –

which can be very widely manifested, in many not overtly sexual ways – makes a dull job sparkle. Inter-sexual social reality is what is most salient.

Women complain that female bosses have favourites and are inconsistent because they deal in personal relationships instead of focusing on the job, whereas women feel they get fair treatment from male bosses. The predominantly personal dimension of women's managerial style leads to sniping or awkwardness; or a sense of superiority and trying to prove a point when giving out work.

Something powerful is at play here. Women have an acute awareness of the separate worlds of the sexes. Underlying the negative feelings women have for same-sex bosses, is that they are aware of the instrumental motivation of women to try to travel up organisational structures, of being more in the company of higher-status men. From the perspective of evolutionary psychology, women don't acquire status, except in the sense of acquiring it indirectly from their long-term mates; so women placing themselves over other women according to the criteria of a male competitive status hierarchy may be seen by their female underlings as incongruous – cheating even. Women's natural predisposition to networking exacerbates this. A female boss is not centred on the workplace as a coalition as are men; instead being more concerned with what she perceives as her 'in-group' of women, most of whom are likely outside the organisation, with whom the women under her may well have no connection.

The women bosses with their favoured women underlings stick together, and the selective bias women have for other women will come out in interviews for promotion. There is an irony that women, as the people women least want to see manage them, will tend to end up with positions of responsibility, thus driving further workplace discord amongst women, and further discrimination against men.

17. Women lack the ruthlessness required to lead large teams

With an in-built strong concern for people's feelings and a preference for being liked over being respected, female bosses are increasingly hampered as they ascend the corporate hierarchy. I've lost count of the number of times senior female executives have delayed firing incompetent employees, believing that miraculous transformations will occur, or that more training courses will turn them into competent people.

18. Women who require role models to inspire them are followers, not leaders

The most frequently cited reason for using positive discrimination to drive up the number of female executive directors in major firms is to provide role models for women to follow. Truly talented and hard-working female executives are generally insulted by the idea of positive discrimination. One, expecting to land a FTSE250 executive directorship within the coming two years, told me:

> 'I hate this notion that women need role models to inspire them. Leaders don't want or need role models, only followers do. And executive directors, above all else, need to be leaders and not followers. Maggie Thatcher didn't need a female role model, did she? I've met numerous women who talked about the need for more role models. Not one of these women had the *slightest* grasp of how business works at senior levels – hardly surprising, as they had no personal experience of it. Campaigning for positive discrimination for women, with the aim of having more female directors, is demeaning to women and ultimately counter-productive.'

19. Women prefer to promote women rather than men

From *The Woman Racket*, a section titled, 'Women's preference for their own sex: serious sex discrimination against men':

> The fourfold female preference for their own sex, and the 'in-group' / 'out-group' differences between men and women means that employers entrusting recruitment to women are likely to get not the best man for the job but more likely a mediocre woman. It also means potential problems of female

performance in the job, irrespective of ability. The upshot for men is serious sex discrimination against them.

In recruitment, whereas women candidates will tend on average not to suffer discrimination – even if the interview panel is all-male – men candidates will probably suffer worst outcomes the greater is the proportion of female interviewers. If the panel is all-women, then not only is this effect at its maximum, but there is no male perspective to counteract it. Women interviewers will prefer women (even aside from any feminist political attitudes, or any acceptance of notions of supposed oppression of women, or pressure through equal-opportunities policies). There would seem to be two complementary reasons for this. First, the interviewer tends to feel a potential personal connection with any and every female applicant, even though she may be a complete stranger – there need be no shared 'in- group' for this to occur, as would be the case for men. Second, prejudicial preference will go relatively unchecked (compared to how men would feel) given that women have a very different sense of 'in-group', and so will be less concerned about the impact of making a decision that may not be in the best interests of the work group...

Performance in the job by female workers will tend to be problematic because of the relative failure to identify with the 'in-group' of fellow workers, and to focus instead on personal connectedness rather than the task at hand. This will reduce efficiency in the workplace directly, but there is also a further impact in that those members of the work group that the top clique of female workers do not feel personally related to, will feel rejected. As a result, they will either become de-motivated, or work more for themselves and competitively against the group. This is the opposite of how male workers would tend to behave. Men experience a mutually reinforcing sense of belonging to a group, and competitiveness on behalf of the group (as well as individual effort within it to try to rise to the top).

The current notion, though, is that women make better employees than men. Men are thought to be 'bolshy' and women compliant. Yet the more rule-based existence of men – apparent right from the days of school playground team sports – makes them likely to be more predictable and reasonable than women. Countless television advertisements (exemplified by the excruciating BT 'work smarter' series, but long ubiquitous), proclaim a contest of male 'dimwits' versus female 'smarties'...

Some think that men are too status-orientated, without seeing that there is a problem with women employees being too person-centred. Both male and female sex-typical behaviours could be regarded either as distractions from or contributions to the work culture, but employers certainly do prefer women (as a 1996 Rowntree report showed). Yet it is men who have the additional clear attributes of being both task-centred and of forming teams within the workplace, rather than personal networks that may well be more connected with life outside – though sometimes female work teams are as effective as male ones...

Conclusive evidence of widescale discrimination against men at the job application stage was uncovered in 2006 by Peter Riach and Judith Rich, 'An Experimental Investigation of Sexual Discrimination in Hiring in the English Labour Market'. They had sent pairs of resumés to employers: one from a mythical applicant called 'Phillip' and another from a no less fictitious 'Emma', differing from each other only in the most minor details, but sufficient to ensure they would not be detected as being identical. The experience, qualifications, age, marital status, socio-economic background – every relevant detail – were as near to identical as could make no difference. They awaited the offer of an interview (or a request for a telephone discussion) or a rejection note (or silence).

Nobody was prepared for the result. Not even the direction of it, let alone the size. It was not women but men who got the fewer offers, and by not a small margin but by a massive factor of *four*. Uncannily, this is precisely the same factor by which women prefer other women to men, as discovered in research into the female social psychology of 'in-group'. Have workplaces completely capitulated to basing their hiring entirely on female prejudice? (HR is a predominantly female profession.)

Women's preference for promoting women over men leads to justifiable resentment among men. It also sends an unfortunate message to women, 'You don't need to be as good as a man to get ahead.'

Men are also more often disadvantaged than women by the irrational or shallow grounds used by some women for accepting or rejecting job applicants. I had heard that some women made decisions on the basis of criteria such as handwriting, but refused to believe it. So I was interested in the following article by the journalist and former magazine editor Rowan Pelling in *The Daily Telegraph* of October 13, 2010:

> Handwriting is as distinguishing a mark of personality and aptitude as a person's voice, manner and qualifications. My reverence for the power of the hand-inked word is so great that I could never love a man whose script was diabolical. The men I know feel just as passionately about a woman's hand. That's why fountain pens make perfect tokens of love.
>
> When I ran my own office, the first thing I would examine when a CV arrived was the handwriting on the envelope. If it was an elegant flow of dark ink, it leapt to the top of the pile; but if there was an ugly scrawl then out it went.

20. *Women perceive the battle for senior positions in gender terms, not individual terms*

Maybe it's attributable to feminism and its focus on gender and power, but women tend to see the battle for senior positions as one facet of 'the battle of the sexes'. This may account for their perceiving a common cause with other women. If so, they're wasting their time and energies. The people who run major businesses have little or no genuine interest in gender politics. All they're interested in is, 'Can this person do the job?' A woman who campaigns for women will unwittingly be sending out the message, 'I may not be much myself, but just look at what a wonderful gender I belong to!' How pathetic is that?

Why would businesses accept positive discrimination for women and thereby appoint women who are *less* capable than available men for senior positions? To do so would be to strike at the heart of the capitalist model of business, and thereby at the heart of a free society. But businesses have contributed to the public's expectation that they act in uncommercial ways. Recent years have seen an explosion in the 'Corporate Social Responsibility' or 'Corporate Responsibility' industries. Firms seek to be more environmentally-friendly than their competitors, more enthusiastic about 'fair trade', gender balance and a range of other left-wing causes. The underlying message is that capitalism needs to be on the defensive, as if being the sole creator of real employment and wealth is not in itself a sufficiently laudable achievement.

Forcing gender balance in the boardrooms of major corporations would be a social engineering experiment – and an irreversible one, possibly – which could well go badly wrong. It is, after all, forcing organisations to adopt a measure to placate feminists *whose ideology is Marxism*. You couldn't make it up, could you? No socialist or communist regime even managed to design and manufacture a car which its citizens – or at least its citizens with the option of buying a car built in another country's private sector – would want.

Measures to promote more gender balance in the boardrooms of major organisations are currently being considered by the coalition government. So what is the position of the leading employers' representative body in the UK, the CBI? The CBI represents employers which collectively employ a third of the country's private sector workers. From their website Cbi.org.uk, a section on 'Policy and lobbying work':

> A core element of the CBI's work is its much-respected lobbying – an ongoing activity allowing members to drive change to the legislative and regulatory framework in which they have to operate, and backed by our 80-strong policy

engine which works full-time on the issues directly affecting business. All government departments can affect business, but the potential impact of legislation isn't always understood by those who devise it. The CBI's unique relationship with business means we know exactly how it can be affected by government legislation, communicating this through our equally unique relationship with government. And our influence is such that government takes notice.

No other business organisation can match our extensive network of contacts with government ministers, MPs, civil servants, advisers, opinion formers and media commentators.

Interested to learn the organisation's position on gender balance in the boardroom, I wrote to the Director-General, Richard Lambert, and received a reply shortly after – appendices 9 and 10. From his reply we learn that the CBI believes 'enforced quotas are not the answer', which is encouraging, but much of the remainder of the letter could have been penned by a militant feminist, including:

Diverse boards have many benefits that include promoting more robust challenge in the boardroom, helping to reduce group-think as well as ensuring companies are in touch with their customers, all important themes in the wake of the financial crisis.

Given the lack of diversity in the boardrooms of Britain's major companies, these views – presented as facts – are speculative to say the least. I wouldn't have been surprised to find them in materials from Harriet Harman or The Fawcett Society. But they come from the Director-General of the country's leading employers' organisation. It would be difficult to imagine a clearer indicator of the country's slow and lazy drift to left-wing habits of thinking over the past decade; and it is, ironically, an example of the very 'group-think' which it claims is present in boards which are not diverse.

If gender balanced boardrooms were ever legislated for in the private sector – a triumph of Marxist ideology in a supposedly free society – the immediate impact might not be negative. The new female directors could be expected to consult widely – as is the female habit – with experienced business people who, by definition, would mostly be men. But over time a female trait would become ever more apparent: risk aversion. The long-term profitability of our major companies could be expected to decline as a result, because in comparison with companies in developing countries which enjoy low costs, companies in developed countries need to be relatively *less* risk averse and more entrepreneurial.

But here's the big question: could the legislation enforcing gender-balanced boards be reversed, even if damage to companies suggested the need to do so? Militant feminist campaigning organisations would be up in arms, denying the possibility of a link between gender balanced boards and reduced profitability. By their very natures feminists can't be swayed by rational arguments, and you couldn't develop an *emotional* argument for reversing gender balanced boardrooms. Hoping for politicians to take a tough decision which would be challenged by half the electorate, women – or at least challenged by women's whining self-appointed representatives at The Fawcett Society and elsewhere – would be optimistic.

The inevitable result of countries legislating for gender balanced boardrooms would be to place the countries in question at an economic disadvantage to countries where companies continued to appoint directors on the grounds of merit. How many citizens would, if given a choice in the matter, accept the risk of a decline in their standard of living as the price of gender balance in the boardroom?

CHAPTER 18

HOW HAVE MILITANT FEMINISTS BECOME SO INFLUENTIAL?

One hears that the 'women of the United States' are up in arms about this or that; the plain fact is that eight fat women, meeting in a hotel parlor, have decided to kick up some dust.
HL Mencken 1880–1956 American journalist, essayist, magazine editor, satirist, critic of American life and culture

Where are the militant feminists among us? – my efforts to interview leading figures promoting the militant feminist agenda – how do a small number of militant feminists manage to wield such a disproportionate influence? – the exhausting Ms Harman

Whilst considering the possibility of writing this book, and during the time it took me to write it, I was aware of an irony. The group of women I am crediting with so much influence – militant feminists – are all but invisible in society. Sticking with the definition of a militant feminist as a person who seeks equality of outcome between men and women in the workplace – regardless of the number of able women wishing to take opportunities available to them – I've never knowingly met one. I spoke to friends and family members, neighbours, and former business associates: they didn't know any militant feminists either, they never had known any to the best of their knowledge, nor could they suggest where I might find an example. My adopted home town, the throbbing metropolis of Bedford, appeared to be a militant feminist-free zone.

In an effort to better understand militant feminists' perspectives on outcomes at senior levels in the business world, I wrote to four people I expected to have some insights into the matter, seeking a meeting and an audio interview. Copies of the letters are provided in the appendices of this book:

Appendix 5 – The Rt Hon Harriet Harman
Appendix 7 – Lord Davies of Abersoch
Appendix 8 – Ceri Goddard, Chief Executive of The Fawcett Society
Appendix 11 – Trevor Phillips, Chair of The Equality and Human Rights Commission

Only Harriet Harman had the courtesy to respond, and that was – surprise, surprise – to decline a meeting. The people most qualified to talk about the influence of militant feminists in modern Britain clearly had no intention of doing so. Why might that be, I wonder?

It's easy to poke fun at the more bizarre manifestations of militant feminist thinking such as 'celebrating fatness' – and I plan to continue doing so, regularly and mercilessly – but in doing so it's all too easy to miss the big picture:

Militant feminists exert an influence on political and business agendas to a degree which is *wildly* disproportionate to their numbers.

How, precisely, do they manage to achieve this? In the remainder of this chapter I speculate on the matter.

Men don't campaign for their collective interests: they have no interest in gender politics

Men have perfectly legitimate collective interests, but because they don't act collectively and campaign for them to be recognised, politicians can safely ignore them. Politicians legislate against men's collective interests in the knowledge that men will just put up with it. To be discriminated against is the lot of men in the modern era; to complain about the situation remains unmanly. So women are free to carry on collectively manipulating men. They can rely on men with left-of-centre political persuasions to support them at all times, or at the very least not challenge them.

Men are starting to recognise that they are being discriminated against in terms of job recruitment and promotion. My hope is that this will, in time, make them interested in gender politics, and a long overdue backlash will finally begin.

Political correctness has triumphed

For all the criticism levelled against political correctness, you might have expected it to wither away and die. But you'd be wrong; it's alive and well and controlling the thinking of many British citizens, and most politicians, on a daily basis. Maybe it's partly the result of 13 years of a dismal Labour administration with the likes of Harriet Harman in senior positions.

The first rule of political correctness is that women are beyond criticism. The second is that their interests must be furthered by any means: given the nature of the perceived injustice, either equality or special treatment will usually suffice.

Men and women are delusional; business people aren't immune

Whilst researching for this book I spoke to a number of former business associates and colleagues, both men and women, who had worked for many years at senior levels in the business world. Without telling them the theses I planned to put forward in the book, I asked them for their general thoughts about the genders at senior levels in business. Talking as if on some form of mental auto-pilot, most said that women were as capable as men of succeeding in senior positions, and they were confident that over time the number of women in Britain's boardrooms would rise inexorably, leading to gender balance in Britain's boardrooms in the fullness of time.

Then I asked them for their *personal* experiences of men and women in business. It turned out, to my surprise, that almost all of them shared my own experience, including:

- women are more interested in work-life balance than men, so they're less interested in competing for senior positions
- women find it more difficult than men to make the tough decisions required in senior-level positions, especially with respect to firing people
- women are more likely than men to suffer adverse reactions to the stress which inevitably accompanies senior roles
- women are more likely than men to bail out of senior positions, partly because they're more likely than men to have the option of doing so
- women are highly risk-averse and loathe to make decisions which might be criticised

I then asked my former colleagues how they might explain the discrepancies between the views they'd earlier expressed about men and women in the workplace, and their personal experience. After considering the question for a time, most of the men said they had assumed their personal experience was untypical. The women said it was an unspoken rule for women to point out and criticise the common failings of men, but not those of women. In the business world this translated into a tendency to claim that women's failings, if and when noticed, were *not* characteristic of women. An example of any 'female typical' characteristic could always be found among some men, thereby neutralising the claim.

Big business has no representation against militant feminism

One organisation above all represents big business in Britain, and has long been considered 'the voice of business' in its dealings with politicians: the CBI, the Confederation of British Industries. It has a President – Helen Alexander – who had a successful career in business. A good start, but then one notes on their website Cbi.org.uk a lady Director whose biography runs as follows:

> [Name supplied] is responsible for leading the CBI's work on employment, employee relations, pensions and diversity. She was previously Head of Employee Relations and Diversity, responsible for the CBI's work on trade union issues, dispute resolution, working time, diversity and family-friendly policies. Prior to this, [name supplied] worked in employee relations and HR Policy at the BBC and as head of Employee Resourcing at the CBI, covering pay and pensions, labour market flexibility, welfare reform and sickness absence.
>
> [Name supplied] is a member of the Ethnic Minority Employment Taskforce, the Fair Employment Enforcement Board and the Employment Tribunal Steering Board. She is also a member of the Social Affairs Committee of BUSINESSEUROPE, the European Employers' Organisation and chairs its Employment and Skills Working Group.

Diversity… family-friendly policies… ethnic minorities… fair employment enforcement… How can an employers' organisation both campaign in these areas and also represent its membership, which will surely be in firm opposition to social engineering agendas such as increasing boardroom diversity and eliminating the gender pay gap? It can't, of course. In this area at least the CBI is not representing but campaigning; which might be fine for its female members, but what about its male members?

No organisations exist to counter the arguments of feminist campaigning organisations
In the absence of such organisations the militant feminists have an open goal to kick into. Woe betide any politician who dared to publicly criticise organisations such as The Fawcett Society. The simple fact is, however, that such organisations have no democratic mandate. Why, then, are they permitted – encouraged, even – to wield such influence on our political processes?

Men are more reasonable than women
Men are by nature more reasonable than women; they know a working balance has to be struck between opposing interests. Women don't have this sense of a need for balance. Their instinct is always to want more: more money, more clothes, more free time, more everything. If my speculation in chapter 2 is correct – that militant feminists have extreme female brains – then we should not be surprised that they are more unreasonable than most women. They will *never* be content.

Harriet Harman exhausted her colleagues
How did Harriet Harman manage to exert her vice-like grip over the Labour administration's gender agenda between 1997 and 2010? I suspect it was largely a matter of personality. She's a sterling example of the sort of women whose long-suffering husbands mutter in a weary tone, 'Yes, dear'.

I doubt if such women know why they generally get what they want in life. Maybe they flatter themselves that they're 'strong'. But the reality is that when faced with the zeal of such women, most people – and almost all men, including myself – rapidly lose the will to live, and will say or do *anything* to stop the relentless torrent of words. 'What's that, Harriet? The boards of Britain's major companies should better reflect the diversity of British citizens in terms of weight and height? Another brilliant idea! How do you keep thinking of them?'

CHAPTER 19

THE EQUALITY ACT 2010: THE TRIUMPH OF HARRIET HARMAN

The worst government is often the most moral. One composed of cynics is often very tolerant and humane. But when fanatics are on top there is no limit to oppression.
HL Mencken 1880–1956 American journalist, essayist, magazine editor, satirist, critic of American life and culture: *Minority Report* (1956)

The speedy introduction of Labour's Equality Bill 2010 – the insidious public sector 'Equality Duty' – the vision that lies at the heart of the current coalition government – coalition politicians' dereliction of duty – transparency, accountability, blah, blah, blah – (legal) positive action v (illegal) positive discrimination: can *you* spot the difference? – two very different objectives: equality of outcome v equality of opportunity

Only a month before a 13-year-long Labour administration came to an end after the May 2010 general election, a piece of legislation received Royal Assent: The Equality Bill 2010. This was surely the crowning glory of Harriet Harman's career, although by the time it was brought into effect by a Commencement Order three months later, she was sitting on the opposition benches.

Much of Ms Harman's evident cheerfulness in opposition is due, I suspect, to the degree with which the left-wing philosophy behind the Act was accepted by the coalition government: not least by the new Prime Minister as we shall see in the next chapter. The Commencement Order which enabled 90 per cent of the Act to be brought into force on 1 October 2010 was made on 5 July 2010, just eight weeks after the formation of the coalition: unseemly haste, you might well think.

The gender-related aspects of the Act, guidance related to them, and associated consultation exercises, all bear militant feminist hallmarks. It is taken as a fact that the gender pay gap results from discrimination against women, and that differences in outcomes directly and proportionately reflect differences in opportunities. A consultation exercise concerning the public sector 'Equality Duty' was started on 19 August 2010 and completed on 10 November 2010. From the Equalities Office website:

> An important part of the Act is the public sector Equality Duty, which has a key role in ensuring that fairness is at the heart of public bodies' work and that public services meet the needs of different groups. The Act also gives ministers the power to impose specific duties, which are legal requirements designed to help public bodies meet their obligations under the public sector Equality Duty.
>
> This consultation seeks your views on our proposals for draft regulations for the specific duties and the list of public bodies that will be subject to the general and specific duties.
>
> This consultation will be of interest to:
>
> - public bodies;
> - those monitoring the performance of public bodies;
> - others who perform public functions; and
> - organisations that are interested in how public services can eliminate discrimination, advance equality and foster good relations.
>
> Comments from other interested parties are also welcome.

Much is made in the associated 72-page consultation document, 'Equality Act 2010: The public sector Equality Duty – Promoting equality through transparency', about the impact that transparency will have on accountability. Back to the consultation document:

The Equality Act 2010 replaced the existing anti-discrimination laws with a single Act. It included a new public sector Equality Duty, replacing the separate public sector equality duties relating to race, disability and sex, and also covering age, sexual orientation, religion or belief, pregnancy and maternity, and gender reassignment more fully. The Equality Duty consists of a general duty, set out in the Act itself, and specific duties imposed through regulations.

The general duty is set out in section 149 of the Act. In summary, those subject to the Equality Duty must have due regard to the need to:

- eliminate unlawful discrimination, harassment, victimisation;
- advance equality of opportunity between different groups;
- foster good relations between different groups.

Section 153 of the Act gives Ministers the power to impose specific duties through regulations. The specific duties are legal requirements designed to help public bodies meet the general duty. A consultation document published in June 2009[1] set out proposals for specific duties, and a policy statement published in January 2010[2] set out the previous Government's proposed approach. We have considered the results of that consultation and the earlier proposals and developed a new approach in line with the Coalition Government's guiding principles of freedom, fairness and responsibility. Our new approach also takes into account the Government's clear aim of replacing top-down interventions from the centre with local democratic accountability driven by transparency and decentralisation.

[1] *Equality Bill: Making it Work – Policy proposals for specific duties: A consultation*
www.equalities.gov.uk/pdf/Specific%20Duties%20Consultation%20Docum
entWEB.pdf

[2] *Equality Bill: Making it work – Policy proposals for specific duties: Policy Statement*
www.equalities.gov.uk/PDF/psdresp_GEO_MakingItWork_acc.pdf

The coalition government's approaches to the issue of increasing equality and fairness are largely those favoured by Ms Harman and her like over many years, but with less central government involvement. Later in the consultation document:

This Government's guiding principles are freedom, fairness and responsibility, and a shared desire to work in the national interest. There are too many barriers to social mobility and equal opportunities in Britain today. We need concerted action from government and public service providers to help tear down the barriers and create a fairer society...

Public sector bodies have huge potential to create a fairer society through the way they deliver their services, the people they recruit, and the jobs and training they offer to their staff. They also have effective levers to encourage business, civil society organisations and other bodies to use their creativity and resources to bring about a lasting change of culture through the way in which they commission and procure services...

The Government is committed to re-distributing power away from Westminster and Whitehall back to local communities. We are intent on liberating public bodies from top-down targets. We need to have faith in those engaged in front-line service delivery to work with local people to identify local priorities and to design services to meet the needs of the people they serve. Central government must give them the freedom to manage their operations in the way that delivers the best outcomes for the public.

These changes put public sector professionals, working together with citizens, in the driving seat, but greater freedom must be accompanied with greater accountability. Not accountability to Whitehall departments or bureaucratic quangos, but to the people who fund and use their services. We do not intend to prescribe how public bodies go about their business, but we will ensure that we put in place the right framework which empowers citizens to scrutinise the data and evidence on which their public services perform. We will do this by bringing data into the daylight – letting people see for themselves the information public bodies are using to make decisions and the data on their performance. Citizens will then be able to judge, challenge, applaud [Author's note: applaud? You couldn't make it up, could you?] and hold to account the public bodies they ultimately pay for. This is the vision that lies at the heart of this Government and guides our approach to the public sector Equality Duty.

If this is a vision, I'm a Pot Noodle. How on earth can citizens hold public bodies to account, if not through their elected representatives? This is an astonishing dereliction of duty on the part of our politicians. The resulting accountability vacuum will be filled, and filled quickly, by special interest groups such as The Fawcett Society. The consultation document goes on to cover, 'Our proposals for specific duties':

> Public bodies will be judged by citizens on the basis of clear information about the equality results they achieve, rather than on whether they have completed a tick-box list of processes... [Author's note: this is highly disingenuous. The 'tick-box list of processes' refers to the need to provide evidence that opportunities have been made equally available to different groups, e.g. men and women. By abandoning this principle, and demanding instead equality of *outcome*, we end up in an incredible position. Taking a theoretical scenario where a number of senior positions are on offer, and applications from men outnumber those from women in the ratio of 10:1, women should – under the equality of outcome principle – still land at least half the jobs; and in practise more than half, as part of the drive to 'improve' the organisation's overall gender balance. Is it just me, or is this utter madness?]
>
> We will require public bodies to publish a range of equality data relating both to their workforces and to the services they provide. Different bodies will necessarily publish different data sets relating to their particular business, but there are some common principles that will guide them in how they publish their data. Publication of data must be done in a way that is open and freely available to third parties, such as community groups and equality campaigners, who can re-use this data to hold public bodies to account. This means that equality data must be pro-actively released in a way that is consistent with the Public Data Principles set out by the Public Sector Transparency Board established by the Prime Minister. These Principles include:
>
> - timeliness;

- fine granularity; [Author's note: I assume this means, 'sufficiently detailed to give feminists *something* to whine about.']
- openness;
- aggregated and anonymised data;
- standardised formats; and
- publication under a standard open licence which allows free re-use (including commercial re-use) of the data for any lawful purpose without further permission...

Where organisations are making slow progress on eliminating discrimination, advancing equality and fostering good relations, arming citizens and civil society groups [Author's note: hmm... it's a long shot, but might the groups include The Fawcett Society, by any chance?] with information which will allow them to apply public pressure to drive a faster pace of change...

We will require public bodies with 150 or more employees to publish data on equality in their workforces... we would expect this to include data on *important inequalities such as the gender pay gap* [Author's italics], the proportion of staff from ethnic minority communities and the distribution of disabled employees throughout an organisation's structure. Public bodies will be required to publish this data at least annually...

As well as ensuring public bodies are transparent about their equality data, we also want them to be transparent about the equality outcomes they are going to work towards. We will require public bodies, as part of their normal business planning process, to set equality outcome objectives, informed by the evidence and data they publish. These objectives should be specific, relevant and above all measurable. This will enable meaningful scrutiny by citizens and other interested groups who will be able to tell, from the equality data, whether a public body is achieving what it set out to achieve. This approach is in line with the government's emphasis on democratic, rather than bureaucratic, accountability.

Elsewhere on the Equalities Office's website – the 'FAQ' section – we are encouraged to believe there will be a distinction between a new weasel term, 'positive action', and 'positive discrimination':

POSITIVE ACTION

When will the positive action provisions of the Equality Act 2010 come into force?

The general positive action provisions (section 158), together with those relating specifically to the selection of candidates by political parties (sections 104 & 105), will come into force on 1 October 2010. Ministers are currently considering the provisions that relate to positive action in recruitment and promotion (section 159).

What exactly is positive action?

The term 'positive action' covers a range of measures [Author's note: er, such as what, exactly?] which organisations can use where those with a 'protected characteristic' (age, disability, gender reassignment, marriage and civil partnership, pregnancy and maternity, race, religion or belief, sex, sexual orientation):

- experience some sort of disadvantage because of that characteristic;
- have particular needs linked to that characteristic; or
- are disproportionately under-represented in a particular activity.

Where any of these conditions apply, positive action can be taken to overcome that disadvantage, meet that need or encourage participation in that activity. Positive action can be taken in relation to a wide group of activities, such as *employment* [Author's italics], education, training and service delivery. Positive action measures can be used to counteract the effects of past discrimination so that people in such groups have equal opportunities to achieve their potential.

Will the Equality Act 2010 allow the use of positive discrimination?

No. Positive discrimination means favouring a particular under-represented or otherwise disadvantaged group solely because they have a particular protected characteristic. Positive discrimination is generally unlawful in the UK and there are currently no plans to change that position.

Does the use of positive action measures mean the introduction of quotas?

No. The Equality Act 2010 does not permit the use of quotas, which would represent a form of positive discrimination and, as such, would be inconsistent with EU law and would go against the merit principle [Author's note: the word 'merit' doesn't appear in the 72-page consultation document we've considered in this chapter.]

What measures are in place to ensure that organisations do not misuse the positive action provisions?

The provisions make clear that any positive action measures taken have to be a *proportionate means* [Author's note: what on earth is the meaning of the term 'proportionate means' in this context?] of:

- achieving the aim of overcoming a disadvantage suffered by persons who share a particular protected characteristic;
- addressing disproportionate under-representation in an activity by persons who share a particular protected characteristic; or
- meeting the specific needs of people with a particular protected characteristic.

Is it a requirement for organisations to use the positive actions provisions?

No. All forms of positive action are entirely voluntary, whether those measures relate to employment, the provision of services or the work of political parties. There is no compulsory requirement for any organisation to use any of the positive action provisions.

Now let me take this slowly for the sake of my sanity:

Positive action (legal)
'Positive action can be taken in relation to a wide range of activities, such as employment…'

Positive discrimination (illegal)
'Positive discrimination means favouring a particular under-represented or otherwise disadvantaged group solely because they have a particular protected characteristic.'

So, what's the difference between positive action and positive discrimination? It's perfectly obvious: there is none. Public sector bodies will have *no choice* but to adopt widespread positive action – positive discrimination – to achieve their equality targets, or they will face criticism from The Equality and Human Rights Commission, The Fawcett Society, and other organisations. In the absence of anyone stopping public sector organisations from adopting positive discrimination, and politicians having declared themselves unaccountable in the matter, the militant feminists will have a field day. We shouldn't hold our breath waiting for the Prime Minister to intervene, for reasons which will become obvious in the next chapter.

The government's policies are hopelessly confused because they pursue two different and often competing objectives: equality of outcome (traditionally a left-of-centre objective) and equality of opportunity (for many years a common objective across the political spectrum). Its instincts are to favour the former over the latter whenever they conflict. Public bodies have been required to comply with the General Duty of the Equality Act from 1 April 2011. From the consultation document:

> The Equality and Human Rights Commission will produce practical guidance 12 weeks before the entry into force of the regulations to explain the requirements of the general and specific duties in more detail and set out what different types and sizes of public bodies need to do to comply. In addition, central government is committed to working to help public bodies understand what they must do in order to implement the Equality Duty. It is essential that there are measures in

place to give public bodies confidence in complying with the Duty, and to ensure that it is effective in helping public bodies to deliver equality *outcomes* [Author's italics].

The Equality Act 2010 was a remarkable triumph for Harriet Harman and militant feminism, and brought to you by the Prime Minister and leader of the Conservative party, David Cameron.

CHAPTER 20

DAVID CAMERON:
HEIR TO HARMAN?

Emotion is a rotten base for politics.
Dick Francis 1920-2010 British horse racing crime writer and retired jockey

The speedy introduction of the Equality Act 2010 – David Cameron and Harriet Harman – does Cameron have a female-pattern brain, and is he a militant feminist? – the scandalous protection of the NHS budget: a triumph of emotion over reason – all-women prospective parliamentary candidate shortlists – only discrimination against men is acceptable – Cameron tries to hook anglers' votes – Cameron appoints a Labour peer to report into the 'lack' of women in Britain's boardrooms – Business Secretary Vince Cable attacks capitalism, with the support of the Prime Minister

What an irony it is that 90 per cent of the Equality Act 2010 – the brainchild of Harriet Harman – came into force as a result of a Commencement Order made by a *Conservative*-led coalition shortly after it assumed power. What better evidence could we have to suggest that David Cameron is not the 'heir to Blair' – as he once termed himself – but in truth the 'heir to Harman'?

I was struck on a number of occasions by scenes on television of David Cameron and Harriet Harman – acting leader of the Labour Party after the party's defeat in the 2010 general election – conversing in the Houses of Parliament. They always seemed very comfortable in each other's company. One day a question occurred to me. Well, two questions, to be precise. Does Cameron have a female-pattern brain, and is he a militant feminist too? The answers to both questions are clearly in the affirmative. Let's look at the evidence.

Cameron invariably argues for what he wants in emotional terms, not rational ones: a sure sign of a female-pattern brain. An illustration of this. It's long been painfully clear to the British public that the National Health Service is in *dire* need of vigorous reform: its inefficiency is legendary. But Cameron has ring-fenced the NHS budget (around £104 billion p.a.) at a time of a national financial emergency. Did Cameron argue for the protection of this budget in rational terms, as we might have hoped? No. He argued for it because of the support it had provided for his late son Ivan, who suffered from cerebral palsy and a severe form of epilepsy, and died at the age of six. Of course this was a tragedy for the family, but should it be used to justify the protection of the NHS's budget? And are we to infer that if the Camerons *hadn't* had a child who required a high level of support from the NHS, Cameron would have been open to reducing the NHS's budget? What sort of a way is this to determine policy?

Cameron's only work experience, before entering politics, was in 'Corporate Affairs', a variety of public relations, with its focus on relationships. The Chartered Institute of Public Relations informs me that 65% of its members are female, 35% male. Cameron's interest in relationships suggests a female pattern brain, as does his relentless focus on image. He's even more image-conscious than former Prime Minister Tony Blair, and his instincts are invariably feminist. In opposition Cameron decided to use legislation *introduced by Harriet Harman* to force women-only prospective parliamentary candidate shortlists onto constituency parties. From an article in *The Independent* of 21 October 2009:

David Cameron provoked a furious row with Tory backbenchers and grassroots members yesterday after reversing his party's opposition to all-women shortlists in a bid to boost the number of female Conservative MPs.

Only Labour has opted for all-women shortlists at previous elections, with past Conservative leaders opposing them as undemocratic. Mr Cameron's U-turn will see all-women shortlists imposed on some constituencies selecting their candidates in the New Year. Aides to Mr Cameron have said he has done all he can to promote women MPs on to the front bench but privately admits that he is hampered by the fact that the party only has 19 sitting female MPs. That number would rise to 60 should the party win a majority at the next election, still only one fifth of its seats.

To the frustration of Conservative Central Office (CCO), local party associations have resisted rules forcing them to give half of the places on their shortlists to women. The system has failed to deliver more female Tory candidates, with men appearing in the last six major selection contests.

Announcing the change in policy at the Speaker's Committee, Mr Cameron said: 'It's my intention, if we continue as we are, that some of those shortlists will be all-women shortlists to help us boost the number of Conservative women MPs,' he said. 'There are many very, very good women on our priority list of candidates who haven't yet been selected and I want to give them the chance to serve in parliament.'

The announcement immediately saw a backlash from Tory backbenchers and grassroots members of the party. Ann Widdecombe, a staunch critic of all-women shortlists, said that it would make some female MPs feel like second-class citizens. 'Women, no matter what their circumstances, must get to Westminster on their own merits and be able to know that when they're sitting in the House of Commons,' she said.

John Strafford, chairman of the Campaign for Conservative Democracy, said that party members were 'spitting blood' about the decision. 'Many constituencies are just beginning to understand what controls central office is imposing on them,' he said.

Tim Montgomerie and Jonathan Isaby, editors of the influential Tory members' website ConservativeHome, also issued a statement opposing the move. 'We feared this would happen,' they stated. 'All women shortlists are fundamentally unConservative and they have no place in a party pledged to meritocracy and localism.'

The use of women-only shortlists had nothing to do with women's merits, and by extension nothing to do with the collective merit of the party's future MPs, nor the quality of future administrations: it had everything to do with the image of the party, and by extension, Cameron himself. It was, in short, a resounding triumph of spin over substance. I resigned my membership of the party upon learning of the proposed adoption of women-only shortlists.

The magazine of *The Daily Telegraph* on 1 May 2010, five days before the general election, included an article by the journalist Mick Brown. A few days previously Brown had accompanied Cameron for a day on the campaign trail in the West Country. The first visit was to a garage in Exeter, owned and run by a woman. Cameron remarked to Brown about his personal staff:

'As you can see, we are an all-woman team. I don't employ a man if I can possibly help it.'

An interesting use of the word 'we' there. Unwittingly, Cameron was confirming that he too has a female-pattern brain. Can you imagine a party leader uttering the following about his or her personal staff?

'As you can see, we are an all-man team. I don't employ a woman if I can possibly help it.'

Of course not: only discrimination against men is acceptable. Men simply don't constitute a group worthy of consideration, although sub-groups of men may; during the hours he spent with Cameron, Mick Brown noticed Cameron scanning a printout of an interview he had recently done with the *Angling Times*. He asked Cameron what the political angle was, to which Cameron replied:

'Well, four million people go fishing, so that's a good start...'

Impressive statesmanship there, I think you'll agree.

Cameron appears to have swallowed the militant feminist agenda hook, line, and sinker. Many people, including myself, voted Conservative in the 2010 general election to ensure the end of the dire influence of Harriet Harman and her kind. But Cameron is happy to promote the militant feminist agenda. From an article titled, 'Inquiry into lack of women in boardroom' in *The Daily Telegraph* of August 3, 2010:

> A Labour peer and respected former banker is to lead a new enquiry into why so few women make it to the top in business. Lord Davies of Abersoch will produce a report into the lack of female representation in Britain's boardrooms that will guide the Coalition's plans for greater equality in the City.
>
> The former chairman of Standard Chartered was one of the few bankers to emerge from the financial crisis with his reputation intact and was made a trade minister by Gordon Brown. David Cameron was similarly impressed and invited Lord Davies, who has been vocal about the lack of women at the top of business, to carry out a study.
>
> The peer believes that Britain would have 750,000 more small firms if women were fully engaged with the business world. 'We need more female entrepreneurs,' he said. 'A quarter of the large FTSE companies don't have women on their boards. [Author's note: how *have* they survived with such a crippling disadvantage?] We should change that. It is all about providing role models.'
>
> Mr Cameron said during the election campaign that he wanted to change the way business worked so that women were more fairly represented. He even indicated that a Tory government would force FTSE companies to have women

making up 50 per cent of their 'long list' when directors were appointed. Lord Davies began some of his work while a minister.

Cameron's appointment of Lord Davies was an astonishing move for a Conservative politician. I wrote to Lord Davies seeking a meeting (appendix 7) but didn't receive a reply.

Cameron was elected leader of the Conservative party in 2005, and throughout the years between then and the 2010 general election he said and did little to suggest his sympathies were anything other than left-wing, to the dismay of many supporters of a traditionally right-of-centre party including myself. Prior to the recession that followed the global banking crisis triggered by Lehman Brothers filing for bankruptcy protection in September 2008 I cannot recall Cameron – nor his friend George Osborne, the Shadow Chancellor of the Exchequer – showing any understanding that the size and influence of the British state should be reduced, something which has long been blindingly obvious to Conservative party supporters. It is clear that the cuts in public spending announced on 20 October 2010 are only to be undertaken because there is no alternative.

On 22 September 2010 the Business Secretary, Vince Cable – a Liberal Democrat – gave a speech at his party's annual conference. Given how left-wing most of the delegates were, it was hardly surprising that he criticised City financiers at some length. But he went much further and attacked capitalism itself. From *The Daily Telegraph* of the following day:

> Mr Cable used his speech to attack capitalism, the free market and bankers. He described City financiers as 'spivs and gamblers' and said they posed more of a threat to Britain than

Bob Crow, the militant trade unionist who had led recent transport strikes...

Mr Cable described the corporate world as 'murky' and said that markets were 'often rigged'. He refused to tone down the comments after previews of the speech caused outrage...

He added, 'The Government's agenda is not one of *laissez-faire*. Markets are often irrational or rigged. So I am shining a harsh light into the murky world of corporate behaviour... Capitalism takes no prisoners and kills competition where it can, as Adam Smith explained over 200 ears ago...

Eamonn Butler, director of the Adam Smith Institute, challenged Mr Cable's interpretation of the Scottish economist's thinking. 'Business Secretary Vince Cable is wrong on capitalism and wrong on Adam Smith', Dr Butler said. 'Unfortunately, we have a Business Secretary who doesn't understand business and who misinterprets the founder of modern economics too. It is not capitalism that kills competition. It is regulation, and regulated capitalism. Adam Smith was perfectly clear. Business people would love to rig the market in their favour. But it is only the power of governments that enables them to do this. Where free competition reigns, businesses cannot keep out competitors.'...

David Buik, of the brokers BGC Partners, said, 'We were hoping that Dr Cable was just pandering to the dissenting coalition voices, but I fear that was not the case. This was a speech by an Opposition spokesman – a typical rant from a left-wing, anti-establishment aficionado, who is wholly against the concept of the free enterprise system, thus dismissing the advantages of the capitalist system. I have to say I am shocked at such an irresponsible speech.'

Downing Street sources said that they were 'perfectly relaxed' about the speech, which they had seen in advance.

Could it be any clearer? The Prime Minister is not only a militant feminist, he's appointed an anti-capitalism Business Secretary too, and supports his utterances. I'll leave the last words in this chapter to Simon Heffer, a columnist with *The Daily Telegraph*. From the 25 September 2010 edition, an article titled, 'Vince is the anti-business secretary':

The great political event of this week was the transition of Vince Cable from a figure of fun to one of absurdity. His attack on capitalism showed that he doesn't understand it. He doesn't understand markets. He doesn't understand banking. He doesn't understand the City. He doesn't really understand economics. Apart from that, he's an absolute genius.

Events at the Lib Dems' conference prompted reactions from their Conservative Coalition partners that ranged from mild shock via distaste to absolute rage. Dr Vince's contribution is in the last category. Not only does he give a worrying display of stupidity as the man charged with presiding over the revival of British business; he also gave the impression that his mad little party is dictating Coalition financial policy, and inflicting on Britain measures that do anything but promote growth and prosperity, but much to parade Dr Vince's socialist conscience.

Many phrases in his speech cry out to be branded the most idiotic. It is fearsomely hard to select the one that actually was, but Dr Vince's assertion that capitalism kills competition is so obtuse that it suggests he must need a step-by-step guide to tying his shoelaces. Capitalism creates competition. It is the alternative system of Soviet-style regulation and restrictions on enterprise that kills it. Dr Vince is clearly wedded to this ideology…

Pure capitalism of the sort Dr Vince detests is also a protection against what he calls 'rigging' markets. What markets does he suggest have been rigged, and how? Under capitalism in its proper sense, rigging of markets is impossible, because rigging is only done by monopoly (which we have perfectly good laws against) and by other forms of anti-capitalist regulation that keep providers of goods and services out of the marketplace. If Dr Vince thinks that this is what happened with banking, whose problems started with a Leftist government bloating the money supply, he is deranged...

I know Dave wants to close down the Conservative party, and he seems to have found, in Dr Vince, the perfect man to help him do it. If the Tory Party is going to let the Lib Dem grumbling appendix control the Government's digestive system, why should it expect anyone who believes in enterprise and prosperity to vote for it next time round?

CHAPTER 21

WHY AREN'T MEN REVOLTING?

In all legends men have thought of women as sublime separately but
horrible in a herd.
G K Chesterton 1874-1936 English writer: 'What's Wrong With the World' (1910)

Women are unfairly taking work from men – feminists are exploiting
men's deference towards women – the real pensions scandal –
discrimination against men is enshrined in the Equality Act 2010 –
Esther Vilar's *The Manipulated Man* – 'The Slave's Happiness' – single
mothers – men are fearful of re-evaluating their position

Men are increasingly finding themselves out of work when
women less experienced and competent than themselves are
landing jobs, often with the able assistance of women in
Human Resources. I've had experience of this myself, bidding
for assignments which have ultimately been awarded to women
with less experience and expertise. If women think men will
put up with being treated like this indefinitely, they're mistaken.
There will be a backlash; what form it will take, it's difficult to
say. Perhaps the backlash will come from other women,
because there's an irony here. Many of the men being deprived
of work are supporting women and children, and the work is
often being carried out by women without such responsibilities.

Despite militant feminists' relentless talk about women's
abuse at the hands of men, including rape, the overwhelming
majority of men are deferential towards women. How much
this has a genetic basis is difficult to say; but certainly most
men are effectively socialised by their mothers, sisters and
others to treat women with deference. And it is this deference
which militant feminists are exploiting in their campaigns.

Men have long been wedded to the idea of bending to women's will in the home, but the habit is proving ruinous for men in the world of work, because there is no limit to what women want. It's a common delusion men have, that if they give women what they ask for, women will be happy. The truth is the opposite. Women's appetites – like men's, to be fair – always increase once satisfied.

Despite their markedly greater longevity, women in the United Kingdom have for many years retired five years earlier than men, at 60. Special treatment for women rather than equality, yet again. The proposed introduction of pension age harmonisation at 66 years of age, in 2020, came as a rare and welcome example of women losing their special treatment. Even if real fairness would have been to allow men to retire years earlier than women, to compensate them for their shorter lifespans. But it was a step, and with nobody campaigning on men's behalf, it was as much as men might expect.

At the heart of the British pensions system is the National Insurance system, through which employed people have long paid a small amount of tax regularly and thereby – over the course of their working lives – build up a full pension entitlement. Because many women do not engage in paid employment, or work part-time in preference to working full-time, they are not entitled to the full pension. For many years women's groups have campaigned against this 'pensions scandal', claiming that women are discriminated against for taking time out of the workplace to help raise children. This completely ignores the reality that many of these women weren't staying at home to raise children, or if they were, they were doing so for only a few years. We saw in an earlier chapter that over 2006/08, 59 per cent of men, and just 39 per cent of women, worked full-time. The figures for part-time work were 6 per cent and 26 per cent respectively. And women are far more likely than men to work part-time throughout their working lives.

A system in which women's pensions were supplemented, to reflect the time they were not in paid employment due to raising children, might have some merit. But can it be right that if a person decides not to undertake paid employment for his or her entire adult life, his or her pension entitlement would be the same as that of someone who had worked constantly for up to half a century? Surely not. That would be special treatment gone mad, wouldn't it? But, because the people in question are mainly women, that's precisely what's going to happen.

The reality of the pension system is that pensions are paid not through taxes paid in the past, but through current tax income. On average men pay markedly higher taxes than women, so the pensions bill – along with all other bills paid for by taxation – falls mainly on men to settle. And so it is that men will be the main payers of a proposed overhaul of the pensions system announced by the government on 24 October 2010. From the following day's *Daily Telegraph*, an article titled 'State pension to be fixed at £140':

> A fixed state pension of £140 is to be proposed by ministers, as part of the biggest shake-up of the system for 50 years. Under the plans, anyone entitled to a state pension would be paid the same amount, providing a boost to women and married couples who lose out under the current system...
>
> The plans are likely to be welcomed by women, many of whom do not qualify for the basic pension because they have not made enough National Insurance contributions after taking time off work to raise a family. It is thought that the new system could be in place before the next general election in 2015, before the pension age for women rises to 66...

> Dr Ros Altmann, a former pensions adviser to the Treasury, said the proposal would be a 'fantastic reform'.

Dr Altmann *would* say that, wouldn't she? Special treatment for women, largely financed by men. Fantastic, indeed. She was quoted again in the following day's edition of the newspaper:

> Ros Altmann, director-general of Saga Group, said, 'This is a quid pro quo for suddenly raising the women's state pension age to 66 in 2020, which will save money but hit women hard. This will give them back something in return.'

Why, one might ask, was there a need to 'give them back something in return'? This isn't about fairness or equality, it's modern politics at its most cynical. The proposed overhaul ticks two of David Cameron's favourite boxes: it gives special treatment to women, and will therefore be a vote winner for him; and it will be mainly financed by men. Why aren't men revolting against this iniquitous proposal? Maybe because they're so used to being manipulated by women, and by those who campaign on their behalf, that they no longer notice it.

Discrimination against men is at the core of The Equality Act 2010. Public sector organisations will have no choice, in the course of 'correcting' the gender balances at senior levels through 'positive action', but to discriminate against men. The outcome will be inevitable: there will be a presumption that senior jobs must go to women unless there are none willing to take on the roles in question. Because competence is less important in the public sector than in the private sector, public sector organisations will become even less effective and efficient over time. What a dismal prospect, and what a price to pay for gender equality. Doubtless militant feminists will think it a price worth paying.

The manipulation of men by women is not a development of the modern era, but it has at least been described by writers in the modern era. We have arrived at the fortieth anniversary of the publication of a book written by Esther Vilar, a German-Argentinian writer who originally trained as a doctor. She is best known for her 1971 book *The Manipulated Man* and its various follow-ups which argue that contrary to common feminist and women's rights rhetoric, women in industrialised cultures are not oppressed, but rather exploit a well-established system of manipulating men. A revised edition appeared in 2008. From its back cover:

> Esther Vilar's classic polemic about the relationship between the sexes caused a sensation on its first publication. In her introduction to this revised edition, Vilar maintains that very little has changed. A man is a human being who works, while a woman chooses to let a man provide for her and her children in return for carefully dispensed praise and sex.
>
> Vilar's perceptive, thought-provoking and often very funny look at the battle between the sexes has earned her severe criticism and even death threats. But Vilar's intention is not misogynistic: she maintains that only if women and men look at their place in society with honesty, will there be any hope for change.

In a new introduction for the 2008 edition, Vilar states that, 'if anything, the female position of power has only consolidated... now, as before, it does not occur to the underprivileged (men) to fight against this grotesque state of affairs.' The book starts with a short chapter, 'The Slave's Happiness':

> The lemon-coloured MG skids across the road and the woman driver brings it to a somewhat uncertain halt. She gets out and finds her left front tyre flat. Without wasting a moment she prepares to fix it: she looks towards the passing cars as if expecting someone. Recognizing this standard

international sign of woman in distress ('weak female let down by male technology'), a station wagon draws up. The driver sees what is wrong at a glance and says comfortingly, 'Don't worry. We'll fix that in a jiffy.' To prove his determination, he asks for her jack. He does not ask if she is capable of changing the tire herself because he knows – she is about thirty, smartly dressed and made-up – that she is not.

Since she cannot find a jack, he fetches his own, together with his other tools. Five minutes later the job is done and the punctured tire properly stowed. His hands are covered with grease. She offers him an embroidered handkerchief, which he politely refuses. He has a rag for such occasions in his tool box. The woman thanks him profusely, apologizing for her 'typically feminine' helplessness. She might have been there till dusk, she says, had he not stopped. He makes no reply and, as she gets back into the car, gallantly shuts the door for her. Through the wound-up window he advises her to have her tire patched at once and she promises to get her garage man to see to it that very evening. Then she drives off.

As the man collects his tools and goes back to his own car, he wishes he could wash his hands. His shoes – he has been standing in the mud while changing the tire – are not as clean as they should be (he is a salesman). What is more, he will have to hurry to keep his next appointment. As he starts the engine he thinks, 'Women! One's more stupid than the next.' He wonders what she would have done if he had not been there to help. He puts his foot on the accelerator and drives off – faster than usual. There is the delay to make up. After a while he starts to hum to himself. In a way, he is happy.

Almost any man would have behaved in the same manner – and so would most women. Without thinking, simply because men are men and women so different from them, a woman will make use of a man whenever there is an opportunity. What else could the woman have done when her car broke down? She has been taught to get a man to help. Thanks to his knowledge he was able to change her tire quickly – and at no cost to herself. True, he ruined his clothes, put his business in jeopardy, and endangered his own life by driving too fast afterwards. Had he found something else wrong with the car, he would have repaired that, too. That is what his knowledge of cars is for. Why should a woman learn to change a flat when the opposite sex (half the world's population) is able and willing to do it for her?

Women let men work, think for them and take on their responsibilities – in fact, they exploit them. Yet, since men are strong, intelligent and imaginative, while women are weak, unimaginative, and stupid, why isn't it men who exploit women? Could it be that strength, intelligence, and imagination are not prerequisites for power but merely qualifications for slavery? Could it be that the world is not being ruled by experts but by beings who are not fit for anything else – by women? And if this is so, how do women manage it so that their victims do not feel themselves cheated and humiliated, but rather believe themselves to be what they are least of all – masters of the universe? How do women manage to instil in men this sense of pride and superiority that inspires them to ever greater achievements?

Why are women never unmasked?

Why indeed? And why are men not revolting against militant feminists, who are intent on harming their interests? After all, positive discrimination for women is simply discrimination against men. If men think about gender politics at all – and very few of them do – they largely buy the myth that women before the modern era were oppressed by men. Maybe they see being oppressed by women as a just punishment for a mythical historical 'wrong'.

Perhaps the most pernicious example of militant feminists harming the interests of men lies in the area of social policy. Harriet Harman and her like are at best indifferent to the traditional family where a man works and supports a wife and children. And what better way to encourage a major departure from the traditional family than to adopt 'child-centric' policies as an excuse to encourage and finance single motherhood? From an article in *The Daily Telegraph* edition of 25 February 2010:

Single mothers are making a 'lifestyle choice' to live alone on state benefits, a report suggested yesterday. Growing numbers are relying on benefits that encourage them 'not to bother' with stable relationships, the Centre for Policy Studies found.

Geoff Dench, who conducted the research, said the circumstances of single mothers had changed as the proportion of lone mothers had grown over the past 20 years. In 1986, just 15 per cent of single mothers with children under 13 had never married or cohabited, but by 2006 that proportion had grown to 57 per cent.

Mr Dench said: 'It seems that lone motherhood is less a result of relationship breakdown, more a lifestyle choice. And the existence of state benefits as a source of economic security seems to be encouraging young mothers not to bother with male resident partners.'

Steve Moxon wrote a chapter titled, 'Excluding the Family: the state as the real absent father' in *The Woman Racket*. In the chapter he comments on the phenomenon of single mothers, including the following:

The one thing the world does not lack is people. Women need no encouragement to have children, and the less encouragement they're given then the more likely are the children they have to be wanted, loved, and well-adjusted as adults – so that they are not actually deleterious to society...

The children of single parents – as research overwhelmingly demonstrates – are much more likely to be social problems and cost the taxpayer further expense; not least when they perpetuate the cycle and become single mothers or feckless fathers who in turn themselves become strangers to their own children.

Why continue to pay women to create social breakdown? It makes less sense than it would to pay men to visit prostitutes to further their corresponding natural inclinations. Nobody in their right mind would suggest such a thing, of course; but the social implications would be incomparably more benign than subsidising women to have children.

Having children is the most obvious personal asset anyone could have; and those who are childless, and especially those who are single and who may be unable to form a partnership, are the truly disadvantaged in any society. The principal attraction that women feel for men is status, and this most easily translates into earnings. Men who earn so little that they are unattractive to most or to nearly all women, form the most disadvantaged subgroup in our own, as in any, society. Yet as a proportion of their income, they more than anyone are forced to pay for single parenthood. They are literally bankrolling a lifestyle for the very women who would not have them in the first place.

Why aren't men revolting against the influence of militant feminists, leaving aside the obvious possibility of sheer apathy? There are no campaigning organisations for them to join with influence equivalent to, for example, The Fawcett Society. One possible explanation is provided by Esther Vilar who, in her new introduction to the second edition of her book, makes the point that in the original edition of the book she underestimated men's fear of re-evaluating their own position:

> Yet the more sovereignty they are losing in their professional lives – the more automatic their work, the more controlled by computers they become, the more that increasing unemployment forces them to adopt obsequious behavior towards customers and superiors – then the more they have to be afraid of a recognition of their predicament. And the more essential it becomes to maintain their illusion that it is not they who are the slaves, but those on whose behalf they subject themselves to such an existence.
>
> As absurd as it may sound: today's men need feminists more than their wives do. Feminists are the last ones who still describe men the way they like to see themselves: as egocentric, power-obsessed, ruthless, and without inhibitions when it comes to satisfying their animalistic instincts. Therefore the most aggressive Women's Libbers find themselves in the strange predicament of doing more to maintain the status quo than anyone else. Without their arrogant accusations the macho man would no longer exist, except perhaps in the movies. If the press didn't stylize men as rapacious wolves, the actual sacrificial lambs of this 'men's

society', men themselves, would no longer flock to the factories so obediently.

CHAPTER 22

ARE WOMEN REVOLTING?

It is not fair to ask of others what you are unwilling to do yourself.
Eleanor Roosevelt 1884-1962 First Lady of the United States 1933-45

Women want less work and more life – women are revolting against militant feminism not by what they say, but through the choices they make

Given women's sense of group solidarity and fear of criticism we cannot expect a significant number of them to object stridently to the machinations of militant feminists, regardless of how adversely their lives are being affected by them.

If and when they're presented with a choice, women seek a 'better' work/life balance, which for women invariably means less work and more life: the *opposite* of the choice militant feminists wish them to make. Women are revolting against militant feminists by not seeking paid employment, preferring to work part-time, or working full-time but with little ambition for promotion. Such is the scale on which women continue to do this, that gender balance in the boardroom cannot be delivered until and unless companies are legally forced to select female executive directors on grounds other than merit. This could only damage the performance of those companies, hamper their job creation capacity, and damage the prosperity of the country. Prices worth paying? Surely not, for either women or men.

We have to ask what support there is among women for gender balance in the boardroom, given that the vast majority of women (in common with the vast majority of men) will never have the ambition for such high office. I've yet to find a women who supports the idea. Women have a more developed sense of 'fair play' than men, and they recognise the iniquity of initiatives designed to give more top roles to women regardless of the proportions of men and women willing and able to perform such roles successfully. They frequently used the term 'demeaning to women' to describe the initiatives.

CHAPTER 23

CONCLUSIONS

You cannot claim both full equality and special dispensation.
William Raspberry 1935- African-American Pulitzer Prize-winning columnist: *Washington Post* 20 September 1989

Crunch time for militant feminism? – feminism is hostile to business – gender balance in the boardroom: an experiment which could have grave consequences – what women need to do to reach the boardroom – a final plea

This is an interesting time for gender politics, and quite possibly a 'crunch time' for militant feminism. In the words of Bertrand Russell, 'All movements go too far'. By alternatively playing the 'equality' and 'special treatment' cards, militant feminists have undermined the credibility of women in general. In seeking to advance women through positive discrimination they are telling the people who run businesses that women cannot be expected to perform as well as men, and telling women they needn't be of equal merit with men to go as far, or further, than them. How can women be taking any inspiration from this sorry state of affairs?

Women may not be openly hostile to their militant feminist sisters, but through the choices they make they are clearly rejecting their ideology. Women appear less inclined with each year that passes to take on the stresses and strains that inevitably accompany senior positions in business.

Feminism is a Marxist ideology and inherently hostile to business. Measures aimed at improving gender balance in the senior reaches of business can only damage business. There is no evidence that greater diversity (of gender or any other attribute) will improve companies' performances. It's a left-wing theory, yet to be tested; if it's ever tested it will fail, as left-wing theories invariably do.

The developed world in general, and its businesses in particular, are overwhelmingly the creations of men, and at the most senior levels businesses remain largely run by men. Those businesses continue to deliver the economic prosperity we've come to expect. To force women into positions of power which few of them want, in the cause of gender balance, would be an experiment in social engineering which could have grave consequences for our economic prospects.

But these are only comments about women and men *in general*. The opportunities for talented and hardworking individual women to progress all the way to the boardroom, should they so choose, have never been better. So, you might reasonably be asking at this stage, when will women start reaching the boardroom in greater numbers? The answer is simple. When women start *acting* like equals with men, instead of seeking special treatment. When women demand to be judged on their personal strengths rather than on their gender's alleged strengths. When women stop believing the feminist fantasies, lies, delusions and myths which are a comfort blanket for them, and start to focus their energies on competing more effectively for senior positions. *Then* more women will make progress into the boardroom. One woman at a time, not *en masse*.

Dear reader, I end with a plea. Let's stop the futile attempts to placate militant feminists through pursuing their agendas. They're a miniscule band of dismal women who should be ignored for all our sakes, and especially for women's sakes.

APPENDIX 1

QUOTATIONS

Democracy never lasts long. It soon wastes, exhausts and murders itself. There was never a democracy that did not commit suicide.
John Adams 1735-1826 second President of the United States, 1797-1801: letter to John Taylor 15 April 1814

My wife was an immature woman . . . I would be home in the bathroom, taking a bath, and she would walk in whenever she felt like it and sink my boats.
Woody Allen 1935- American screenwriter, film director, actor, comedian, writer, musician and playwright

The sadness of the women's movement is that they don't allow the necessity of love. See, I don't personally trust any revolution where love is not allowed.
in *California Living* 14 May 1975
Maya Angelou 1928- American novelist and poet

We can aspire to anything, but we don't get it just 'cause we want it. I would rather spend my life close to the birds than waste it wishing I had wings.
Eli Attie Writer and political operative House MD, *Dying Changes Everything* (2008)

Publishers are in business to make money, and if your books do well they don't care whether you are male, female, or an elephant.
Margaret Atwood 1939- Canadian novelist: Graeme Gibson *Eleven Canadian Novelists* (1973)

Whatever you do, keep clear of thin women. They're trouble.
Alan Ayckbourn 1939- English dramatist: *A Small Family Business* (1987)

Women – one half of the human race at least – care fifty times more for a marriage than a ministry.
Walter Bagehot 1826-77 English economist and essayist: *The English Constitution* (1867)

Love... the delightful interval between meeting a beautiful girl and discovering that she looks like a haddock.
John Barrymore 1882-1942 American actor

All that is beautiful and noble is the result of reason and calculation.
Charles Baudelaire 1821-67 French poet and critic: *The Painter of Modern Life* (1863)

People keep asking me if I'll marry again. It's as if after you've had one car crash you want another.
Stephanie Beacham 1947- British television, film and theatre actress

What makes equality such a difficult business is that we only want it with our superiors.
Henry Becque 1837-99 French dramatist and critic: *Quelles littéraires* (1890)

It is better to marry than to burn.
I Corinthians 7:9

[Author's note: it's not much of a choice though, is it?]

It is better to dwell in a corner of the housetop than with a brawling woman in a wide house.
Proverbs 21:9

A continual dropping in a very rainy day and a contentious woman are alike.
Proverbs 27:15

But God hath chosen the foolish things of the world to confound the wise; and God hath chosen the weak things of the world to confound the things which are mighty.
New Testament, St. Paul in *I Corinthians* 1:27
The Bible (Authorised Version)

Female, n. One of the opposing, or unfair, sex.
Ambrose Bierce 1842-1914 American journalist and satirist: *The Devil's Dictionary* (1911)

Women have no wilderness in them,
They are provident instead,
Content in the tight hot cell of their hearts
To eat dusty bread.
Louise Bogan 1897-1970 American poet: 'Women' (1923)

Politics are usually the executive expression of human immaturity.
Vera Brittain 1893-1970 English writer: *Rebel Passion* (1964)

All that is necessary for the triumph of evil women is that good women do nothing.
  on The Rt Hon Harriet Harman MP, a British feminist politician, and her like
  Mike Buchanan 1957- British writer

The so-called conservative, uncomfortably disdainful of controversy, seldom has the energy to fight his battles, while the radical, so often a member of the minority, exerts disproportionate influence because of his dedication to his cause.

Conservatism is the tacit acknowledgement that all that is finally important in human experience is behind us; that the crucial explorations have been undertaken, and that it is given to man to know what are the great truths that emerged from them.
  William F Buckley Jr 1925-2008 American conservative author and commentator: *God and Man at Yale* (1951)

It is a general popular error to imagine the loudest complainers for the public to be the most anxious for its welfare.
  Edmund Burke 1729-97 Anglo-Irish statesmen, author, political theorist and philosopher: *Observations on a late Publication on the Present State of the Nation* (1769)

Woman suffrage: I will vote for it when women have left off making a noise in the reading room of the British Museum, when they leave off wearing high head-dresses in the pit of a theatre, and when I have seen as many as twelve women in all catch hold of the strap or bar on getting into an omnibus.
  Samuel Butler 1835-1902 English novelist and writer: *Selections of the Note-Books from Samuel Butler* (1930)

| Question to Lord Carrington: | If Mrs Thatcher were run over by a bus . . . ? |
| Lord Carrington: | It wouldn't dare. |

  during the Falklands War
  Russell Lewis *Margaret Thatcher* (1984)
  Lord Carrington 1919- British Conservative politician, Foreign Secretary 1979-82

The ladies walking by the car were attractive on the whole – the area had a high 'totty count', we agreed – and our spirits started to lift. Paul quipped, 'Will you look at the melons on that! Must have cost her £3,000, and we get the benefit!'
  Mike Buchanan *Two Men in a Car* (2008), St. Tropez, France, August 2007

Why are we having such an enjoyable time? Easy. Not having wives or girlfriends telling us what to do!

Mike Buchanan *Two Men in a Car* (2008), remark to the author, France, August 2007

Just heard my Aunt has been diagnosed with dementia. Upsetting news, but on the bright side I suppose I should be grateful for the £50 I get for my birthday every week.

text message to the author and others, 21 December 2009

A man walks into a shop selling Xmas trees and selects a six-foot-tall one. The shop assistant asks, 'Are you going to put it up yourself?' at which the man looks shocked and replies, 'No, you sick pervert, I'm going to put it up in the living room!'

text message to the author and others, 23 December 2009

It's only adultery if you get caught!

Paul Carrington 1950- Martial arts expert, security man, thrice married (to Yugoslavian, Italian and Ugandan women), thrice divorced, single, eternal optimist, singer-songwriter, socialist, the author's chauffeur in his travelogue *Two Men in a Car (a businessman, a chauffeur, and their holidays in France)*, and one of eight guitarists – Thunderin' Paul Carrington – whose life stories are related in the author's *Guitar Gods in Beds. (Bedfordshire: a heavenly county)*

She is so clearly the best man among them.

of Margaret Thatcher
diary, 11 February 1975
Barbara Castle 1910-2002 British Labour politician

I don't believe in astrology; I'm a Sagittarian and we're sceptical.

Sir Arthur C Clarke 1917-2008 English science fiction writer

All men have an equal right to the free development of their faculties; they have an equal right to the impartial protection of the state; but it is not true, it is against all the laws of reason and equity, it is against the eternal nature of things, that the indolent man and the laborious man, the spendthrift and the economist, the imprudent and the wise, should obtain and enjoy an equal amount of goods.

Victor Cousin 1792-1867 French philosopher

You've got to get married, haven't you? You can't go through life being happy.

Colin Crompton 1931-1985 English stand-up comedian: *Laugh with the Comedians* (1971)

My wife and I were happy for 20 years. Then we met.

Rodney Dangerfield 1921-2004 American comedian and actor

The feminist movement seems to have beaten the manners out of men, but I didn't see them put up a lot of resistance.
Clarissa Theresa Philomena Aileen Mary Josephine Agnes Elsie Trilby Louise Esmerelda Dickson Wright 1947- English celebrity chef. Trained as a lawyer, she became the youngest woman ever to be called to the Bar: *Mail on Sunday*, 24 September 2000

Women's suffrage will, I believe, be the ruin of our Western civilisation. It will destroy the home, challenging the headship of men laid down by God. It may come in your time – I hope not in mine.
John Dillon 1851-1927 Irish nationalist politician c.1912, to a deputation led by Hanna Sheehy Skeffington: Diana Norman *Terrible Beauty* (1987)

What is a communist? One who hath yearnings
For equal division of unequal earnings.
Ebenezer Elliott 1781-1849 English poet: 'Epigram' (1850)

If you can react the same way to winning and losing, that is a big accomplishment. That quality is important because it stays with you the rest of your life.
Chris Evert 1954- attractive American tennis player of the female persuasion

It would be equally correct to say that sheep are born carnivorous, and everywhere they nibble grass.
 commenting on Rousseau's 'Man was born free, and everywhere he is in chains'
Émile Faguet 1847-1916 French writer and critic

No amount of artificial reinforcement can offset the natural inequalities of human individuals.
Henry P Fairchild 1815-99 American Marxist sociologist

I listen to feminists and all these radical gals – most of them are failures. They've blown it. Some of them have been married, but they married some Casper Milquetoast who asked permission to go to the bathroom. These women just need a man in the house. That's all they need. Most of the feminists need a man to tell them what time of day it is and to lead them home. And they blew it and they're mad at all men. Feminists hate men. They're sexist. They hate men – that's their problem.
Jerry Falwell 1933-2007 American Baptist cleric, televangelist and conservative commentator

The most perfect equality of rights can never exclude the ascendant of superior minds.
Adam Ferguson 1723-1818 Scottish philosopher and historian: *History of Civil Society* (1823)

If at first you don't succeed, try, try again. Then quit. No use being a damned fool about it.
W C Fields 1880-1946 American humorist (attributed)

Let's assume that each person has an equal opportunity, not to become equal, but to become different. To realise whatever unique potential of body, mind and spirit he or she possesses.
John Fischer 1930- Belgian pianist, composer and visual artist

I want an old-fashioned house
With an old-fashioned fence
And an old-fashioned millionaire.
Marve Fisher American songwriter: 'An Old-Fashioned Girl' (1954 song)

If I were alive in Ruben's time, I'd be celebrated as a model. Kate Moss would be used as a paint brush.
Dawn French 1957- British comedy actress: in *Sunday Times* 13 August 2006

The great question that has never been answered and which I have not yet been able to answer, despite my 30 years of research into the feminine soul, is 'What does a woman want?'
Sigmund Freud 1856-1939 Austrian neurologist who founded the psychoanalytic school of psychology

Few trends could so thoroughly undermine the very foundations of our free society as the acceptance by corporate officials of a social responsibility other than to make as much money for their stockholders as possible.
Milton Friedman 1912-2006 American economist and statistician: *Capitalism and Freedom* (1962)

I'll not listen to reason... Reason always means what someone else has got to say.
Elizabeth Gaskell 1810-65 English novelist: *Cranford* (1853)

If you tell a lie big enough and keep repeating it, people will eventually come to believe it. The lie can be maintained only for such time as the State can shield the people from the political, economic and/or military consequences of the lie. It thus becomes vitally important for the State to use all of its powers to repress dissent, for the truth is the mortal enemy of the lie, and thus by extension, the truth is the greatest enemy of the State.
Joseph Goebbels 1897-1945 German politician and Propaganda Minister in Nazi Germany 1933-45

There is nothing more frightful than ignorance in action.
Johann Wolfgang von Goethe 1749-1832 German writer of books of poetry, drama, literature, theology, philosophy, humanism and science

The market is not an invention of capitalism. It has existed for centuries. It is an invention of civilisation.
Mikhail Gorbachev 1931- Last head of state of the Soviet Union, serving from 1988 until its collapse in 1991

Women are frightening. If you get to forty as a man, you're quite battle-scarred.
Hugh Grant 1960- English actor and film producer

Capitalism is based on self-interest and self-esteem; it holds integrity and trustworthiness as cardinal virtues and makes them pay off in the marketplace, thus demanding that men survive by means of virtue, not vices. It is this superlatively moral system that the welfare statists propose to improve upon by means of preventative law, snooping bureaucrats, and the chronic goad of fear.
Alan Greenspan 1926- American economist, Chairman of the Federal Reserve of the United States 1987-2006: *The Assault on Integrity* (1963)

Women say they want a man who knows what a woman's worth. That's a pimp.
Rich Hall 1954- American stand-up comedian and writer

America is now given over to a damned mob of scribbling women.
Nathaniel Hawthorne 1804-64 American novelist

Your liberal is an eternal sixteen-year-old, forever rebellious, forever oblivious to the nasty realities of life, forever looking *forward* to some impossible revolution in human nature.
Tony Hendra 1941- English satirist and writer: *The Book of Bad Virtues* (1995)

My mother drew a distinction between achievement and success. She said that, 'achievement is the knowledge that you have studied and worked hard and done the best that is in you. Success is being praised by others, and that's nice, too, but not as important or satisfying. Always aim for achievement and forget about success.'
Helen Hayes 1900–93 American actress

The most essential gift for a writer is a built-in, shock-proof shit detector. This is the writer's radar, and all great writers have had it.
Paris Review spring 1958
Ernest Hemingway 1899–1961 American novelist

There is nothing wrong with discontent at having a modest place in the scheme of things. That very discontent produced the ambition that built the culture of yesterday and today. But the discontent of those times was accompanied by discipline, willingness to work hard, and ready acceptance of a competitive society.

The worst aspect of what gets called 'political correctness' these days is the erosion of the intellectual confidence needed to sort out, and rank, competing values.
William A Henry III 1950-1994 American cultural critic and author: *In Defence of Elitism* (1994)

By means of shrewd lies, unremittingly repeated, it is possible to make people believe that heaven is hell – and hell heaven. The greater the lie, the more readily it will be believed by the great masses.
Adolf Hitler 1889-1945 Austrian-born German politician, leader of the National Socialist German Workers Party: *Mein Kampf* (1925-26)

When people are free to do as they please, they usually imitate each other. Originality is deliberate and forced, and partakes of the nature of a protest.
Passionate State of Mind (1955)

They who lack talent expect things to happen without effort. They ascribe failure to a lack of inspiration or ability, or to misfortune, rather than to insufficient application. At the core of every true talent there is an awareness of the difficulties inherent in any achievement, and the confidence that by persistence and patience something worthwhile will be realized. Thus talent is a species of vigor.
Eric Hoffer 1902–83 American social writer and philosopher

What has always made the state a hell on earth has been precisely that man has tried to make it his heaven.
Friedrich Hölderlin 1770-1843 German poet

Three minutes' thought would suffice to find this out; but thought is irksome and three minutes is a long time.
AE Housman 1859–1936 English poet: *D Iunii Iuvenalis Saturae* (1905) preface

If the first law of American corporate life is that deadwood floats, the corresponding rule of liberation-talk is that hot air expands.

The all-pervasive claim to victimhood tops off America's long-cherished culture of therapeutics. To seem strong may only conceal a rickety scaffolding of denial, but to be vulnerable is to be invincible.
Robert Hughes *Culture of Complaint* (1993)

The right to be heard does not automatically include the right to be taken seriously.
Hubert Humphrey 1911-78 American Democratic politician

That all men are equal is a proposition which, at ordinary times, no sane individual has ever given his assent.

At least two-thirds of our miseries spring from human stupidity, human malice and those great motivators and justifiers of malice and stupidity: idealism, dogmatism and proselytising zeal on behalf of religious or political ideas.
Aldous Huxley 1894-1963 English humanist, pacifist, poet, travel writer, film script writer

One almost begins to feel that the reason some women worked feverishly to get into men's clubs is to have a respite from the womanised world feminists have created.
Carol Iannone American conservative writer and literary critic: *Good Order* (1994) ed. Brad Miner 'The Feminist Perversion'

The strongest man in the world is he who stands alone.

The majority never has right on its side. Never I say! That is one of the social lies that a free, thinking man is bound to rebel against. Who makes up the majority in any given country? Is it the wise men or the fools? I think we must agree that the fools are in a terrible overwhelming majority, all the wide world over. But, damn it, it can surely never be right that the stupid should rule over the clever!
Henrik Ibsen 1828-1906 19th century Norwegian playwright, theatre director: *An Enemy of the People* (1882)

I believe that political correctness can be a form of linguistic fascism, and it sends shivers down the spine of my generation who went to war against fascism.
P D James 1920- English writer of detective stories: in *Paris Review* 1995

I find that the harder I work, the more luck I seem to have.
Thomas Jefferson 1743–1826 American Democratic-Republican Party co-founder and statesman, political philosopher

Science may have found a cure for most evils; but it has found no remedy for the worst of them all – the apathy of human beings.
Helen Keller 1880-1968 American deaf blind author, political activist and lecturer

Marxian Socialism must always remain a portent to the historians of Opinion – how a doctrine so illogical and so dull can have exercised the minds of men, and, through them, the events of history.
John Maynard Keynes 1883-1946 English economist: *The End of the Laissez-Faire* (1926)

How beautiful maleness is, if it finds its right expression.
DH Lawrence 1885-1930 English author, poet, playwright, essayist and literary critic

All God's children are not beautiful. Most of God's children are, in fact, barely presentable.
Fran Lebowitz 1950- American author: *Metropolitan Life* (1978)

Hilary Clinton said in her book it was a challenge to forgive Bill, but she figured if Nelson Mandela could forgive, she could give it a try. Isn't that amazing? I didn't know Clinton hit on Mandela's wife.
Jay Leno 1950– American comedian and television host

There's only one real sin, and that is to persuade oneself that the second-best is anything but the second-best.
Doris Lessing 1919– British novelist and short-story writer

Feminine intuition, a quality perhaps even rarer in women than in men.
Ada Leverson 1862-1933 British writer and novelist: quoted in *The Feminist Companion to Literature in English* ed. Virginia Blaine and others (1990)

She's the sort of woman who lives for others – you can always tell the others by their haunted expressions.
CS Lewis 1898-1963 English scholar, religious writer and novelist: *The Screwtape Letters* (1942)

The notion that every problem can be studied as such with an open and empty mind, without preconception, without knowing what has already been learned about it, must condemn men to a chronic childishness.
Walter Lippmann 1889-1974 American journalist: address to the American Association for the Advancement of Science, University of Pennsylvania, 29 December 1940

The quality of a person's life is in direct proportion to their commitment to excellence, regardless of their chosen field of endeavour.
Vincent T Lombardi (1930–70) American football coach

There's a rule, I think. You get what you want in life, but not your second choice too.

Alison Lurie 1926- American novelist: *Real People* (1969)

The human race progresses because and when the strongest human powers and the highest human faculties lead it . . . if all the ruling classes of today could be disposed of in a single massacre, and nobody left but those who at present call themselves the workers, these workers would be as helpless as a flock of shepherdless sheep.

William Hurrell Mallock 1849-1923 English author: *Aristocracy and Evolution* (1892)

I'm a writer first and a woman after.

Katherine Mansfield 1888–1923 New Zealand-born short-story writer: letter to John Middleton Murray, July 1917

I like a woman with a head on her shoulders. I hate necks.

Steve Martin 1945– American actor, comedian, writer, playwright, producer, musician, and composer

Women's Liberation is just a lot of foolishness. It's the men who are discriminated against. They can't bear children. And no-one's likely to do anything about that.

Golda Meir 1878-1978 Israeli stateswoman, Prime Minister 1969-74: in *Newsweek* 23 October 1972

What makes many men feel unhappy under capitalism is the fact that capitalism grants to each the opportunity to attain the most desirable positions which, of course, can only be attained by a few.

Daydreams of a 'fair' world which would treat him according to his 'real worth' are the refuge of all those plagued by a lack of self-knowledge.

Ludwig von Mises 1881-1973 Austrian economist, philosopher and author: *The Anti-Capitalist Mentality* (1956)

I have never had any great esteem for the generality of the fair sex, and my only consolation for being of that gender has been the assurance it gave me of never being married to anyone amongst them.

Lady Mary Wortley Montagu 1689-1762 English aristocrat and writer: letter to Mrs Calthorpe of 7 December 1723

I suppose true sexual equality will come when a general called Anthea is found having an unwise lunch with a young, unreliable model from Spain.

John Mortimer 1923-2009 English novelist, barrister, and dramatist: *The Spectator*, 26 March 1994

If men were shouted down for being sexist when they used the word 'postman', then asking if there was any chance of a quick shag seemed like a bit of a non-starter.
John O'Farrell 1962– British author, broadcaster, and comedy scriptwriter

Political language – and with variations this is true of all political parties, from Conservatives to Anarchists – is designed to make lies sound truthful and murder respectable, and to give an appearance of solidity to pure wind.
George Orwell 1903-1950 English novelist, journalist, literary critic, poet: *Decline of the English Murder and other essays* (1965) title essay, written 1946

I love men, even though they're lying, cheating scumbags.
Gwyneth Paltrow 1972- American actress

It is our national joy to mistake for the first-rate, the fecund rate.
review of Sinclair Lewis *Dodsworth:* in *New Yorker* 16 March 1929

I hate women. They get on my nerves.
quoted in *Women's Wicked Wit* ed. Michelle Lovric (2000)
RE Drennan *Wit's End* (1973)

Oh, life is a glorious cycle of song,
A medley of extemporanea;
And love is a thing that can never go wrong;
And I am Marie of Romania.
'Comment'
Dorothy Parker 1893–1967 American critic and humorist

For the mind does not require filling like a bottle, but rather, like wood, it only required kindling to create in it an impulse to think independently and an ardent desire for the truth.
Plutarch 46–120 Greek philosopher and biographer: *Moralia*

Sometimes I'm charmed by the fact that there are women with whom you can discuss the theory of light all evening, and at the end they will ask you what is your birth sign.
Roman Polanski 1933- French-born and resident Polish film director, producer, writer and actor

Marxism is only an episode – one of the many mistakes we have made in the perennial and dangerous struggle for building a better and a freer world.
Sir Karl Popper 1902-94 Austrian and British philosopher: *The Open Society and its Enemies* (rev. ed. 1952)

Properly, we should read for power. Man reading should be man intensely alive. The book should be a ball of light in one's hand.
Ezra Pound 1885–1972 American poet

You won't learn much about capitalism at a university. How could you? Capitalism is a matter of risks and rewards, and a tenured professor doesn't have much to do with either.
Jerry Pournelle 1933- American science fiction writer, essayist and journalist

Capitalism is a social system based on private ownership of the means of production. It is characterized by the pursuit of material self-interest under freedom and it rests on a foundation of the cultural influence of reason.
George Reisman 1937- American economist: *A Treatise on Economics* (1996)

There are two theories about arguing with women. Neither one works.
Roy Rogers 1911-98 American singer and cowboy actor

A book is a version of the world. If you do not like it, ignore it; or offer your own version in return.
O Magazine April 2003
Salman Rushdie 1947– Indian-born British novelist

Every man, wherever he goes, is encompassed by a cloud of comforting convictions, which move with him like flies on a summer day.

One should as a rule respect public opinion in so far as is necessary to avoid starvation and to keep out of prison, but anything that goes beyond this is voluntary submission to an unnecessary tyrant.

Envy is the basis of democracy.

To be without some of the things you want is an indispensable part of happiness.
The Conquest of Happiness (1930)

Man is a credulous animal, and must believe something; in the absence of good grounds for belief, he will be satisfied with bad ones.
Unpopular Essays (1950)

Men fear thought as they fear nothing else on earth – more than ruin – more even than death . . . Thought is subversive and revolutionary, destructive and terrible, thought is merciless to privilege, established institutions, and comfortable habit. Thought looks into the pit of hell and is not afraid. Thought is great and swift and free, the light of the world, and the chief glory of man.

Many people would sooner die than think; In fact, they do so.

If a man is offered a fact which goes against his instincts, he will scrutinise it closely, and unless the evidence is overwhelming, he will refuse to believe it. If, on the other hand, he is offered something which affords a reason for acting in accordance to his instincts, he will accept it even on the slightest evidence. The origin of myths is explained in this way.

It has been said that man is a rational animal. All my life I have been searching for evidence which could support this.

The whole problem with the world is that fools and fanatics are always so certain of themselves, but wiser people so full of doubts.

Passive acceptance of the teacher's wisdom is easy to most boys and girls. It involves no effort of independent thought, and seems rational because the teacher knows more than his pupils; it is moreover the way to win the favour of the teacher unless he is a very exceptional man. Yet the habit of passive acceptance is a disastrous one in later life. It causes man to seek and to accept a leader, and to accept as a leader whoever is established in that position.

Few people can be happy unless they hate some other person, nation, or creed.

The fact that an opinion has been widely held is no evidence whatever that it is not utterly absurd; indeed in view of the silliness of the majority of mankind, a widespread belief is more likely to be foolish than sensible.

All movements go too far.
Lord Bertrand Russell 1872-1970 Nobel Prize-winning British philosopher, logician, mathematician, historian, free trade champion, pacifist and social critic

The skill of writing is to create a context in which other people can think.
Edwin Schlossberg 1945– American designer, author, and artist

Clemenceau once said that war is too important to be left to the generals. When he said that, 50 years ago, he may have been right . . . but now, war is too important to be left to the politicians. They have neither the time, the training, nor the inclination for strategic thought . . . And I can no longer sit around and allow Communist subversion, Communist corruption, and Communist infiltration of our precious bodily fluids.
Col Jack Ripper commander of Burpleson AFB to Group Capt Mandrake (**Peter Sellers**): *Dr Strangelove* 1964 film

Pay no attention to what the critics say. No statue has ever been put up to a critic.
Jean Sibelius 1865–1957 Finnish composer: quoted in Bengt de Törne *Sibelius: A Close Up* (1937)

When intellectuals discover that the world does not behave according to their theories, the conclusion they invariably draw is that the world must be changed. It must be awfully hard to change theories.
syndicated column, 10 December 1985

Much of the social history of the Western world over the past three decades has involved replacing what worked with what sounded good. In area after area – crime, education, housing, race relations – the situation has gotten worse after the bright new theories were put into operation. The amazing thing is that this history of failure and disaster has neither discouraged the social engineers nor discredited them.
Is Reality Optional? (1993)
Thomas Sowell 1930– African-American economist and social commentator

I don't think I'll get married again. I'll just find a woman I don't like and give her a house.
Rod Stewart 1945- British singer-songwriter and musician

When a true genius appears in the world, you may know him by this sign, that the dunces are all in confederacy against him.
Jonathan Swift 1667–1745 Anglo-Irish poet and satirist: *Thoughts on Various Subjects* (1711)

Like Johnson's friend Edwards, I too have tried to be a Marxist but common sense kept breaking in.
AJP Taylor 1906-90 British historian: *Journal of Modern History* (1977)

There is a demand in these days for men who can make wrong appear right.
Terence 185-159BC Roman playwright

This I set down as a positive truth. A woman with fair opportunities and without a positive hump, may marry whom she likes.
William Makepeace Thackeray 1811-1863 English novelist: *Vanity Fair* (1847-8)

No woman will in my time be Prime Minister or Chancellor or Foreign Secretary – not the top jobs. Anyway I wouldn't want to be Prime Minister. You have to give yourself 100%.
on her appointment as Shadow Education Spokesman: in *Sunday Telegraph* 26 October 1969

Economics are the method; the object is to change the soul.
Sunday Times 3 May 1981

To wear your heart on your sleeve isn't a very good plan; you should wear it inside, where it functions best.

Europe will never be like America. Europe is a product of history. America is a product of philosophy.

The problem with socialism is that eventually you run out of other people's money.

You may have to fight a battle more than once to win it.
Margaret Thatcher 1925- British Conservative politician, Leader of the Conservative Party 1975-90, Prime Minister of the United Kingdom 1979-90

If a man does not keep pace with his companions, perhaps it is because he hears a different drummer. Let him step to the music which he hears, however measured or far away.
Henry Thoreau 1817-62 American author, poet, naturalist, tax resister, development critic, surveyor, historian, philosopher, and leading transcendentalist: *Conclusion* (1854)

99% of the adults in this country are decent, honest, hard-working, honest Americans. It's the other lousy 1% that gets all the publicity and gives us a bad name. But then . . . we elected them.
Lily Tomlin 1939- American actress, comedian, writer and producer

I'm in favour of liberalised immigration because of the effect it would have on restaurants. I'd let just about everybody in, except the English.
Calvin Trillin 1935– American journalist, humorist, food writer, poet, memoirist, and novelist

There is no road to wealth so easy and respectable as that of matrimony.
Doctor Thorne (1858)

Equality is a doctrine to be forgiven when he who preaches it is striving to raise others to his own level.
North America (1862)

Men don't know women, or they would be harder to them.
Lady Ongar in *The Claverings* (1867)
Anthony Trollope 1815-82 English novelist

The average man's a coward.
Adventures of Huckleberry Finn (1884)

We have no thoughts of our own, no opinions of our own: they are transmitted to us, trained into us.
A Connecticut Yankee in King Arthur's Court (1889)

Noise proves nothing. Often a hen who has merely laid an egg cackles as if she had laid an asteroid.

When in doubt tell the truth.
Following the Equator (1897)

Mankind is governed by minorities, seldom or never by majorities. It suppresses its feelings and its beliefs and follows the handful that makes the most noise. Sometimes the noisy handful is right, sometimes wrong, but no matter, the crowd follows it.
The Mysterious Stranger (1910)

It seems a great pity they allowed Jane Austen to die a natural death.
Mark Twain 1835-1910 American author and humorist

The Queen is most anxious to enlist every one who can speak or write to join in checking this mad, wicked folly of 'Woman's Rights', with all its attendant horrors, on which her poor feeble sex is bent, forgetting every sense of womanly feeling and propriety.
Queen Victoria 1819-1901 Queen of the United Kingdom of Great Britain and Ireland 1837-1901: letter to Theodore Martin, 29 May 1870

Almost everything I ever did, even as a scientist, was in the hope of meeting a pretty girl.
James D Watson 1928- Nobel Prize-winning American molecular biologist, geneticist, and zoologist

I believe that inequalities of wealth and position are inevitable and that it is therefore meaningless to discuss the advantages of their elimination.
Evelyn Waugh 1903-66 English novelist: *Mexico: An Object Lesson* (1939)

An office party is not, as is sometimes supposed, the Managing Director's chance to kiss the tea-girl. It is the tea-girl's chance to kiss the Managing Director, however bizarre an ambition this may seem to anyone who has seen the Managing Director face on.

Katharine Whitehorn 1928- British photographic model for advertisement for the energy drink Lucozade, writer, journalist, editor and broadcaster: *Roundabout* (1962) 'The Office Party'

One must have a heart of stone to read the death of Little Nell without laughing.

Oscar Wilde 1854–1900 Anglo-Irish dramatist and poet

Unable obtain bidet. Suggest handstand in shower.

cabled response to his wife's cabled complaint from Paris just after the Second World War, that her accommodation did not have a bidet, and could he arrange to have one sent to her?

Billy Wilder 1906–2002 American film director and writer

A man is designed to walk three miles in the rain to phone for help when the car breaks down – and a women is designed to say 'you took your time' when he comes back dripping wet.

Victoria Wood 1953- British writer and comedienne: *Up to You, Porky – The Victoria Wood Sketch Book* (1985)

A democracy cannot exist as a permanent form of government. It can only exist until the voters discover that they can vote themselves largesse from the public treasury. From that moment on, the majority always votes for the candidates promising the most benefits from the public treasury with the result that a democracy always collapses over lousy fiscal policy, always followed by a dictatorship. The average of the world's great civilizations before they decline has been 200 years. These nations have progressed in this sequence: From bondage to spiritual faith; from faith to great courage; from courage to liberty; from liberty to abundance; from abundance to selfishness; from selfishness to complacency; from complacency to apathy; from apathy to dependency; from dependency back again to bondage.

Alexander Fraser Tytler, **Lord Woodhouselee** 1747-1813 British lawyer and writer: 'Cycle of Democracy' (1770)

Quit now, you'll never make it. If you disregard this advice, you'll be halfway there.

David Zucker 1947- American film director, producer and screenwriter

APPENDIX 2

THE EMPATHY QUOTIENT (EQ) QUESTIONNAIRE

Read each statement very carefully and rate how strongly you agree or disagree with it.

1.	I can easily tell if someone else wants to enter a conversation	strongly agree	slightly agree	slightly disagree	strongly disagree
2.	I prefer animals to humans	strongly agree	slightly agree	slightly disagree	strongly disagree
3.	I try to keep up with the current trends and fashions	strongly agree	slightly agree	slightly disagree	strongly disagree
4.	I find it difficult to explain to others things that I understand easily, when they don't understand it first time	strongly agree	slightly agree	slightly disagree	strongly disagree
5.	I dream most nights	strongly agree	slightly agree	slightly disagree	strongly disagree
6.	I really enjoy caring for other people	strongly agree	slightly agree	slightly disagree	strongly disagree
7.	I try to solve my own problems rather than discussing them with others	strongly agree	slightly agree	slightly disagree	strongly disagree
8.	I find it hard to know what to do in a social situation	strongly agree	slightly agree	slightly disagree	strongly disagree
9.	I am at my best first thing in the morning	strongly agree	slightly agree	slightly disagree	strongly disagree

10. People often tell me that I went too far in driving my point home in a discussion	strongly agree	slightly agree	slightly disagree	strongly disagree
11. It doesn't bother me too much if I am late meeting a friend	strongly agree	slightly agree	slightly disagree	strongly disagree
12. Friendships and relationships are just too difficult, so I tend not to bother with them	strongly agree	slightly agree	slightly disagree	strongly disagree
13. I would never break a law, no matter how minor	strongly agree	slightly agree	slightly disagree	strongly disagree
14. I often find it difficult to judge if something is rude or polite	strongly agree	slightly agree	slightly disagree	strongly disagree
15. In a conversation, I tend to focus upon my own thoughts rather than on what my listener might be thinking	strongly agree	slightly agree	slightly disagree	strongly disagree
16. I prefer practical jokes to verbal humour	strongly agree	slightly agree	slightly disagree	strongly disagree
17. I live for today rather than the future	strongly agree	slightly agree	slightly disagree	strongly disagree
18. When I was a child, I enjoyed cutting up worms to see what would happen	strongly agree	slightly agree	slightly disagree	strongly disagree
19. I can pick up quickly if someone says one thing but means another	strongly agree	slightly agree	slightly disagree	strongly disagree
20. I tend to have very strong opinions about morality	strongly agree	slightly agree	slightly disagree	strongly disagree

21. It is hard for me to see why some things upset people so much	strongly agree	slightly agree	slightly disagree	strongly disagree
22. I find it easy to put myself in somebody else's shoes	strongly agree	slightly agree	slightly disagree	strongly disagree
23. I think that good manners are the most important thing a parent can teach their child	strongly agree	slightly agree	slightly disagree	strongly disagree
24. I like to do things on the spur of the moment	strongly agree	slightly agree	slightly disagree	strongly disagree
25. I am good at predicting how someone will feel	strongly agree	slightly agree	slightly disagree	strongly disagree
26. I am quick to spot when someone is feeling awkward or uncomfortable	strongly agree	slightly agree	slightly disagree	strongly disagree
27. If I say something that someone else is offended by, I think that that's their problem, not mine	strongly agree	slightly agree	slightly disagree	strongly disagree
28. If anyone asked me if I liked their haircut, I would reply truthfully, even if I didn't like it	strongly agree	slightly agree	slightly disagree	strongly disagree
29. I can's always see why someone should have felt offended by a remark	strongly agree	slightly agree	slightly disagree	strongly disagree
30. People often tell me that I am very unpredictable	strongly agree	slightly agree	slightly disagree	strongly disagree
31. I enjoy being the centre of attention at any social gathering	strongly agree	slightly agree	slightly disagree	strongly disagree

32. Seeing people cry doesn't really upset me	strongly agree	slightly agree	slightly disagree	strongly disagree
33. I enjoy having discussions about politics	strongly agree	slightly agree	slightly disagree	strongly disagree
34. I am very blunt, which some people take to be rudeness, even though this is unintentional	strongly agree	slightly agree	slightly disagree	strongly disagree
35. I don't tend to find social situations confusing	strongly agree	slightly agree	slightly disagree	strongly disagree
36. Other people tell me I am good at understanding how they are feeling and what they are thinking	strongly agree	slightly agree	slightly disagree	strongly disagree
37. When I talk to people, I tend to talk about their experiences rather than my own	strongly agree	slightly agree	slightly disagree	strongly disagree
38. It upsets me to see an animal in pain	strongly agree	slightly agree	slightly disagree	strongly disagree
39. I am able to make decisions without being influenced by people's feelings	strongly agree	slightly agree	slightly disagree	strongly disagree
40. I can't relax until I have done everything I had planned to do that day	strongly agree	slightly agree	slightly disagree	strongly disagree
41. I can easily tell if someone else is interested or bored with what I am saying	strongly agree	slightly agree	slightly disagree	strongly disagree
42. I get upset if I see people suffering on news programmes	strongly agree	slightly agree	slightly disagree	strongly disagree

43. Friends usually talk to me about their problems as they say that I am very understanding

    strongly agree   slightly agree   slightly disagree   strongly disagree

44. I can sense if I am intruding, even if the other person doesn't tell me

    strongly agree   slightly agree   slightly disagree   strongly disagree

45. I often start new hobbies but quickly become bored with them and move on to something else

    strongly agree   slightly agree   slightly disagree   strongly disagree

46. People sometimes tell me that I have gone too far with teasing

    strongly agree   slightly agree   slightly disagree   strongly disagree

47. I would be too nervous to go on a big rollercoaster

    strongly agree   slightly agree   slightly disagree   strongly disagree

48. Other people often say that I am insensitive, though I don't always see why

    strongly agree   slightly agree   slightly disagree   strongly disagree

49. If I see a stranger in a group, I think that it is up to them to make an effort to join in

    strongly agree   slightly agree   slightly disagree   strongly disagree

50. I usually stay emotionally detached when watching a film

    strongly agree   slightly agree   slightly disagree   strongly disagree

51. I like to be very organised in day-to-day life and often make lists of the chores I have to do

    strongly agree   slightly agree   slightly disagree   strongly disagree

52. I can tune in to how someone else feels rapidly and intuitively

    strongly agree   slightly agree   slightly disagree   strongly disagree

53. I don't like to take risks	strongly agree	slightly agree	slightly disagree	strongly disagree
54. I can easily work out what another person might want to talk about	strongly agree	slightly agree	slightly disagree	strongly disagree
55. I can tell if someone is masking their true emotion	strongly agree	slightly agree	slightly disagree	strongly disagree
56. Before making a decision I always weigh up the pros and cons	strongly agree	slightly agree	slightly disagree	strongly disagree
57. I don't consciously work out the rules of social situations	strongly agree	slightly agree	slightly disagree	strongly disagree
58. I am good at predicting what someone will do	strongly agree	slightly agree	slightly disagree	strongly disagree
59. I tend to get emotionally involved with a friend's problems	strongly agree	slightly agree	slightly disagree	strongly disagree
60. I can usually appreciate the other person's viewpoint, even if I don't agree with it	strongly agree	slightly agree	slightly disagree	strongly disagree

How to Score Your EQ

Score two points for each of the following items if you answered 'strongly agree' and one point if you answered 'slightly agree': 1, 6, 19, 22, 25, 26, 35, 36, 37, 38, 41, 42, 43, 44, 52, 54, 55, 57, 58, 59, 60.

Score two points for each of the following items if you answered 'strongly disagree' and one point if you answered 'slightly disagree': 4, 8, 10, 11, 12, 14, 15, 18, 21, 27, 28, 29, 32, 34, 39, 46, 48, 49, 50.

The following items are not scored: 2, 3, 5, 7, 9, 13, 16, 17, 20, 23, 24, 30, 31, 33, 40, 45, 47, 51, 53, 56.

Simply add up all the points you have scored to obtain your total EQ score.

How to Interpret Your EQ Score

0-30 = **low** (most people with Asperger Syndrome or high-functioning autism score about 20)

33-52 = **average** range (most women score about 47 and most men score about 42)

53-63 is **above average**

64-80 is **very high**

80 = **maximum**

Details on the norms, validity, reliability and other statistical issues relating to this test and the next are given in the original articles published in the scientific journals cited in Simon Baron-Cohen's *The Essential Difference* (2003).

APPENDIX 3

THE SYSTEMISING QUOTIENT (SQ) QUESTIONNAIRE

Read each statement very carefully and rate how strongly you agree or disagree with it.

1.	When I listen to a piece of music, I always notice how it's structured	definitely agree	slightly agree	slightly disagree	definitely disagree
2.	I adhere to common superstitions	definitely agree	slightly agree	slightly disagree	definitely disagree
3.	I often make resolutions, but find it hard to stick to them	definitely agree	slightly agree	slightly disagree	definitely disagree
4.	I prefer to read non-fiction than fiction	definitely agree	slightly agree	slightly disagree	definitely disagree
5.	If I were buying a car, I would want to obtain specific information about its engine capacity	definitely agree	slightly agree	slightly disagree	definitely disagree
6.	When I look at a painting, I do not usually think about the technique involved in making it	definitely agree	slightly agree	slightly disagree	definitely disagree
7.	If there was a problem with the electrical wiring in my home, I'd be able to fix it myself	definitely agree	slightly agree	slightly disagree	definitely disagree
8.	When I have a dream, I find it difficult to remember precise details about the dream the next day	definitely agree	slightly agree	slightly disagree	definitely disagree

9. When I watch a film, I prefer to be with a group of friends, rather than alone	definitely agree	slightly agree	slightly disagree	definitely disagree
10. I am interested in learning about different religions	definitely agree	slightly agree	slightly disagree	definitely disagree
11. I rarely read articles or Web pages about new technology	definitely agree	slightly agree	slightly disagree	definitely disagree
12. I do not enjoy games that involve a high degree of strategy	definitely agree	slightly agree	slightly disagree	definitely disagree
13. I am fascinated by how machines work	definitely agree	slightly agree	slightly disagree	definitely disagree
14. I make a point of listening to the news each morning	definitely agree	slightly agree	slightly disagree	definitely disagree
15. In maths, I am intrigued by the rules and patterns governing numbers	definitely agree	slightly agree	slightly disagree	definitely disagree
16. I am bad about keeping in touch with old friends	definitely agree	slightly agree	slightly disagree	definitely disagree
17. When I am relating a story, I often leave out details and just give the gist of what happened	definitely agree	slightly agree	slightly disagree	definitely disagree
18. I find it difficult to understand instruction manuals for putting appliances together	definitely agree	slightly agree	slightly disagree	definitely disagree
19. When I look at an animal, I like to know the exact species it belongs to	definitely agree	slightly agree	slightly disagree	definitely disagree

20. If I were buying a computer, I would want to know exact details about its hard drive capacity and processor speed

   definitely agree   slightly agree   slightly disagree   definitely disagree

21. I enjoy participating in sport

   definitely agree   slightly agree   slightly disagree   definitely disagree

22. I try to avoid doing household chores if I can

   definitely agree   slightly agree   slightly disagree   definitely disagree

23. When I cook, I do not think about exactly how different methods and ingredients contribute to the final product

   definitely agree   slightly agree   slightly disagree   definitely disagree

24. I find it difficult to read and understand maps

   definitely agree   slightly agree   slightly disagree   definitely disagree

25. If I had a collection (e.g. CDs, coins, stamps), it would be highly organised

   definitely agree   slightly agree   slightly disagree   definitely disagree

26. When I look at a piece of furniture, I do not notice the details of how it was constructed

   definitely agree   slightly agree   slightly disagree   definitely disagree

27. The idea of engaging in 'risk-taking' activities appeals to me

   definitely agree   slightly agree   slightly disagree   definitely disagree

28. When I learn about historical events, I do not focus on exact dates

   definitely agree   slightly agree   slightly disagree   definitely disagree

29. When I read the newspaper, I am drawn to tables of information, such as football league scores or stock market indices

   definitely agree   slightly agree   slightly disagree   definitely disagree

30. When I learn a language, I become intrigued by its grammatical rules — definitely agree / slightly agree / slightly disagree / definitely disagree

31. I find it difficult to learn my way around a new city — definitely agree / slightly agree / slightly disagree / definitely disagree

32. I do not tend to watch science documentaries on television or read articles about science and nature — definitely agree / slightly agree / slightly disagree / definitely disagree

33. If I were buying a stereo, I would want to know about its precise technical features — definitely agree / slightly agree / slightly disagree / definitely disagree

34. I find it easy to grasp exactly how odds work in betting — definitely agree / slightly agree / slightly disagree / definitely disagree

35. I am not very meticulous when I carry out D.I.Y. — definitely agree / slightly agree / slightly disagree / definitely disagree

36. I find it easy to carry on a conversation with someone I've just met — definitely agree / slightly agree / slightly disagree / definitely disagree

37. When I look at a building, I am curious about the precise way it was constructed — definitely agree / slightly agree / slightly disagree / definitely disagree

38. When an election is being held, I am not interested in the results for each constituency — definitely agree / slightly agree / slightly disagree / definitely disagree

39. When I lend someone money, I expect them to pay me back exactly what they owe me — definitely agree / slightly agree / slightly disagree / definitely disagree

40. I find it difficult to understand information the bank sends me on different investment and savings systems	definitely agree	slightly agree	slightly disagree	definitely disagree
41. When travelling by train, I often wonder exactly how the rail networks are coordinated	definitely agree	slightly agree	slightly disagree	definitely disagree
42. When I buy a new appliance, I do not read the instruction manual very thoroughly	definitely agree	slightly agree	slightly disagree	definitely disagree
43. If I were buying a camera, I would not look carefully into the quality of the lens	definitely agree	slightly agree	slightly disagree	definitely disagree
44. When I read something, I always notice whether it is grammatically correct	definitely agree	slightly agree	slightly disagree	definitely disagree
45. When I hear the weather forecast, I am not very interested in the meteorological patterns	definitely agree	slightly agree	slightly disagree	definitely disagree
46. I often wonder what it would be like to be someone else	definitely agree	slightly agree	slightly disagree	definitely disagree
47. I find it difficult to do two things at once	definitely agree	slightly agree	slightly disagree	definitely disagree
48. When I look at a mountain, I think about how precisely it was formed	definitely agree	slightly agree	slightly disagree	definitely disagree
49. I can easily visualise how the motorways in my region link up	definitely agree	slightly agree	slightly disagree	definitely disagree

50. When I'm in a restaurant, I often have a hard time deciding what to order — definitely agree / slightly agree / slightly disagree / definitely disagree

51. When I'm in a plane, I do not think about the aerodynamics — definitely agree / slightly agree / slightly disagree / definitely disagree

52. I often forget the precise details of conversations I've had — definitely agree / slightly agree / slightly disagree / definitely disagree

53. When I am walking in the country, I am curious about how the various kinds of trees differ — definitely agree / slightly agree / slightly disagree / definitely disagree

54. After meeting someone just once or twice, I find it difficult to remember precisely what they look like — definitely agree / slightly agree / slightly disagree / definitely disagree

55. I am interested in knowing the path a river takes from its source to the sea — definitely agree / slightly agree / slightly disagree / definitely disagree

56. I do not read legal documents very carefully — definitely agree / slightly agree / slightly disagree / definitely disagree

57. I am not interested in understanding how wireless communications works — definitely agree / slightly agree / slightly disagree / definitely disagree

58. I am curious about life on other planets — definitely agree / slightly agree / slightly disagree / definitely disagree

59. When I travel, I like to learn specific details about the culture of the place I am visiting — definitely agree / slightly agree / slightly disagree / definitely disagree

60.	I do not care to know the names of the plants I see	definitely agree	slightly agree	slightly disagree	definitely disagree

How to Score Your SQ

Score two points for each of the following items if you answered 'definitely agree' and one point if you answered 'slightly agree': 1, 4, 5, 7, 13, 15, 19, 20, 25, 29, 30, 33, 34, 37, 41, 44, 48, 49, 53, 55.

Score two points for each of the following items if you answered 'definitely disagree' and one point if you answered 'slightly disagree': 6, 11, 12, 18, 23, 24, 26, 28, 31, 32, 35, 38, 40, 42, 43, 45, 51, 56, 57, 60.

The following items are not scored: 2, 3, 8, 9, 10, 14, 16, 17, 21, 22, 27, 36, 39, 46, 47, 50, 52, 54, 58, 59.

Simply add up all the points you have scored to obtain your total SQ score.

How to Interpret Your SQ Score

0-19 = **low**

20-39 = **average** range (most women score about 24 and most men score about 30)

40-50 = **above average** (most people with Asperger Syndrome or high-functioning autism score in this range).

51-80 = **very high** (three times as many people with Asperger Syndrome score in this range, compared to typical men, and almost no women score in this range)

80 = **maximum**

Details on the norms, validity, reliability and other statistical issues relating to this test and the previous one are given in the original articles published in the scientific journals cited in Simon Baron-Cohen's *The Essential Difference* (2003).

APPENDIX 4

HARRIET HARMAN:
A BIOGRAPHY

Human beings are perhaps never more frightening than when they are
convinced beyond doubt that they are right.
Laurens Van der Post 1906-96 Afrikaner author, farmer, war hero, political adviser to
British heads of government, close friend of Prince Charles, godfather of Prince William,
educator, journalist, humanitarian, philosopher, explorer and conservationist: *The Lost
World of the Kalahari* (1958)

From Wikipedia in September 2010:

Harriet Ruth Harman (born 30 July 1950) is a British Labour Party
politician, who is the Member of Parliament (MP) for Camberwell and
Peckham, and was MP for the predecessor Peckham constituency from
1982 to 1997. She has been the Leader of the Labour Party and Leader
of the Opposition since 11 May 2010, but will step down when a
permanent leader is elected in September 2010.

She was previously the Member of Parliament for Peckham from a by-
election in 1982 until its abolition. In 2007, she became the Deputy
Leader and Party Chair of the Labour Party, and served in the Cabinet as
Leader of the House of Commons, Lord Privy Seal, and Minister for
Women and Equality from 2007 to 2010. Following the resignation of
Gordon Brown as Prime Minister and Labour Leader, Harman became
Party Leader and replaced Conservative Party Leader David Cameron
(who became Prime Minister) as Leader of the Opposition. She serves in
both roles until the Labour party elects a permanent Leader. She is also
the current female MP with the longest period of continuous service in
the House of Commons.

She was educated at the independent St Paul's Girls' School and the
University of York, where she gained a BA in Politics. Between 1978 and
1982, she was legal officer for the National Council for Civil Liberties
and as such was found in contempt of court by Mr Justice Park in the
important civil liberties case Harman v The Home Office (the conviction
for contempt being upheld on appeal) before becoming MP for
Peckham in a by-election in 1982. However, Ms Harman won the day
when she took her case to the European Court of Human Rights in

Strasbourg and successfully argued that the prosecution had breached her right to freedom of expression. In the field of public law, Harman v United Kingdom is still a well-known case that is cited in textbooks...

In the by-election held on 28 October 1982, she was elected Member of Parliament for Southwark, Peckham with a majority of 3,931 votes. She became Labour's front-bench spokeswoman for social services in 1984, and then health in 1987. After the 1992 general election she entered the Shadow Cabinet as Shadow Chief Secretary to the Treasury (1992–1994); and later served as Shadow Employment Secretary (1994–1995), Shadow Health Secretary (1995–1996) and Shadow Social Security Secretary (1996–1997). Harman is a committed feminist, having said, 'I am in the Labour Party because I am a feminist. I am in the Labour Party because I believe in equality.' Because of her unabashed feminism, her detractors have given her the nickname 'Harriet Harperson' [Author's note: also 'Harridan Harman' and 'Mad Hattie'].

After Labour's victory in the 1997 general election, she became Secretary of State for Social Security and was given the task of reforming the Welfare State. During this time, her more notable policies included introducing a minimum income guarantee and winter fuel payments for the elderly. It was later ruled that the fuel payments policy breached European sex discrimination laws due to the fact men were forced to wait five years longer to receive them than women. The policy was amended so both sexes qualified at age 60. Harman was sacked from the position in 1998...

Harman made a return to the front bench after the 2001 general election, with her appointment to the office of Solicitor General, thus becoming the first female Solicitor General. In accordance with convention, she was appointed as Queen's Counsel, although she was never a barrister, had no rights of audience in the higher courts, did not obtain them and never presented a case during her time as Solicitor General, or at all.

After the 2005 general election, she became a Minister of State in the Department for Constitutional Affairs with responsibilities including constitutional reform, legal aid and court processes. On 16 March 2006, Harman relinquished her ministerial responsibilities for electoral administration and reform of the House of Lords. She stated that this was to avoid any potential conflict of interest after her husband Jack Dromey, the Treasurer of the Labour Party, announced that he would be investigating a number of loans made to the Labour Party that had not been disclosed to party officers. She retained her other responsibilities.

Harman announced her intention to stand for Deputy Leadership of the Labour Party when John Prescott stood down. On 27 November

2006 Patrick Wintour reported that she had commissioned an opinion poll that had found that she would be more popular with the electorate than any of the other likely candidates. She used this point to argue that she should become the next Deputy Prime Minister in an interview with the BBC.

Harman did not have the support of any major unions, and helped to fund her campaign for deputy leadership by taking out a personal loan of £10,000 and a £40,000 extension to her mortgage. Harman failed to report some donations and loans on time, and was subject to an Electoral Commission inquiry for breaches of electoral law. The commission said that her 'failure to report on time is a serious matter' though the case was not handed over to the police.

On 24 June 2007 in a close contest Harman was elected Deputy Leader of the Labour Party. Alan Johnson had led in all but the first of the previous rounds, but when second-preference votes had been redistributed after the fourth round, Harman stood elected with 50.43% of the vote to Johnson's 49.56%.

Harman is known as a long term supporter of Gordon Brown and regarded as a personal friend. On 28 June 2007, she was appointed to sit in newly appointed Prime Minister Gordon Brown's Cabinet as Leader of the House of Commons, Lord Privy Seal and Minister for Women and Equality (combining these post with the Deputy Leader and Chair of the Labour Party). However, unlike the previous Deputy Leader of the Labour Party, John Prescott, Harman was not given the title of 'Deputy Prime Minister'...

Harman attacked the Conservative Party at the 2007 Labour Party Conference 2007, referring to them as the 'nasty party' and suggesting that there would be little competition at the next election.

In April 2008, Harman's blog was 'hacked' and changed to state that she had joined the Conservative Party. Harman later admitted when questioned by Sky News that the incident was a result of her using 'Harriet' and 'Harman' as her username and password. [Author's note: you couldn't make it up, could you?]

Following Gordon Brown's resignation as prime minister and Leader of the Labour Party on 11 May 2010, Harman, as Deputy Leader of the Party, automatically became the acting Leader of the Party as well as the Leader of the Opposition in the House of Commons.

As part of a proposed Equality Bill in 2010, Harman announced a consultation on changing the existing discrimination laws, which included options for Reverse Discrimination in employment. Under the proposals, employers would be legally allowed to discriminate in favour of a job candidate on the basis of their race or gender where the candidates were otherwise equally qualified. Employers would not be required to use these powers, but would be able to do so without the threat of legal action for discriminatory practices. Harman has stated that this proposal would not simply involve discrimination against white males, and that men will benefit in some circumstances; for example if a school wanted to balance a predominantly female workforce by discriminating in favour of employing a male teacher.

The white paper also proposed measures to end age discrimination, promote transparency in organisations and introduce a new equality duty on the public sector. These changes, if made, could face a challenge under Article 14 of the European Convention on Human Rights, which prohibits discrimination on the basis of sex, race, colour, language, religion and on several other criteria. Michael Millar, writing in *The Spectator* was of the opinion that, 'The Equality Bill before parliament today gives employers the right to choose an ethnic minority candidate or female candidate over a white male, specifically because they are an ethnic minority or female.' Some commentators, however, such as Graham Kirby, writing for the blogging site 'The Samosa', have defended the act as essentially meritocratic and necessary.

Harman also commissioned a report on allowing political parties to draw up all-black shortlists designed to increase the number of black MPs in Westminster. A further report proposed extending the arrangement allowing all-women shortlists beyond 2015 which will fail to have any impact in the 2010 General Election. These proposals are supported by members of the three major parties, though no others allow discrimination in their shortlists. Inside the Labour Party, Harman has said she does 'not agree with all-male leaderships' because men 'cannot be left to run things on their own'; and that, consequently, one of Labour's top two posts should always be held by a woman.

She has backed plans for an increase in the number of homosexual MPs, and has suggested that 39 openly gay MPs should be in the next Parliament. The target is based on an official estimate that six per cent of Britain is homosexual; however, such targets have been criticised for failing to take account of gay MPs who prefer to keep their sexuality private…

During the nomination round of the 2010 Labour Leadership Contest, she backed Diane Abbott, MP for Hackney North and Stoke Newington. She later said that this was to prevent the election from being all-male. She stated that she intends to remain neutral throughout the contest and that 'This is a very crucial period and we have got five fantastic candidates. All of them would make excellent leaders of the party.' [Author's note: yeah, right.]

Harman has received criticism from the right wing and conservative press for her perceived views on families. Erin Pizzey criticised the views expressed by Harman and other leading female Labour figures in the 1990 IPPR report 'The Family Way'. Writing in the *Daily Mail*, Pizzey accused the report of being a 'staggering attack on men and their role in modern life' as a result of its stating, 'it cannot be assumed that men are bound to be an asset to family life or that the presence of fathers in families is necessarily a means to social cohesion'. In May 2008 an interview she gave to think tank Civitas Harman stated that marriage was irrelevant to government policy and that there was 'no ideal type of household in which to bring up children'.

In 1996 Harman sent her younger son Joseph to St Olave's Grammar School, Orpington after sending her eldest son Harry to a grant-maintained school. This appeared to go against the spirit of the pledge by David Blunkett not to increase selective education. Harman attempted to explain: 'This is a state school that other children in my son's class will be going to... And admission is open to every child in Southwark irrespective of money or who their parents are'. [Author's note: when asked to comment on this matter, Deputy Prime Minister John Prescott famously remarked, 'I'm not going to defend any fucking hypocrites'.]

In 2003, Harman was fined £400 and banned from driving for seven days after being convicted of driving at 99 mph (159 km/h) on a motorway, 29 mph (47 km/h) above the speed limit. The size of the fine was described as lenient by the Automobile Association given that Harman's salary at the time was £125,000 per year.

On 7 April 2007, Harman was issued with a £60 fixed penalty notice and given three penalty points on her licence for driving at 50 mph (80 km/h) in a portion of the A14 in Suffolk that had a temporary 40 mph (64 km/h) limit. Harman paid the fine several months late and avoided appearing at Ipswich magistrates court. A Labour Party source said of her failure to pay the fine: 'She made an innocent mistake. She forgot to pay on time because she was spending all her time on the deputy leadership contest touring the country.' [Author's note: so much for women and multitasking...] In April 2008 Harman was again caught breaking the speed limit, this time in a 30 mph zone. She received a further 3 points on her driving licence for the offence.

On 8 January 2010 Harman pleaded guilty to driving without due care and attention in relation to an incident on 3 July where she struck another vehicle whilst driving using a mobile phone. She had previously 'strongly refuted' the allegations and had claimed she would 'deny the charges'. Harman was fined £350, ordered to pay £70 costs, a £15 victim surcharge and had three points added to her licence. A second charge of driving whilst using a mobile phone was withdrawn and no action was taken over claims she had left the scene without exchanging registration and insurance details. A spokesperson said, 'Ms Harman is pleased that it has been established that this was not a "hit-and-run" accident as portrayed in some media reports. It was a parking incident and no damage was done.' Road safety organisations such as Brake condemned the leniency of the punishment and decision to drop the charge of driving whilst using a mobile phone, however the judge defended the decision stating that 'Ms Harman's guilty plea to driving without due care and attention included her admitting that she had been using a mobile phone at the time.' [Author's note: we truly live in a mad world. Ms Harman admitted to using a mobile phone whilst driving, so, er, she wasn't charged with the offence.] As a result of the case Harman became the first serving Cabinet minister in memory to plead guilty to a criminal offence.

In November 2007 it emerged that property developer David Abrahams's secretary Janet Kidd had donated £5,000 to Harman's successful deputy leadership bid. After an investigation by *The Mail on Sunday* newspaper into other donations made by people associated with Abrahams, and Prime Minister Gordon Brown's assertion that all such monies would be returned, Harman issued a statement saying she accepted the donation on 4 July 'in good faith', had registered the monies with the Electoral Commission and the Register of Members' Interests, and that she was 'not aware of any funding arrangements... between David Abrahams and Janet Kidd'. Harman was interviewed on the BBC Radio 4 PM programme on 27 November 2007 and was evasive when asked to confirm or deny that her campaign team had contacted Kidd soliciting money and was unable to answer this question directly, preferring to change the subject. On 28 November the BBC's Nick Robinson reported on his blog that Ms Harman had now revealed that her team 'may' have asked Kidd for a donation...

In January 2009, Harman proposed a rule change to exempt MPs' expenses from the Freedom of Information Act. Her parliamentary order aimed to remove 'most expenditure information held by either House of Parliament from the scope of the Freedom of Information Act'. It meant that, under the law, journalists and members of the public would no longer be entitled to learn details of their MP's expenses. Labour MPs were to be pressured to vote for this measure by use of a three line whip. Her proposal was withdrawn when the Conservative Party said they would vote against, and an online campaign by mySociety. The failure of the motion led to the disclosure of expenses of British Members of Parliament.

In March 2009 Harman was criticised for anti-male bias over the issue of the impact of the recession. After a government report suggested that women were twice as likely to lose their jobs as men and feared losing their jobs more than men, Harman stated 'we will not allow women to become the victims of this recession'. However, some statistics contradicted her position, including the Office for National Statistics report on the issue which stated 'the economic downturn in 2008 has impacted less on women in employment than men' According to the ONS men were losing their jobs at twice the rate of women. The Government Equalities Office insisted the ONS figures did not render pointless its efforts to help women.

In June 2009 Sir Michael Scholar, head of the UK Statistics Authority, wrote to Harman to warn her that different headline figures used by the ONS and Government Equalities Office with regards to pay differentiation between men and women might undermine public trust in official statistics. The GEO's headline figure was 23%, which was based on median hourly earnings of all employees, not the 12.8%, based on median hourly earnings of full-time employees only, used by the ONS. Scholar wrote: 'It is the Statistics Authority's view that use of the 23% on its own, without qualification, risks giving a misleading quantification of the gender pay gap'. The Equalities Office rejected his criticism, saying: 'With women representing over three-quarters of the part-time workforce, we believe this figure gives the fullest picture of the country's gender pay gap.'

APPENDIX 5

THE FIRST LETTER TO
THE RT HON HARRIET HARMAN MP

The Rt Hon Harriet Harman
Member of Parliament for Camberwell and Peckham, Deputy Leader of
the Labour Party, Labour Party Chair, Minister for Women and Equality,
Leader of the House of Commons, and The Lord Privy Seal
House of Commons
London SW1A 0AA

26 April 2009

Dear Ms Harman,

I am writing a book about marriage in the developed world in the
modern era, *The Fraud of the Rings*. In this book, I reflect that marriage is
but one of the ways in which women advantage themselves at the
expense of men, aided and abetted by a number of groups with vested
interests. This has always been the case, and presumably will remain so
while women campaign effectively for 'women's interests', and men fail
to campaign for *their* interests.

The purpose of this letter is to request a meeting to discuss what I see
as one of the more contentious aspects of New Labour policy, namely
the move from seeking equality of opportunity for women (which I
applaud) to equality of outcome (which I believe no government should
try to dictate). Women are 'under-represented' at senior levels in many
walks of life though exercising *choices*, as outlined so well by Susan Pinker
in her book *The Sexual Paradox*. Government policy completely
disregards this reality, and it's about time it didn't.

I should like to (audio) record an interview with you on these matters –
half an hour should suffice. I would, of course, be happy to meet you at
a time and location of your choosing. I attach an excerpt from my book
on this matter.

Yours etc.

EXCERPT FROM BOOK

When you look for it, it's not difficult to find examples of women working together to advance their interests at the expense of men. Let's start with The Rt Hon Harriet Harman QC MP, Member of Parliament for Camberwell and Peckham, Deputy Leader of the Labour Party, Labour Party Chair, Minister for Women and Equality, Leader of the House of Commons, and The Lord Privy Seal. She must have the largest business card on the planet.

In the foreword of the paper *Women's Changing Lives: Priorities for the Ministers for Women – One Year On Progress Report*, presented to Parliament in July 2008, Harriet Harman wrote the following:

> A modern democracy must be fair and equal. The government has fought for equal representation and it's because of this that we have record levels of women MPs, as well as more black and Asian MPs and councillors than ever before. But we need more women and more black, Asian and minority ethnic MPs and councillors to make our democracy truly representative.
>
> That's why in March I announced that political parties will be able to use all-women shortlists for the next five elections.

Wow. So through government diktat, for the next 22 or so years I – and every other man in the United Kingdom – could be stopped from becoming a prospective MP *solely on the grounds of gender*, regardless of our fitness for the office. And the least competent female candidate would *automatically* be deemed more worthy of public office than the most competent otherwise electable male candidate.

Response from Harriet Harman's assistant diary secretary:

'Unfortunately the Minister will not be able to grant your request due to heavy diary commitments at the time.'

APPENDIX 6

THE SECOND LETTER TO
THE RT HON HARRIET HARMAN MP

The Rt Hon Harriet Harman QC MP
Member of Parliament for Camberwell and Peckham
House of Commons
London SW1A 0AA

8 June 2010

Dear Ms Harman,

I explored gender differences at considerable length in one of my books
– *The Fraud of the Rings* – and as is my custom I'm giving away the books
I used in my researches to worthy causes. I cannot think of a more
worthy recipient of a book written by a Canadian psychologist than your
good self. It's Susan Pinker's *The Sexual Paradox*, which I have the
pleasure of enclosing.

I was sorry that you did not put yourself forward for leadership of the
party. I was planning to write a book which had as a core element your
sweeping to victory in 2015.

Yours etc.

Response: none received, surprisingly

APPENDIX 7

THE LETTER TO
LORD DAVIES OF ABERSOCH

The (Rt Hon the) Lord Davies of Abersoch
House of Lords
London SW1A 0PW

6 August 2010

Dear Lord Davies,

It was with a heavy heart that I read the article 'Inquiry into lack of women in boardroom' in *The Daily Telegraph* of Tuesday 3 August. There is not a lack of women in boardrooms. If anything, women are *over-*represented both in boardrooms and in the senior reaches of business and the public sector, due to positive discrimination. Most women are more interested in being happy than being powerful, and that's not going to change any time soon.

Anyone who reads a book by the Canadian-American psychologist Susan Pinker, *The Sexual Paradox*, can be in no doubt that women's representation at senior levels in organisations is down to the choices they make. I understand that over 90% of mechanical engineering graduates are male, while over 90% of psychology graduates are female. Why is the 'shortage' of female engineers deemed to be a problem while the 'shortage' of male psychologists isn't? We keep hearing that the problem is a shortage of role models for women. It's not true. Women have had role models for *decades*.

I enclose your complimentary signed and numbered copy of my book *The Marriage Delusion: the fraud of the rings?* and would refer you in particular to the material on women in the workplace in chapter 3 (p.36) and in chapter 7 (p.62), along with the material on Harriet Harman including Appendix 2 (p.218), and the story of her wielding a .44 Magnum revolver (p.57).

I should like to meet up with you for an audio interview so that I might better understand (for a forthcoming book) how the myth of women being under-represented in the boardroom continues to survive, even when Ms Harman is no longer in power. It seems to me that the militant feminist agenda remains completely unchallenged in British political circles.

Yours etc.

Response from Lord Davies: none received

APPENDIX 8

THE LETTER TO THE CHIEF EXECUTIVE OF THE FAWCETT SOCIETY

Ceri Goddard
Chief Executive
The Fawcett Society
1-3 Berry Street
London EC1V 0AA

1 September 2010

Dear Ms Goddard,

I am writing a book about feminism in the modern era, and I am writing to you about a phenomenon that has long baffled me: the continuing struggle for equality of gender outcome in the workplace – in well-paid, low-risk lines of work in comfortable surroundings, at least – as opposed to equality of opportunity, which women have long enjoyed in this country.

It is obvious to any rational person that the genders are very different, and why should this reality not play out in the fields of work, politics etc. as it does in other fields? I understand that over 90% of engineering graduates from British universities are men, while over 90% of psychology graduates are women. Why is the former deemed a problem to be addressed – *Woman's Hour* has been covering it with monotonous regularity since 1737, I believe – while the latter is not?

It's certainly not an issue of a lack of role models. I've been hearing the role model argument for *decades* during which there have been more female role models than you could shake a stick at. If Margaret Thatcher isn't regarded as an inspiring role model for women – as a science graduate, research chemist, barrister, and surely the greatest peacetime prime minister of the 20th century – then who could be?

I should like to meet you for an audio interview so that I might better understand your perspectives on equality of outcome in the workplace.

I'm sure my book's readers would find them interesting, and perhaps your secretary could call my secretary, Sharon Smith (xxxxx xxxxxx, sharon@xxxxxx) to arrange a suitable date and time?

Yours etc.

Response from Ceri Goddard: none received

APPENDIX 9

THE LETTER TO THE DIRECTOR-GENERAL OF THE CBI

Richard Lambert
Director-General
CBI
Centre Point
103 New Oxford Street
London WC1A 1D4

2 October 2010

Dear Mr Lambert,

After 33 years working as an executive in the private sector, I took early retirement in January 2010 to focus full-time on writing and publishing. I'm currently working on a book which includes material on women in the workplace, and exposes the absurdity of seeking 'gender balance' in the boardroom, a provision in the 2010 Equality Act, albeit one still under consideration by the government. I was dismayed to learn in August that David Cameron had appointed Lord Davies of Abersoch, a *Labour* peer, to look into the matter. I wrote to him (attached) but received no reply.

My experience throughout 33 years in business was that women interested in the most senior roles in business were hugely outnumbered by the number or men who were interested, and this didn't change over time. The idea that women need more role models is quite ridiculous. One need only read three books (two of them written by women) to understand why women are not interested in senior executive roles: *The Sexual Paradox* by the psychologist Susan Pinker, *The Female Brain* by the neuropsychiatrist Professor Louann Brizendine, and *The Essential Difference* by Professor Simon Baron-Cohen.

Enforcing gender balance in the boardroom would inevitably weaken our major companies, and I am keen to do what I can to fight it, through my book. I would be grateful to learn your – or the CBI's – views on the matter, for inclusion in the book, and would ask for this before the end of October. Thank you.

Yours etc.

Response from Richard Lambert: next page

APPENDIX 10

THE LETTER FROM THE DIRECTOR-GENERAL OF THE CBI

Mr Mike Buchanan
<address>

18 October 2010

Dear Mr Buchanan,

Thank you for your letter regarding Lord Davies' review on board gender equality. I was interested to read your perspective on this subject, but while I agree that enforced quotas are not the answer, I do believe there is a need to increase board diversity in the UK through workable, business-led initiatives.

Board diversity, including gender diversity, can help to drive corporate governance and this is something explicitly referred to in the FRC's[1] revised UK Corporate Governance Code[2]. Diverse boards have many benefits that include promoting more robust challenge in the boardroom, helping to reduce group-think[3] as well as ensuring companies are in touch with their customers[4], all important themes in the wake of the financial crisis.

We at the CBI believe therefore that board gender equality, as part of a wider drive for board diversity, is key to ensuring appropriate corporate governance is exercised in the future.

Yours etc.

Author's notes:

[1] Financial Reporting Council
[2] The code came into force for major companies for accounting periods starting after 29 June 2010. The only reference in the code to diversity states, 'The search for board candidates should be conducted, and appointments made, on merit, against objective criteria and with due regard for the benefits of diversity on the board, including gender'.

Nowhere in the code does it state what the supposed benefits of diversity for major companies' boards are. And what does 'due regard' mean in this context? If this is evidence-based guidance, then I'm a jam doughnut.

[3] Feminist group-think is used here to claim a benefit of a reduction in board group-think: what a delicious irony.

[4] I am not aware of any evidence for such claimed benefits. Given the current lack of diversity in major companies' boards, they are at best untested assertions; and given that the assertions are frequently put forward by militant feminists, we can confidently expect them – if ever tested in the real business world – to prove hopelessly flawed.

APPENDIX 11

THE LETTER TO THE CHAIR OF THE EQUALITY AND HUMAN RIGHTS COMMISSION

Trevor Phillips
Chair
The Equality and Human Rights Commission
3 More London
Riverside Tooley Street
London SE1 2RG

12 October 2010

Dear Mr Phillips,

I have read with interest the material relating to the 'gender pay gap' in your triennial report, 'How Fair is Britain?', and failed to find even a suggestion in its 750 pages that the gender pay gap – even if we restrict our analysis to full-time workers – might be attributable to women freely exercising education and career choices with an understanding that the result could be lower income over the course of their working lives. Such an explanation doesn't accord with the feminist vision of women as victims, of course, and I wasn't surprised to see that The Fawcett Society was one of the organisations that had provided you with 'invaluable assistance'.

Anyone who reads a book by the Canadian-American psychologist Susan Pinker, *The Sexual Paradox*, can be in no doubt that women's representation in different lines of work, and at senior levels in organisations, is down to the choices they make freely. I understand that over 90% of mechanical engineering graduates are male, while over 90% of psychology graduates are female. Why is the 'shortage' of female engineers deemed to be a problem while the 'shortage' of male psychologists isn't? We keep hearing that the problem is a shortage of role models for women. It's not true. Women have had role models for *decades.*

I should like to meet up with you for an audio interview so that I might better understand (for my forthcoming seventh book) how the myth of women being under-represented at senior levels in the public and private sectors (other than voluntarily) continues to survive, likewise how the 'occupational segregation' you cite in your report is a manifestation of anything other than women exercising freedom of choice in their education and lines of employment, as well as in their choice of full-time or part-time work, which are surely good things? It seems to me that the militant feminist agenda remains completely unchallenged in British public debate. I look forward to hearing from you shortly, and arranging a time and date for the interview.

Yours etc.

Response from Trevor Phillips: none received

APPENDIX 12

THE LETTER TO
THE RT HON THERESA MAY MP
(AND HER RESPONSE)

The Rt Hon Theresa May MP
Home Secretary and Minister for Women & Equalities
House of Commons
London SW1A 0AA

24 November 2010

Dear Mrs May,

David and Goliatha: David Cameron – heir to Harman?
I had the pleasure of working for the Conservatives (as an interim executive at CCHQ, over 2006-2008) and I now have pleasure in enclosing your complimentary copy of my seventh book, *David and Goliatha*. I started the book in 2009 as a protest against the dire influence on our public life of militant feminists such as Harriet Harman. Following the election I've been dismayed to see her dismal philosophies enshrined in legislation with the Commencement Order which brought 90 per cent of her Equality Bill (2010) into force.

The consultation period relating to the document 'Equality Act 2010: The public sector Equality Duty – Promoting equality through transparency' has now passed. Doubtless you will have had formal representations from bodies such as The Fawcett Society, presenting militant feminist perspectives. You will have had few if any from organisations pointing out that the gender pay gap is the result of men and women freely making choices with regards to their working lives; and that one of the reasons women are 'under-represented' in the senior reaches of organisations is that they are far less inclined than men to seek or remain in such jobs.

Perhaps the most invidious provision of the Act is the introduction of the concept of 'positive action', by means of which public sector organisations will meet their 'Equality Duty'. Whatever the weasel words associated with positive action might be in the Act and associated guidance, it will surely result in positive discrimination – for women in particular – and discrimination is illegal under British and EU law. Might I ask, do you personally support the concept of positive action in this context?

Yours etc.

Response: in a letter Theresa May wrote, 'My approach to these issues is set out in a speech I recently gave, available here:

www.equalities.gov.uk/ministers/speeches-1/equalities_strategy_speech.aspx

[Author's note: the link leads to the text of a speech given by Mrs May on 17 November 2010 titled, 'Political Correctness won't lead to equality'.]

REFERENCES AND
FURTHER READING

Andreae, Simon (2000), *The Secrets of Love and Lust* (London: Abacus).

Baron-Cohen, Simon (2003), *The Essential Difference* (London: Allen Lane).

Barrett, Louise, and Dunbar, Robin, and Lycett, John (2002), *Human Evolutionary Psychology* (Basingstoke and New York: Palgrave).

Belenky, Mary Field, and Clinchy, Blythe McVicker, and Goldberger, Nancy Rule, and Tarule, Jill Mattuck (1986), *Women's Ways of Knowing: The Development of Self, Voice, and Mind* (New York: Perseus Books).

Bernstein, Richard (1994), *Dictatorship of Virtue: Multiculturalism and the Battle for America's Future* (New York: Alfred A Knopf).

Brizendine, Louann (2007), *The Female Brain* (London: Bantam Press).

Browne, Anthony (2006), *The Retreat of Reason: Political Correctness and the Corruption of Public Debate in Modern Britain* (London: The Institute for the Study of Civil Society [Civitas]).

Buchanan, Mike (2010), *David and Goliatha: David Cameron – heir to Harman?* (Bedford: LPS publishing).

Buchanan, Mike (2010), *The Fraud of the Rings* (Bedford: LPS publishing).

Cooper, Joel (2007), *Cognitive Dissonance: Fifty Years of a Classic Theory* (London: Sage Publications).

Hall, Judy (2003), *The Crystal Bible: A Definitive Guide to Crystals* (London: Octopus).

Harman, Harriet (1993), *20th Century Man, 21st Century Woman: How Both Sexes Can Bridge The Century Gap* (London: Vermillion).

Masterson, Dick (2008), *Men Are Better Than Women* (New York: Simon & Schuster).

Moxon, Steve (2008), *The Woman Racket* (Exeter: Imprint Academic).

Nathanson, Paul, and Young, Katherine K (2001), *Spreading Misandry: The Teaching of Contempt of Men in Popular Culture* (Quebec City: McGill-Queen's University Press).

Newcomb, Jacky (2008), *Angel Kids: Enchanting Stories of True-Life Guardian Angels and 'Sixth-Sense' Abilities in Children* (London: Hay House).

Patai, Daphne, and Koertge, Noretta (2003), *Professing Feminism* (Plymouth: Lexington Books).

Pinker, Steven (2003), *The Blank Slate: The Modern Denial of Human Nature* (London: Penguin).

Pinker, Susan (2008), *The Sexual Paradox: Men, Women, and the Real Gender Gap* (New York: Scribner).

Price, Katie (2008), *Pushed to the Limit* (Salt Lake City: Century).

Sommers, Christina Hoff (1994), *Who Stole Feminism? How Women Have Betrayed Women* (New York: Simon & Schuster).

Vilar, Esther (1971), *The Manipulated Man* (Germany: C Bertelsman Verlag).

Weldon, Fay (2006), *What Makes Women Happy* (London: HarperCollins).

INDEX OF CITED PUBLICATIONS

INDEX

Lightning Source UK Ltd.
Milton Keynes UK
UKHW020045300320
361040UK00004B/38